McGraw-Hill's

500 Physical Chemistry Questions

Also in McGraw-Hill's 500 Questions Series

McGraw-Hill's 500 American Government Questions: Ace Your College Exams
McGraw-Hill's 500 College Algebra and Trigonometry Questions: Ace Your College Exams
McGraw-Hill's 500 College Biology Questions: Ace Your College Exams
McGraw-Hill's 500 College Calculus Questions: Ace Your College Exams
McGraw-Hill's 500 College Chemistry Questions: Ace Your College Exams
McGraw-Hill's 500 College Physics Questions: Ace Your College Exams
McGraw-Hill's 500 Differential Equations Questions: Ace Your College Exams
McGraw-Hill's 500 European History Questions: Ace Your College Exams
McGraw-Hill's 500 French Questions: Ace Your College Exams
McGraw-Hill's 500 Linear Algebra Questions: Ace Your College Exams
McGraw-Hill's 500 Macroeconomics Questions: Ace Your College Exams
McGraw-Hill's 500 Microeconomics Questions: Ace Your College Exams
McGraw-Hill's 500 Organic Chemistry Questions: Ace Your College Exams
McGraw-Hill's 500 Philosophy Questions: Ace Your College Exams
McGraw-Hill's 500 Precalculus Questions: Ace Your College Exams
McGraw-Hill's 500 Psychology Questions: Ace Your College Exams
McGraw-Hill's 500 Spanish Questions: Ace Your College Exams
McGraw-Hill's 500 U.S. History Questions, Volume 1: Ace Your College Exams
McGraw-Hill's 500 U.S. History Questions, Volume 2: Ace Your College Exams
McGraw-Hill's 500 World History Questions, Volume 1: Ace Your College Exams
McGraw-Hill's 500 World History Questions, Volume 2: Ace Your College Exams
McGraw-Hill's 500 MCAT Biology Questions to Know by Test Day
McGraw-Hill's 500 MCAT General Chemistry Questions to Know by Test Day
McGraw-Hill's 500 MCAT Organic Chemistry Questions to Know by Test Day
McGraw-Hill's 500 MCAT Physics Questions to Know by Test Day

McGraw-Hill's 500 Physical Chemistry Questions

Ace Your College Exams

Richard Langley

McGraw Hill

New York Chicago San Francisco Lisbon London Madrid Mexico City
Milan New Delhi San Juan Seoul Singapore Sydney Toronto

The McGraw-Hill Companies

1 2 3 4 5 6 7 8 9 10 QFR/QFR 1 9 8 7 6 5 4 3 2

ISBN 978-0-07-178961-5
MHID 0-07-178961-8

e-ISBN 978-0-07-178962-2
e-MHID 0-07-178962-6

Library of Congress Control Number 2012948975

This book is printed on acid-free paper.

CONTENTS

Introduction vii

PART 1 THERMODYNAMICS

Chapter 1 **Thermodynamics and Equations of State 3**
Questions 1–29

Chapter 2 **The First Law of Thermodynamics 7**
Questions 30–60

Chapter 3 **The Second Law and the Third Law of Thermodynamics 13**
Questions 61–85

Chapter 4 **Fundamental Equations of Thermodynamics 17**
Questions 86–113

Chapter 5 **Chemical Equilibria 21**
Questions 114–139

Chapter 6 **Phase Equilibria 27**
Questions 140–169

Chapter 7 **Electrochemical Equilibria 31**
Questions 170–200

PART 2 QUANTUM MECHANICS

Chapter 8 **Quantum Theory 37**
Questions 201–225

Chapter 9 **Atomic Structure 41**
Questions 226–254

Chapter 10 **Molecular Structure 45**
Questions 255–271

Chapter 11 **Molecular Symmetry 47**
Questions 272–285

Chapter 12 **Rotational and Vibrational Spectra 49**
Questions 286–309

Chapter 13 **Electronic Spectra 53**
Questions 310–329

Chapter 14 **Magnetic Resonance Spectra 57**
Questions 330–343

Chapter 15 **Statistical Mechanics 59**
Questions 344–373

Chapter 16 **Molecular Interactions 63**
Questions 374–385

PART 3 **KINETICS**

Chapter 17 **Kinetic Theory of Gases 67**
Questions 386–410

Chapter 18 **The Rates of Chemical Reactions 71**
Questions 411–433

Chapter 19 **The Kinetics of Complex Reactions 75**
Questions 434–453

PART 4 **OTHER TOPICS**

Chapter 20 **Macromolecules 81**
Questions 454–470

Chapter 21 **The Solid State 85**
Questions 471–488

Chapter 22 **Processes at Solid Surfaces 87**
Questions 489–500

Answers 91

INTRODUCTION

How to Use This Book

There are several factors that you should be aware of when using this book. A quick perusal of this introduction will save you time, as there are many shortcuts and helpful hints included in the next few paragraphs.

Mathematical Background

Physical chemistry is a mathematics-intensive course. In general, the minimum background is two semesters of college-level calculus. Some of the solutions in this text do not require this level of expertise, but there will be cases . . . .

The solutions in this text will be short and to the point. For this reason, long mathematical proofs are not present. The object of this text is to maximize the concentration of information you need to solve physical chemistry problems. In addition, each problem is a "stand-alone" problem, which means there will be no reference to other problems and each problem will contain a definition of all terms present. This will occur even when two or more problems rely on the same information.

In general, there will be only one problem of each type per chapter unless a different substance leads to a different answer. For example, polar molecules behave differently than nonpolar molecules; therefore, there may need to be a problem dealing with a polar molecule and another problem dealing with a nonpolar molecule. Similar problems may appear in different chapters because different textbooks present the material in different chapters.

It will help you to work through the solutions as you go through this book. The optimum method for doing this is to work through the problem then look over the solution as presented, *and*, later, attempt to work through the problem without looking at the solution.

It will help you to have a calculator (preferably scientific) to work the problems. When using the calculator, do not make the freshman chemistry mistake of reporting that 2.0 mL/3.0 = 0.66666667 mL.

In addition, problems requiring several steps may appear to give different results due to intermediate rounding. Ideally, multiple rounding should average to the "correct" answer. In reality, this seldom occurs, and the final answer may be a little higher or lower than the "correct" value. If you get an answer that does not match the value reported in the solution, make sure it is not the result of multiple rounding.

Some very long calculations may be done "by parts." This means that the equation was too long to work in one line. To avoid leaving out important material, only part of the calculation is solved at a time until achieving the final answer.

Certain concepts are applicable to more than one chapter. For this reason, problems on a particular concept may appear in more than one chapter. One reason for this complication is that a particular concept will appear in different chapters in different textbooks.

Definitions

While simply repeating definitions is not the purpose of this text, knowing definitions is exceedingly important to solving physical chemistry problems. For example, being able to repeat the definition of an adiabatic system may help a little, but knowing that the term means that certain quantities are constant and others are related is not only significant but also useful.

Conversions

A physical chemistry course deals with a wide variety of concepts. Measurements used for different concepts require different units. Relating these units requires a large number of conversions. Many physical chemistry texts include tables containing these conversions. You may need to look these up as necessary. If you are having problems with calculations, express all of the given quantities in SI base units (kilograms, meters, seconds, kelvins, moles, amperes, and candelas) or closely related units (joules and pascals).

The symbols for many variables, such as T for temperature and t for time, are usually consistent. Not all texts are consistent with the symbols for other variables. Every attempt will be made to make the meaning of each symbol apparent in each problem.

Many physical chemistry texts do not include "trivial" conversions such as the switch from milliliters to liters. In some cases, this may lead to confusion (hopefully not); therefore, all conversions (including "trivial" conversions) will be present in the solutions. This includes "simple" multiplier conversions such as centimeters to meters. All multiplier conversions will be done exactly the same way. For example, the prefix centi- (c) means 0.01, so the conversion will use the relationship 1 cm = 0.01 m instead of 100 cm = 1 m.

The solutions in many physical chemistry texts are very loose with significant figures (compared to those in general chemistry). In some cases, extra significant figures will be retained for intermediate answers. In general, keep this in mind and watch what your textbook/instructor does. Remember, physical chemistry laboratory courses are more observant of the rules for significant figures.

Data

Traditionally, the working of problems in physical chemistry requires access to a number of data sources. To add this information to this book would increase the length by several thousand pages. There are three good alternatives. First, if you are using this text as a supplement to another physical chemistry text, use the tables in that text. Another useful source is the *CRC Handbook of Chemistry and Physics*. Finally, the National Institute of Standards and Technology (NIST) website is invaluable (http://webbook.nist.gov/).

Over the years, there has been a redetermination of a number of reported values. In some cases, advancements in technology lead to measurements that are more precise (better). New developments in science often lead to alternate methods for the determination of values. Because science is advancing, values will change, and you may find different values for some items. Do not assume that these values are erroneous, but rather the result of differences in experimental methods with the newer value probably being the better value. You should adjust the calculations/answers to accommodate the data available.

"Condensed" Solutions

Throughout this text, solutions to problems will use a "condensed" format. This procedure shortens the solution and minimizes repetition and recopying. The following "trivial" problem illustrates this approach.

> A sample of an ideal gas has a volume of 2.00 quarts under a pressure of 475 torr and at a temperature of 315 K. How many moles of gas are in the sample?

The "regular" approach is to convert the volume into liters, the pressure into atmospheres, and enter the results into the ideal gas equation with $R = 0.0821$ L atm/mol K.

$$\text{Volume} = V = (2.00\ \text{qt})\left(\frac{1\ \text{L}}{1.057\ \text{qt}}\right) = 1.89\ \text{L}$$

$$\text{Pressure} = P = (475\ \text{torr})\left(\frac{1\ \text{atm}}{760\ \text{torr}}\right) = 0.625\ \text{atm}$$

$$\text{Moles} = n = \frac{PV}{RT} = \frac{(0.625\ \text{atm})(1.89\ \text{L})}{\left(0.0821\ \dfrac{\text{L atm}}{\text{mol K}}\right)(315\ \text{K})} = 4.57 \times 10^{-2}\ \text{mol}$$

In some cases, it is possible to do part of the work in your head; however, this will not always be the case.

The "condensed" approach, used in this book, enters the given information into the ideal gas equation, which, technically, solves the problem, and then adds the conversions onto the end of the calculation.

$$\text{Moles} = n = \frac{PV}{RT} = \frac{(475\ \text{torr})(2.00\ \text{qt})}{\left(0.0821\ \frac{\text{L atm}}{\text{mol K}}\right)(315\ \text{K})}\left(\frac{1\ \text{atm}}{760\ \text{torr}}\right)\left(\frac{1\ \text{L}}{1.057\ \text{qt}}\right)$$

$$= 4.57 \times 10^{-2}\ \text{mol}$$

This approach gives the same answer with less work and minimizes the chances of adding an unnecessary conversion or miscopying an intermediate number.

References

Solution manuals, such as this one, are sources that show how to work problems, which illustrate the concepts introduced in textbooks. The purpose of solution manuals is not to introduce concepts or to teach you the underlying theories. Therefore, you may need to consult other texts to learn these concepts. Two useful texts are the following:

I. Levine, *Physical Chemistry*, 6th ed., McGraw-Hill, New York, 2009

C. W. Garland, J. W. Nibler, and D. P. Shoemaker, *Experiments in Physical Chemistry*, 8th ed., McGraw-Hill, New York, 2009

Should you need information on problem-solving techniques or more basic chemical concepts, the following two texts may prove useful to you.

M. S. Silberberg, *Chemistry: The Molecular Nature of Matter and Change*, 6th ed., McGraw-Hill, New York, 2012

J. T. Moore and R. H. Langley, *Chemistry for the Utterly Confused*, 1st ed., McGraw-Hill, New York, 2007

McGraw-Hill's

500 Physical Chemistry Questions

PART 1

Thermodynamics

CHAPTER 1

Thermodynamics and Equations of State

1. In general chemistry courses, students learn that the value of the gas constant (R) is 0.0820578 L atm mol^{-1} K^{-1}. Determine the value of the gas constant in SI base units.

2. A system consisting of two connected gas bulbs of equal volume is immersed in a boiling water bath at 373 K. At this temperature (T), the pressure (P) in the bulbs is 0.750 atm. Rearrangement of the system places one bulb in an ice-water bath (273 K), whereas the other bulb remains in the boiling water bath. What is the new pressure in the system?

3. A sample of an ideal gas is compressed isothermally from 275 mL to 75.0 mL. If the initial pressure was 1.00 bar, what was the final pressure?

4. How many moles of an ideal gas are in a 1,725-mL container at 25°C if the pressure is 675 torr?

5. A tank has a volume of 1,250 L and is filled with air with a relative humidity of 55% at 298 K. Assuming ideal behavior, what is the mass of the water in the tank? At this temperature, the vapor pressure of water is 23.8 torr.

6. Dry ice (solid carbon dioxide) sublimes at 195 K (T). If the pressure is 1.10 atm (P), what is the density of the carbon dioxide gas in grams per liter?

7. A 1.00-L (V) sample of an unknown gas had a pressure of 0.750 atm (P) at an unknown temperature. The addition of 0.0100 mol of hydrogen gas followed by cooling of the container to 298 K (T) returned the pressure to its original value. Determine the original temperature of the sample.

8. A gas mixture has a density of 1.25 g L^{-1} at 298 K (T) and 1.00 atm (P). Assuming ideal behavior, what is the average molar mass of the gas in the mixture?

9. At 372 K (T), the vapor of a volatile liquid filled a Dumas bulb at a pressure of 0.975 atm (P). Upon cooling, the bulb was found to contain 0.3375 g of liquid. The volume of the bulb was 0.110 L (V). What was the molar mass of the volatile liquid?

10. A vacuum system has a pressure of 5.0×10^{-10} atm (P) at 298 K (T). The volume of the system is 1.375 L (V). Assuming ideal behavior, how many molecules of gas remain in the system?

11. The vapor pressure of water at 308 K (T) is 41.2 torr (P). What is the concentration of the water vapor in moles (n) per liter (M)?

12. A 1.00-L (V) sample of steam collected at 389 K (T) and at a pressure of 1.00 atm (P) was condensed to form 0.578 g of water. What was the compressibility factor (Z) of the steam?

13. At 273 K (T) and 100 atm (P), the compressibility factor (Z) is 0.783 for methane gas. What is the volume (V) of 15.0 mol (n) of methane gas at 273 K and 100 atm?

14. A sample of hydrogen gas is collected over water at 30°C. If the pressure of the system is 757.5 torr, what is the partial pressure of the hydrogen gas?

15. Using the van der Waals equation, calculate the pressure (P) exerted by a 2.00-mol (n) sample of chlorine gas confined in a volume (V) of 0.500 L at a temperature (T) of 345 K.

16. The van der Waals constants for methane are $a = 2.25$ L^2 atm mol^{-2} and $b = 0.0428$ L mol^{-1}. Determine the molecular diameter of methane.

17. What is the average translational energy per mole (E_{trans}) for a sample of helium gas at 298 K (T)?

18. What is the root-mean-square speed (v_{rms}) for helium gas at 298 K (T)?

19. Calculate the total force (F) on the wall of a container if 1.00 mol helium atom strikes the wall with a root-mean-square speed of 1.363×10^3 m s^{-1}.

20. An object can escape from Earth's gravitational field by traveling at a velocity greater than escape velocity (1.1×10^4 m s^{-1}). A gas can escape from Earth if its root-mean-square velocity (U_{rms}) is greater than the escape velocity. Determine the temperature at which the root-mean-square velocity of a helium atom is equal to the escape velocity.

21. Poiseuille's flow experiment is one method for measuring the viscosity of a gas. In one experiment, a sample of gas, at 25°C, passed through a 2.000-mm-diameter tube with a length of 1.000 m. While passing through the tube, the pressure of the gas dropped from 1.007 bar to 1.000 bar. After 100.0 s, 90.00 mL of gas, measured at 1.000 bar, passed through the tube. Determine the viscosity of the gas at this temperature.

22. The Knudsen method uses effusion to determine the vapor pressure of a substance. In one experiment, a sample of a beryllium was heated to 1,575 K. After 960.0 s, 9.00 mg of the metal had effused through a 3.20-mm-diameter hole. Determine the vapor pressure of the metal.

23. How much energy (E) does a 75-W light bulb generate in 1.00 h?

24. An electric heater heats a 25-g block of aluminum. The heater supplies 25 W of power for 15 s, and the temperature of the block increases by 17 K. What is the molar heat capacity at constant pressure ($\overline{C}_p$) of aluminum?

25. Determine the heat capacity at constant pressure (C_p) for an ideal monatomic gas.

26. Determine the heat capacity at constant volume (C_v) for an ideal monatomic gas.

27. The molar heat capacities ($\overline{C}_p$) of substances vary with temperature. The general function for determining the molar heat capacity is $(\overline{C}_p) = (a + bT + cT^2)R$, where T is the temperature and a, b, and c are constants that depend on the identity of the substance. For example, in the case of nitrogen gas, $a = 3.245$, $b = 7.108 \times 10^{-4}$ K^{-1}, and $c = -4.06 \times 10^{-8}$ K^{-2} for temperatures in the range 300–1,500 K. What is the heat capacity of nitrogen at 1,500 K?

28. The bond energies for a nitrogen–nitrogen triple bond, a hydrogen–hydrogen bond, and a nitrogen–hydrogen bond are 941, 436, and 393 kJ mol^{-1}, respectively. Using the bond energies, calculate the enthalpy change for the following reaction:

$$N_2(g) + 3\ H_2(g) \rightarrow 2\ NH_3(g)$$

29. It is possible to construct a barometer using liquid gallium in place of mercury. This barometer will work at higher temperatures than a mercury barometer and contains the significantly less toxic gallium. Determine the atmospheric pressure (P), in pascals, when the gallium barometer has a height (h) of 1,696.0 mm of gallium at 32.4°C and the acceleration of gravity (g) is 9.8067 m s^{-2}. The density (ρ) of liquid gallium at this temperature is 6.0930 g/mL.

CHAPTER 2

The First Law of Thermodynamics

30. Work (w) takes many forms, and one of these forms is pressure–volume work ($w = -P\Delta V$). A sample containing 5.00 mol (n) of an ideal gas at 1.00 bar (P_1) and 325 K (T) is compressed at constant temperature by a constant pressure of 10.0 bar (P_2). Determine the amount of pressure–volume work, in joules, required for this process.

31. How much work, in joules, is necessary to transport 2.50 mol of electrons from the anode to the cathode if the potential difference is 0.25 V?

32. The surface area of a drop of water is 8.0×10^{-5} m^2. If the surface tension of water is 0.072 N/m, how much work, in joules, is necessary to exactly double the surface area?

33. A stretched piece of an elastic polymer exerts a force of 1.75 N. How much work, in joules, is necessary to stretch the polymer by 2.54 cm?

34. The relationship $w_{rev} = nRT \ln\left(\frac{P_2}{P_1}\right)$ gives the work involved in the irreversible compression or expansion of an ideal gas. Determine the reversible work (w_{rev}), in joules, for the expansion of 7.00 mol (n) of an ideal gas from 10.0 bar (P_1) to 2.00 bar (P_2) at a constant temperature of 315 K (T).

35. A sample of an ideal monatomic gas expanded adiabatically and reversibly. The initial molar volume of the gas was 24.45 L mol^{-1} at 1.00 bar and 298.2 K (T_1). After the expansion, the molar volume of the gas was 48.90 L mol^{-1} and the temperature was 187.8 K (T_2). Calculate the work (w) done during the expansion.

36. The relationship $w_{irrev} = -P_2(V_2 - V_1)$ gives the work involved in the irreversible compression or expansion of an ideal gas. Determine the irreversible work (w_{irrev}), in joules, for the expansion of 7.00 mol (n) of an ideal gas from 10.0 bar (P_1) to 2.00 bar (P_2) at a constant temperature of 315 K (T).

37. A 2.00-mol (n) sample of oxygen gas expands reversibly and isothermally from 1.00 atm (P_1) to 0.200 atm (P_2) at 298 K (T). How much work (w_{rev}) was done during this expansion?

38. A 5.00-L (V_1) container is filled with a sample of an ideal gas at 15.0 atm (P_1) and 298 K. A valve is opened and the gas undergoes an isothermal expansion into the atmosphere. The external pressure is 1.00 atm ($P_2 = P_{ex}$) and the temperature is 298 K. How much work (w), in liter-atmospheres, did the expanding gas do?

39. A 2.00-mol (n) sample of benzene vaporizes at its normal boiling point of 353 K (T). Calculate the reversible work for this process.

40. The irreversible expansion of a gas does 1.47×10^4 J of work (w_{irrev}). How much heat (q_{irrev}) is absorbed during this expansion?

41. The reversible expansion of a gas does 2.95×10^4 J of work (w_{rev}). How much heat (q_{rev}) is absorbed during this expansion?

42. Determine the standard enthalpy change ($\Delta H_{rxn}°$) for the following reaction at 298 K:

$$2\ Pb(NO_3)_2(s) \rightarrow 2\ PbO(s) + 4\ NO_2(g) + O_2(g)$$

43. A sample of an ideal gas expanded adiabatically and reversibly. The initial molar volume of the gas was 24.45 L mol^{-1} ($\bar{V}_1$) at 1.00 bar (P_1) and 298.2 K. After the expansion, the molar volume of the gas was 48.90 L mol^{-1} ($\bar{V}_2$). What was the pressure (P_2) of the gas after the expansion?

44. A sample of an ideal gas expanded adiabatically and reversibly. The initial molar volume of the gas was 24.45 L mol^{-1} ($\bar{V}_1$) at 1.00 bar and 298.2 K (T_1). After the expansion, the molar volume of the gas was 48.90 L mol^{-1} ($\bar{V}_2$). What was the temperature (T_2), in kelvin, of the gas after the expansion?

45. The combustion of pentane in a constant-volume calorimeter produces 3,515 kJ mol^{-1} ($\Delta U_{rxn}°$) at 298.15 K (T). What is the value of $\Delta H_{rxn}°$ for the following reaction?

$$C_5H_{12}(g) + 8\ O_2(g) \rightarrow 5\ CO_2(g) + 6\ H_2O(l)$$

46. The molar volume of silver (V) is 1.03×10^{-5} m^3 mol^{-1}, the coefficient of thermal expansion (α) for silver is 5.8×10^{-5} K^{-1}, and the compressibility (β) of silver is 7.9×10^{-12} Pa^{-1}. Determine the value of ($C_P - C_V$) for silver at 298 K (T).

47. Calculate C_P, the heat capacity at constant pressure, for water vapor. Assume the vibrational contribution to C_P is 20%.

48. Calculate C_P, the heat capacity at constant pressure, for hydrogen cyanide. Assume the vibrational contribution to C_P is 20%.

49. Determine the heat absorbed, ΔH, when 1 mol of carbon monoxide gas is heated from 298 K (T_1) to 425 K (T_2). The relationship for the heat capacity at constant pressure (in J mol^{-1} K^{-1}) is $C_P = a + bT + cT^2$, with $a = 26.9$, $b = 7.0 \times 10^{-3}$, and $c = -8.2 \times 10^{-7}$.

50. A 10.00-g sample (m) of lead metal was heated to 75.00°C (T_i). This sample was placed in contact with a 17.00-g sample (m) of magnesium metal at 15.00°C (T_i). The C_P of lead metal is 0.127 J/g°C, and the C_P of magnesium metal is 1.024 J/g°C. Assuming no heat is lost to the surroundings, what was the final temperature (T_f) of the two metals?

51. Determine the heat of formation for propane gas given the following thermochemical equations:

(A) $C(gr) + O_2(g) \rightarrow CO_2(g)$ $\Delta H = -394$ kJ mol^{-1}

(B) $C_3H_8(g) + 5\ O_2(g) \rightarrow 3\ CO_2(g) + 4\ H_2O(l)$ $\Delta H = -2{,}222$ kJ mol^{-1}

(C) $H_2(g) + ½\ O_2(g) \rightarrow H_2O(l)$ $\Delta H = -286$ kJ mol^{-1}

52. Determine the heat evolved (ΔH_{T_2}) when ethanol freezes at constant pressure at 148 K (T_2). The enthalpy of crystallization (ΔH_{T_1}) of ethanol at 156 K (T_1) is −4.90 kJ mol^{-1}, and the values of C_P are 0.112 kJ mol^{-1}K^{-1} and 0.111 kJ mol^{-1}K^{-1} for liquid and solid ethanol, respectively.

53. The standard heat of formation of liquid ethanol is –278 kJ mol^{-1} [$\Delta H_f°$(liquid)] and the standard heat of formation of ethanol vapor is –235 kJ mol^{-1} [$\Delta H_f°$(gas)]. Determine the heat of vaporization (ΔH_{vap}) for ethanol.

54. The heat of combustion of propane gas is –2,222 kJ mol^{-1} (ΔH_{com}). Determine the heat of formation of propane [$\Delta H_f°$(propane)] if the heats of formation of carbon dioxide gas and liquid water are –394 kJ mol^{-1} and –286 kJ mol^{-1}, respectively. The reaction is

$$C_3H_8(g) + 5\ O_2(g) \rightarrow 3\ CO_2(g) + 4\ H_2O(l) \qquad \Delta H = -2{,}222\ \text{kJ mol}^{-1}$$

55. At 298 K (T), the enthalpy of formation (ΔH) for gaseous nitric acid is –134 kJ mol^{-1}. Calculate the change in the internal energy (ΔE) for this reaction:

$$1/2\ H_2(g) + 1/2\ N_2(g) + 3/2\ O_2(g) \rightarrow HNO_3(g)$$

56. A sample of 1.00 mol of an ideal diatomic gas is in a system containing a movable system. Calculate the temperature change (ΔT) resulting from the addition of 75.0 J of heat (q) and the application of 225 J of work (w).

57. Determine the final temperature (T_2) of a 1.00-mol sample of helium gas after it has undergone a reversible adiabatic compression from 44.8 L (V_1) to 22.4 L (V_2). Assume the initial temperature (T_1) was 298 K and that the heat capacity ($\bar{C}_v$) is constant and equal to 12.6 J mol^{-1} K^{-1}.

58. A 10.0-g sample of a solid with a molar mass of 74.5 g mol^{-1} is dissolved in 90.0 g of water. At 15°C, the enthalpy of solution is 3.24 kJ, and at 25°C the enthalpy of solution is 2.93 kJ. The value of C_P for the solid is 50.2 J °C^{-1} mol^{-1}, and the value of C_P for water is 75.3 J °C^{-1} mol^{-1}. Determine the value of the heat capacity of the solution in J °C^{-1}.

59. The standard heat of reaction (q_v) for the following reaction is -4.810×10^3 kJ mol^{-1} at constant volume and 298 K:

$$C_7H_{16}(l) + 11\ O_2(g) \rightarrow 7\ CO_2(g) + 8\ H_2O(l)$$

Estimate the heat of reaction at constant pressure (q_p).

60. Determine the enthalpy change for the following reaction

$$2\ C(gr) + 3\ H_2(g) \rightarrow C_2H_6(g)$$

by using the following information:

C–C bond energy = 348 kJ mol^{-1}

H–H bond energy = 436 kJ mol^{-1}

C–H bond energy = 413 kJ mol^{-1}

Heat of vaporization of C(gr) = 718 kJ mol^{-1}

CHAPTER 3

The Second Law and the Third Law of Thermodynamics

61. What is the work (w_{rev}) associated with the isothermal reversible expansion of 1.00 mol (n) of an ideal gas, at 298.15 K (T), from 5.00 L (V_1) to 15.00 L (V_2)?

62. What is the q_{surr} (heat change of the surroundings) associated with the isothermal reversible expansion of 1.00 mol of an ideal gas, at 298.15 K, from 5.00 L to 15.00 L? The value of w_{rev} for this process is -2.72×10^3 J.

63. An experimental internal combustion engine operates as a Carnot engine with an efficiency of 50.0%. How much energy (E) will this engine generate for work from 1.0 gallon of gasoline? A gallon of gasoline will generate about 1.4×10^8 J.

64. What is the efficiency (E) of an engine that operates between 273 K (T_l) and 373 K (T_h)?

65. Determine the Gibbs ($\Delta G°$) free energy change for the following reaction at 298 K:

$$CuO(s) + 2\ HCl(g) \rightarrow CuCl_2(s) + H_2O(g)$$

66. Determine the molar entropy ($\Delta\bar{S}$) of vaporization of butane in J mol^{-1} K^{-1}. The molar heat of vaporization ($\Delta\bar{H}$) of liquid butane is 22.9 kJ mol^{-1}, and the boiling point is 289 K (T).

67. What is the change in the molar Gibbs free energy ($\Delta\bar{G}$) for the conversion of liquid water at 288 K to ice at 288 K (T)? The vapor pressure of water at 288 K is 2.121×10^{-5} Pa (P_1), and the vapor pressure of ice at 288 K is 1.925×10^{-5} Pa (P_2).

68. What is the entropy change (ΔS) associated with the isothermal reversible expansion of 1.00 mol (n) of an ideal gas, at 298.15 K, from 5.00 L (V_1) to 15.00 L (V_2)?

69. What is the change in the entropy of the surroundings (ΔS_{surr}) associated with the isothermal reversible expansion of 1.00 mol of an ideal gas, at 298.15 K (T), from 5.00 L to 15.00 L? The value of entropy change for this process is 9.13 J K^{-1}, and $q_{surr} = -2.72 \times 10^3$ J.

70. What is the change in the entropy (ΔS) of the surroundings and the system associated with the isothermal reversible expansion of 1.00 mol of an ideal gas, at 298.15 K, from 5.00 L to 15.00 L? The entropy change of the system is 9.13 J K^{-1}, and the entropy change of the surroundings is −9.13 J K^{-1}.

71. A sample of neon gas is cooled from 325 K (T_1) to 175 K (T_2). At the same time, the pressure increases from 1.00 bar (P_1) to 7.50 bar (P_2). What is the molar entropy change ($\Delta \bar{S}$) for the neon gas?

72. A sample containing 1.00 mol of helium gas is mixed with 2.00 mol of neon gas. Assuming both gases are behaving ideally, what is the entropy of mixing?

73. Using the data in the following table, calculate the entropy of formation (ΔS) for CaO(s) at 298.15 K.

Component	$S°$
Ca(s)	41.4 J mol^{-1} K^{-1}
O_2(g)	205.0 J mol^{-1} K^{-1}
CaO(s)	39.8 J mol^{-1} K^{-1}

74. Lanthanum metal undergoes a solid-state phase transition from the α-form to the β-form at 583 K (T_{trans}). The enthalpy of transition (ΔH_{trans}) is 397 J mol^{-1}. Calculate the total entropy change accompanying the transition of 1.00 mol of lanthanum if the cooling bath is at 298 K (T_{bath}) and 1.00 atm.

75. Will the following reaction proceed spontaneously at 298 K?

$$Cu_2O(s) + H_2(g) \rightarrow 2\ Cu(s) + H_2O(g)$$

76. The entropy change for the following reaction is 32 J mol^{-1} K^{-1} at 298 K:

$$Cu_2O(s) + H_2(g) \rightarrow 2\ Cu(s) + H_2O(g)$$

The heat capacities ($C_P°$) for the substances in this reaction are 64 J mol^{-1} K^{-1} for Cu_2O(s), 24 J mol^{-1} K^{-1} for Cu(s), 29 J mol^{-1} K^{-1} for H_2(g), and 34 J mol^{-1} K^{-1} for H_2O(g). What is the entropy change at 498 K?

77. The coefficient of thermal expansion (α) for thulium metal is 1.16×10^{-5} K^{-1}, and the density of thulium metal is 9.32×10^3 kg m^{-3}. Calculate the change in the entropy of the system (ΔS_{system}) when 1.00 mol of solid thulium expands isothermally from 250.0 atm (P_1) to 1.0 atm (P_2).

78. A sample containing 1.00 mol (n) of liquid ammonia at 273 K (T_1) is cooled to liquid ammonia at 240 K (T_2). The process is done irreversibly by placing the sample in liquid nitrogen at 77 K. The heat capacity relationship for ammonia gas is $C_P = 24.6$ J mol^{-1} K^{-1} + (3.75×10^{-2} J mol^{-1} K^{-2})T – (1.38×10^{-6} J mol^{-1} K^{-3})T^2, and the heat of vaporization (ΔH_{vap}) is 23.4 kJ mol^{-1}. What is the value of the entropy change (ΔS) for this process?

79. How much does the entropy (ΔS) of a metal increase when heated from 0 K (T_1) to 75 K (T_2) at constant pressure? Over this range, the expression for the heat capacity, in J mol^{-1} K^{-1}, is $C_P = -0.096T + 0.010T^2 - 7.9 \times 10^{-5}T^3$.

80. At 20 K, the heat capacity (C_P) of uranium metal is 3.04 J mol^{-1} K^{-1}. Assuming the metal obeys the Debye third power law, what is the standard absolute entropy (ΔS) of uranium metal at 20 K?

81. Estimate the zero-point entropy for dinitrogen oxide.

82. Exactly 1,000 J of heat (q_{rev}) was reversibly transferred to a piece of platinum at 273.15 K from a thermal reservoir at 273.16 K (T). What was ΔS_{system} for this process?

83. Determine the entropy of vaporization (ΔS) for europium metal in J mol^{-1} K^{-1}. The heat of vaporization (ΔH) of europium is 176 kJ mol^{-1} at 1,712 K (T).

84. Two blocks of silver each containing 2.00 mol (n) of silver are brought into contact. One block is initially at 373.15 K (T_h), and the other block is initially at 273.15 K (T_c). What is the change in entropy (ΔS) for the system? The heat capacity (C_P) of silver is 25.35 J mol^{-1} K^{-1}.

85. Chlorine consists of two isotopes, 75.77% ^{35}Cl and 24.23% ^{37}Cl. Calculate the entropy change for preparation of a mixture of these two isotopes.

CHAPTER 4

Fundamental Equations of Thermodynamics

86. Calculate the change in the molar internal energy ($\Delta\bar{U}$), in J mol^{-1}, for the isothermal expansion of methane gas from 2.00 L (V_1) to 10.00 L (V_2). The values of the van der Waals constants for methane are $a = 2.22$ L^2 bar mol^{-2} and $b = 0.0428$ L mol^{-1}.

87. One mole of water vapor undergoes a compression to liquid water at 373 K (T). The process is reversible, isothermal, and isobaric. What is the work (w) for this process?

88. An ideal gas undergoes an isothermal expansion into a connected evacuated vessel at 315 K. During the expansion, the pressure drops from 7.50 bar to 2.50 bar, and the volume increases from 2.50 L to 7.50 L. Calculate the molar enthalpy change ($\Delta\bar{H}$).

89. An ideal gas undergoes an isothermal expansion into a connected evacuated vessel at 315 K (T). During the expansion, the pressure drops from 7.50 bar (P_1) to 2.50 bar (P_2), and the volume increases from 2.50 L (V_1) to 7.50 L (V_2). Calculate the molar Gibbs free energy change ($\Delta\bar{G}$).

90. An ideal gas undergoes an isothermal expansion into a connected evacuated vessel at 315 K (T). During the expansion, the pressure drops from 7.50 bar to 2.50 bar, and the volume increases from 2.50 L to 7.50 L. The molar Gibbs free energy, $\Delta\bar{G}$, is -2.88×10^3 J mol^{-1}, and the enthalpy, $\Delta\bar{H}$, is 0. Calculate the molar entropy change ($\Delta\bar{S}$).

91. Calculate the value of ΔG_f for mercury vapor at 298.15 K and 15.0 bar (P). The value of ΔG_f° for mercury vapor is 31.8 kJ mol^{-1} at 298.15 K (T).

92. Calculate the value of ΔG_f for liquid mercury at 298.15 K and 15.0 bar (P_2). The value of $\Delta G_f°$ for mercury vapor is 0.00 kJ mol^{-1} at 298.15 K. The density of liquid mercury at 298.15 K is 13.59 g cm^{-3}.

93. Calculate the fugacity (f) of carbon dioxide gas at 75.0 bar (P) and 273 K (T). The van der Waals constants for carbon dioxide are $a = 3.54$ L^2 bar mol^{-2} and $b = 0.0427$ L mol^{-1}.

94. The activity (a) of liquid mercury at 298 K (T) is defined to be 1. Assuming the molar volume of liquid mercury is constant, what is the activity of liquid mercury at 75.0 bar (P)? The molar volume of mercury ($\overline{V}$) is 0.0148 L mol^{-1}.

95. Calculate the molar entropy change ($\Delta\overline{S}$) for the isothermal expansion of methane gas from 2.00 L ($\overline{V}_1$) to 10.00 L ($\overline{V}_2$). The values of the van der Waals constants for methane are $a = 2.22$ L^2 bar mol^{-2} and $b = 0.0428$ L mol^{-1}.

96. Using the data in the following table, calculate the standard Gibbs energy of formation for CaO(s) at 298.15 K.

Component	$\Delta H_f°$	$S°$
Ca(s)	0 kJ mol^{-1}	41.4 J mol^{-1} K^{-1}
O_2(g)	0 kJ mol^{-1}	205.0 J mol^{-1} K^{-1}
CaO(s)	−635.5 kJ mol^{-1}	39.8 J mol^{-1} K^{-1}

97. The following equation shows the disproportionation of copper(I) ions:

$$2\ Cu^+(aq) \rightarrow Cu^{2+}(aq) + Cu(s)$$

At 298 K (T), the enthalpy change ($\Delta H°$) for this process is −78.6 kJ, and the Gibbs free energy change ($\Delta G°$) is −35.3 kJ. What is the entropy change ($\Delta S°$) for this process in joules per kelvin?

98. Determine the Gibbs free energy change ($\Delta G°$) for the vaporization of liquid sodium given that the enthalpy change ($\Delta H°$) for the process is 105.27 kJ mol^{-1} and the entropy change ($\Delta S°$) for the process is 91.06 J mol^{-1} K^{-1}. The boiling point of sodium is 1,156 K (T).

99. A sample of nitrogen gas undergoes isothermal compression from 20.20 L (V_1) to 3.00 L (V_2). The 2.00-mol (n) sample was initially at 298 K (T) and at a pressure of 1.00 bar. Assume the gas behaves ideally. What is the Gibbs free energy (ΔG) change in joules?

100. A sample of neon gas initially at 298 K (T_1), 1.00 bar (P_1), and 25.25 L (V_1) expands into an evacuated chamber ($P_{ext} = 0$). The final volume was 50.50 L (V_2). Assume the neon behaves ideally. Determine the change in the entropy (ΔS), in J mol^{-1} K^{-1}, for the system.

101. A sample of neon gas initially at 298.15 K (T_1), 1.00 bar (P_1), and 25.25 L (V_1) expands into an evacuated chamber ($P_{ext} = 0$). The final volume was 50.50 L (V_2). Assume the neon behaves ideally. The entropy change (ΔS) for this process was 5.7632 J mol^{-1} K^{-1}. Determine the change in the Helmholtz free energy (ΔA), in joules per mole.

102. For an unknown gas at 298.15 K (T) and 1.00 bar (P_1), $\Delta G_f^\circ = -32.76$ kJ mol^{-1}. Calculate ΔG_f, in kilojoules per mole, at 7.50 bar (P_2).

103. The vapor pressure of supercooled water at 263 K (T) is 2.828×10^{-3} atm (P_2), and the vapor pressure of ice at the same temperature is 2.565×10^{-3} atm (P_1). Determine the ΔG_{fus}, in kilojoules per mole, for water at this temperature.

104. The standard heat of solution (ΔH) for sodium hydroxide dissolving in water is −45.8 kJ mol^{-1}. The standard Gibbs free energy of formation (ΔG_f°) of solid sodium hydroxide is −379.4 kJ mol^{-1}, and the value of the standard Gibbs free energy of formation (ΔG_f°) for aqueous sodium hydroxide is −419.1 kJ mol^{-1}. What is the entropy change (ΔS), in joules per mole, when sodium hydroxide dissolves in water at 298 K (T)?

105. The activity of 1.00 mol (n) of a substance changes from 4.31 (a_1) to 1.27 (a_2) at 298 K (T). What is the change in the Gibbs free energy (ΔG) in kilojoules per mole?

106. Determine the pressure (P) for an ideal gas for which $\Delta G - \Delta G^\circ = 2.482$ kJ mol^{-1}. Assume the temperature is 298.15 K (T).

107. A solution is 0.00100 m in potassium chloride and 0.00150 m in potassium sulfate. What is the ionic strength (I) of this solution? (The symbol "m" stands for molality.)

108. A solution is 0.00100 m in potassium chloride and 0.00150 m in potassium sulfate. The ionic strength of this solution is 0.00550 m. Assume the Debye–Hückel coefficient is 0.5116 for this solution. Calculate the activity coefficient (γ_{K^+}) for the potassium ion. (The symbol "m" stands for molality.)

109. One mole of water vapor undergoes a compression to liquid water at 373 K. At this temperature and 1.00 atm, the molar heat of vaporization ($\Delta\bar{H}$) of water is 40.69 kJ mol^{-1}. The work (w) for this process is −3.10 kJ mol^{-1}. The process is reversible, isothermal, and isobaric. What is the change in the molar internal energy ($\Delta\bar{E}$) for this process?

110. One mole of water vapor undergoes a compression to liquid water at 373 K (T). At this temperature and 1.00 atm, the molar heat of vaporization ($\Delta\bar{H}$) of water is 40.69 kJ mol^{-1}. The process is reversible, isothermal, and isobaric. What is the change in the molar entropy ($\Delta\bar{S}$) for this process?

111. Using fugacities, calculate the Gibbs free energy change (ΔG) for the compression of 1.00 mol (n) of ammonia gas, at 473 K (T), from 25 atm to 300 atm. The fugacity of ammonia at 25 atm (f_1) and 473 K is 23.9 atm, and the fugacity of ammonia at 300 atm and 473 K is 193 atm (f_2).

112. The standard enthalpy of formation ($\Delta H°$) of HBr(aq) is −121 kJ mol^{-1}. What is the standard enthalpy of formation of Br^-(aq)?

113. At 800 K (T), the molar volume ($\Delta\bar{V}$) of copper is 7.26×10^{-6} m^3 mol^{-1}, the coefficient of thermal expansion (α) for copper is 6.00×10^{-5} K^{-1}, and the coefficient of isothermal compression (κ) is 3.23×10^{-11} kg m s^{-1}. What is the heat capacity difference ($C_p - C_v$) for copper at 800 K?

CHAPTER 5

Chemical Equilibria

114. Write the general expression for the equilibrium constant (K) for the following reaction:

$$C(graphite) + 2\ N_2O(g) \leftrightarrows CO_2(g) + 2\ N_2(g)$$

115. The equilibrium constant for the following reaction is 0.335 at 1,000 K:

$$2\ SO_3(g) \leftrightarrows 2\ SO_2(g) + O_2(g)$$

What is the value of the equilibrium constant for the following reaction at the same temperature?

$$4\ SO_3(g) \leftrightarrows 4\ SO_2(g) + 2\ O_2(g)$$

116. The equilibrium constant for the following reaction is 0.335 at 1,000 K:

$$2\ SO_3(g) \leftrightarrows 2\ SO_2(g) + O_2(g)$$

What is the value of the equilibrium constant for the reverse reaction?

117. The equilibrium constant (K) for the following reaction is 0.335 at 1,000 K (T):

$$2\ SO_3(g) \leftrightarrows 2\ SO_2(g) + O_2(g)$$

What is the value of the standard Gibbs energy for the reaction?

118. The standard Gibbs free energy ($\Delta G_{rxn}°$) for the following equilibrium reaction is 2.6 kJ mol^{-1}:

$$H_2(g) + I_2(g) \leftrightarrows 2\ HI(g)$$

A gas mixture containing 2.00 bar of hydrogen gas (P_{H_2}), 2.00 bar of iodine vapor (P_{I_2}), and 0.500 bar of hydrogen iodide (P_{HI}) is in a sealed container at 398 K (T). Will more hydrogen iodide form?

119. The standard Gibbs free energy ($\Delta G_{rxn}°$) for the following equilibrium reaction is 2.6 kJ mol^{-1}:

$$H_2(g) + I_2(g) \leftrightarrows 2\,HI(g)$$

A gas mixture containing 0.500 bar of hydrogen gas (P_{H_2}), 0.500 bar of iodine vapor (P_{I_2}), and 2.00 bar of hydrogen iodide (P_{HI}) is in a sealed container at 398 K (T). Will more hydrogen iodide form?

120. Dinitrogen trioxide is an unstable compound that exists in equilibrium with nitrogen oxide and nitrogen dioxide. A 1.312-g sample (m) of dinitrogen trioxide quickly reaches an equilibrium pressure of 0.8885 bar (P) in an 0.7500-L (V) container at 298.15 K (T). What is the average molar mass at equilibrium?

121. Dinitrogen trioxide is an unstable compound that exists in equilibrium with nitrogen oxide and nitrogen dioxide. A 1.312-g sample of dinitrogen trioxide quickly reaches an equilibrium pressure of 0.8885 bar in an 0.7500-L container at 298.15 K. The average molar mass at equilibrium is 48.81 g mol^{-1} (M). What is the extent of reaction (ξ)?

122. Dinitrogen trioxide is an unstable compound that exists in equilibrium with nitrogen oxide and nitrogen dioxide. A 1.312-g sample of dinitrogen trioxide quickly reaches an equilibrium pressure of 0.8885 bar ($P_{N_2O_3}$) in an 0.7500-L container at 298.15 K. The extent of reaction (ξ) is 0.5573 at equilibrium. What is the value of K?

123. Dinitrogen trioxide is an unstable compound that exists in equilibrium with nitrogen oxide and nitrogen dioxide. Calculate K_p for this reaction at 298.15 K (T). The standard Gibbs energies of formation for these compounds, in kilojoules per mole, are $N_2O_3(g) = 139.3$, $NO(g) = 86.7$, and $NO_2(g) = 51.8$.

124. Dinitrogen trioxide is an unstable compound that exists in equilibrium with nitrogen oxide and nitrogen dioxide. The equilibrium constant, K_p, equals 0.7182 at 298.15 K. What is the value of K_c at this temperature?

125. The standard Gibbs energy ($\Delta G_{rxn}°$) change for the following reaction is 12.7 kJ mol^{-1} at 298 K (T):

$$C(graphite) + Cu_2O(s) \leftrightarrows CO(g) + 2\ Cu(s)$$

What is the value of K?

126. The following system is in equilibrium with all three components present:

$$2\ CO(g) \leftrightarrows C(graphite) + CO_2(g)$$

How many degrees of freedom are there?

127. The following system is in equilibrium with only CO and CO_2 present:

$$2\ CO(g) \leftrightarrows C(graphite) + CO_2(g)$$

How many degrees of freedom are there?

128. Carbon monoxide gas is introduced to a container containing an excess of sulfur. The initial pressure of the carbon monoxide is 2.000 atm. The system comes to equilibrium, and the total pressure is 1.030 atm. Determine the value of K_p for the following reaction at this temperature:

$$2\ CO(g) + S(s) \leftrightarrows 2\ C(s) + SO_2(g)$$

129. At elevated temperatures, it is possible to induce the following decomposition equilibrium:

$$2\ CrSO_4(s) \leftrightarrows Cr_2O_3(s) + SO_2(g) + SO_3(g)$$

In one experiment, after the establishment of equilibrium, the total pressure in the system was 1.20 atm. What is the value of K_p at this temperature?

130. At elevated temperatures, it is possible to induce the following decomposition equilibrium:

$$2\ CrSO_4(s) \leftrightarrows Cr_2O_3(s) + SO_2(g) + SO_3(g)$$

The value of K_p is 0.36 at a certain temperature. In one experiment, some solid chromium(II) sulfate was introduced to a container at temperature and with a partial pressure of sulfur trioxide of 1.00 atm. What are the partial pressures of each gas after the establishment of equilibrium?

131. The mole fraction of bromine is 0.0600 in a solution of bromine in carbon tetrachloride at 273 K. At this temperature, the vapor pressure of pure carbon tetrachloride is 33.9 torr, and the vapor pressure of pure bromine is 125 torr. The partial pressure of carbon tetrachloride above the solution is 33.3 torr, and the partial pressure of bromine is 7.90 torr. What are the activity coefficients of bromine and carbon tetrachloride?

132. The mole fraction of bromine is 0.0600 in a solution of bromine in carbon tetrachloride at 273 K. At this temperature, the activity coefficients for carbon tetrachloride and for bromine are 1.04 and 1.05, respectively. What are the activities of bromine and carbon tetrachloride?

133. At 1,000 K, the equilibrium constant for the following equilibrium is 3.76×10^{-5}:

$$I_2(g) \leftrightarrows 2\ I(g)$$

If the initial concentration of $I_2(g)$ is 0.500 M, what are the equilibrium concentrations of $I_2(g)$ and $I(g)$?

134. The standard Gibbs free energy change ($\Delta G°$) for the following process is -9.00 kJ mol^{-1}:

$$NaCl(s) \rightarrow Na^+(aq) + Cl^-(aq)$$

At 298 K (T), the solubility of sodium chloride is 15.0 M. Calculate the solubility product constant, K_{sp}, for NaCl.

135. The solubility product constant for sodium chloride is 37.8 at 298 K. At 298 K, the solubility of sodium chloride is 5.35 M. Calculate the mean ionic activity coefficient for NaCl.

136. A 1.00-L container initially contained 0.431 atm of $S_2(g)$ and 27.5 g of solid carbon. The system was at 500 K. The equilibrium partial pressure of $S_2(g)$ was 0.414 atm. What is the value of K_p at 500 K? The equilibrium was

$$C(gr) + S_2(g) \leftrightarrows CS_2(g)$$

137. For the following equilibrium, $K_p = 0.041$ at 500 K. What is the value of K_c?

$$C(gr) + S_2(g) \leftrightarrows CS_2(g)$$

138. At elevated temperatures, nitrogen and oxygen exist in equilibrium with nitrogen oxide. The equilibrium is

$$N_2(g) + O_2(g) \leftrightarrows 2\ NO(g)$$

At 1,900 K (T_1), the value of the equilibrium constant (K_1) is 2.31×10^{-4}, and the value of the equilibrium constant (K_2) is 6.86×10^{-4} at 2,100 K (T_2). Calculate the enthalpy change ($\Delta H°$) for the equilibrium.

139. At elevated temperatures, nitrogen and oxygen exist in equilibrium with nitrogen oxide. The equilibrium is

$$N_2(g) + O_2(g) \leftrightarrows 2\ NO(g)$$

At 1,900 K (T_1), the value of the equilibrium constant is 2.31×10^{-4} (K_1). The enthalpy change($\Delta H°$) for the equilibrium is 181 kJ mol^{-1}. What is the value of K_2 at 2,000 K (T_2)?

CHAPTER 6

Phase Equilibria

140. At 20°C, *n*-pentane has a vapor pressure of 0.573 bar (P_1^*) and *n*-hexane has a vapor pressure of 0.157 bar (P_2^*). Determine the equation for the bubble point line.

141. At 20°C, *n*-pentane has a vapor pressure of 0.573 bar (P_1^*) and *n*-hexane has a vapor pressure of 0.157 bar (P_2^*). Determine the equation for the dew point line.

142. At 20°C, *n*-pentane has a vapor pressure of 0.573 bar (P_1^*) and *n*-hexane has a vapor pressure of 0.157 bar (P_2^*). If the mole fraction of *n*-pentane in the solution is 0.550 (x_1), what are the partial pressures of *n*-pentane and *n*-hexane?

143. At 20°C, *n*-pentane has a vapor pressure of 0.573 bar (P_1^*) and *n*-hexane has a vapor pressure of 0.157 bar (P_2^*). If the mole fraction of *n*-pentane in the solution is 0.550 (x_1), what is the mole fraction (y_1) of *n*-pentane in the vapor?

144. At 20°C, *n*-pentane has a vapor pressure of 0.573 bar (P_1^*) and *n*-hexane has a vapor pressure of 0.157 bar (P_2^*). The mole fraction of *n*-pentane in the solution is 0.550 (x_1), the partial pressure (P_1) is 0.315 bar for *n*-pentane, and the partial pressure (P_2) is 0.0706 bar for *n*-hexane. Determine the activities of each component.

145. At 20°C, *n*-pentane has a vapor pressure of 0.573 bar (P_1^*) and *n*-hexane has a vapor pressure of 0.157 bar (P_2^*). A solution has a mole fraction of *n*-pentane of 0.550 (x_1) at 20°C. [This makes 0.450 the mole fraction (x_2) of *n*-hexane.] If the partial pressure of the *n*-pentane above this solution is 0.295 bar and the partial pressure of *n*-hexane is 0.0606 bar, what are the activity coefficients (γ_i) of *n*-pentane and *n*-hexane for the solution?

146. Calculate the change in the boiling point of ammonia, at the normal boiling point (239.82 K = T), per pascal change in the atmospheric pressure $\left(\frac{dP}{dT}\right)$. The molar heat of vaporization of ammonia at the normal boiling point is 23.33 kJ mol^{-1} (ΔH_{vap}). (The normal boiling point is the boiling point at 1.01235 bar.) The molar volume of liquid ammonia is 0.02495 L mol^{-1} ($\bar{V}_l$) and the molar volume of ammonia gas at the boiling point is 19.79 L mol^{-1} ($\bar{V}_g$).

147. Determine the change in pressure necessary to change the freezing point of ammonia by 1°C $\left(\frac{dP}{dT}\right)$. The molar heat of fusion of ammonia at the normal boiling point is 5.66 kJ mol^{-1} (ΔH_{fus}). The freezing point of ammonia is 195.42 K (T). This problem requires the reciprocal of the densities, which for liquid ammonia is 0.02498 L mol^{-1} ($\bar{V}_l$) and for solid ammonia is 0.02082 L mol^{-1} ($\bar{V}_s$).

148. The freezing point of liquid ammonia is 195.42 K (T_{fus}) and the enthalpy of fusion ($\Delta H_{fus}°$) is 5.66 kJ mol^{-1}. Determine the value of the freezing point constant (K_f) for liquid ammonia.

149. Determine the vapor pressure of hydrazine (N_2H_4) at 298.15 K (T).

150. The Henry's law constant (K_i) for oxygen gas dissolving in water at 25°C is 4.40 × 10^4 bar. At this temperature, the density of water is 997.05 g L^{-1}. If the partial pressure of oxygen over the water is 1.00 bar (P_i), what is the concentration of oxygen in the solution in moles per liter?

151. The osmotic pressure (∏) of a solution containing 11.0 g of polystyrene per liter of benzene is 1018 Pa at 298 K. Assuming the solution is ideal, what is the average molar mass of the polystyrene?

152. It is possible to purify water through a process known as reverse osmosis. Reverse osmosis requires the application of a pressure greater than the osmotic pressure (∏) to force pure liquid through a semipermeable membrane. Assuming seawater in the Persian Gulf is approximately 1 M and at a temperature (T) of about 300 K, what is the minimum pressure required to force reverse osmosis?

153. Reverse osmosis requires the application of a pressure greater than the osmotic pressure (∏) to force pure liquid through a semipermeable membrane. The osmotic pressure of seawater in the Persian Gulf is approximately 25 atm. How much work (w) is necessary to isolate 1 mol of pure water?

154. A solution of 4.00 g of a carbohydrate in 0.275 L (V) of solution has an osmotic pressure (Π) of 0.0132 atm at 298 K (T). What is the molar mass of the carbohydrate?

155. A solution, at 298 K, contains 1.263 mol of ethanol ($n_{C_2H_5OH}$) in 1.737 mol of water (n_{H_2O}). The volume (V) of the solution is 102.20 mL. If the molar volume of water ($\overline{V}_{H_2O}$) at this temperature is 16.98 mL mol^{-1}, what is the molar volume of ethanol ($\overline{V}_{C_2H_5OH}$)?

156. Calculate the vapor pressure of an aqueous solution where the mole fraction of a nonvolatile solute is 0.0300 and the temperature is 35°C. The vapor pressure of pure water at 35°C is 42.2 torr.

157. At 373 K (T) and 1.00 atm, the molar volume of water vapor ($\overline{V}_g$) is 30.20 L and the molar volume of liquid water ($\overline{V}_l$) is 0.0188 L. The molar heat of vaporization ($\Delta\overline{H}_{vap}$) of water is 40.69 kJ mol^{-1}. What is the change in the boiling point of water per change in the pressure (dT/dP)?

158. At 1.00 atm, the boiling point of n-octane is 399 K. At the boiling point, the molar heat of vaporization ($\Delta\overline{H}_{vap}$) of n-octane is 3.498×10^4 J mol^{-1}. Estimate the vapor pressure of n-octane at 375 K.

159. Determine the mole fraction of benzene (X_B) in a benzene–toluene mixture that boils at 363 K and 1.00 atm (P_{soln}). At 363 K, the vapor pressure of pure benzene ($P°_B$) is 1.34 atm and the vapor pressure of pure toluene ($P°_T$) is 0.534 atm.

160. It requires 53.2 s (Δt_{20}) for ethanol, at 20°C, to flow through an Ostwald viscometer. At 40°C, it requires 36.8 s (Δt_{40}) for the same quantity of ethanol to flow through the viscometer. The viscosity of ethanol (η_{20}) at 20°C is 1.200×10^{-3} Pa s. What is the viscosity of ethanol (η_{40}) at 40°C? The density of ethanol at 20°C (ρ_{20}) is 0.789 g cm^{-3} and the density (ρ_{40}) at 40°C is 0.772 g cm^{-3}.

161. A sample of 40.0 g of a nonelectrolyte in 0.100 kg of water has a freezing point (T_f) of −3.50°C. The freezing point depression constant (K_f) is 1.86°C/m for water. What is the molar mass of the solute?

162. The boiling point elevation, ΔT, of an 0.630 m KCl solution in water is 0.60°C. The boiling point elevation constant, K_b, for water is 0.52°C/m. What is the value of the van't Hoff factor, i, for this solution?

163. The melting point of pure silver is 1,235 K (T°) and the heat of fusion, ΔH_{fus}, is 11.3 kJ mol^{-1}. What is the melting point (T_m) of a copper–silver alloy with a mole fraction (x) of 0.950 silver?

164. A mixture of methylene chloride and water will separate into two layers. Each layer is a saturated solution. Determine the values of c, p, and f for the system.

165. Boron nitride (BN) has two crystalline modifications. One form has the diamond structure with a density of 3.45 g cm^{-3}, and the other form has the graphite structure with a density of 2.10 g cm^{-3}. It is possible to convert the graphite form to the diamond form through the application of pressure. The standard Gibbs energy change for this process is −2.900 kJ mol^{-1} at P_1 = 1.00 bar. Assuming the densities are independent of pressure, calculate the equilibrium pressure (P_2) for this conversion at 298.15 K (T).

166. There are two allotropes of tin. These allotropes are gray tin (α) and white tin (β). Heating of gray tin above 286.4 K and 1.00 bar (P) leads to its conversion to white tin. The heat of transition (ΔH) is 2.238×10^3 J mol^{-1}, and the molar volumes ($\bar{V}$) of gray tin and white tin are 2.06×10^{-5} m^3 and 1.62×10^{-5} m^3, respectively. What is the work (w) done when 1.00 mol (n) of tin undergoes this phase transition from gray to white at 286.4 K and 1.00 bar?

167. There are two allotropes of tin. These allotropes are gray tin (α) and white tin (β). Heating of gray tin above 286.4 K and 1.00 bar leads to its conversion to white tin. The heat of transition (ΔH) is 2.238×10^3 J mol^{-1}, and the molar volumes ($\bar{V}$) of gray tin and white tin are 2.06×10^{-5} m^3 and 1.62×10^{-5} m^3, respectively. The work (w) done when 1.00 mol (n) of tin undergoes this phase transition from gray to white at 286.4 K and 1.00 bar is 0.440 J. What is the change in the internal energy (ΔE) of the system for this transition?

168. There are two allotropes of tin. These allotropes are gray tin (α) and white tin (β). Heating of gray tin above 286.4 K (T) and 1.00 bar leads to its conversion to white tin. The heat of transition (ΔH) is 2.238×10^3 J mol^{-1}, and the molar volumes ($\bar{V}$) of gray tin and white tin are 2.06×10^{-5} m^3 and 1.62×10^{-5} m^3, respectively. What is the change in the entropy (ΔS) of the system for this transition?

169. There are two allotropes of tin. These allotropes are gray tin (α) and white tin (β). Heating of gray tin above 286.4 K (T) and 1.00 bar leads to its conversion to white tin. The heat of transition (ΔH) is 2.238×10^3 J mol^{-1}, and the molar volumes ($\bar{V}$) of gray tin and white tin are 2.06×10^{-5} m^3 and 1.62×10^{-5} m^3, respectively. What is the change in the Gibbs free energy (ΔG) of the system for this transition?

Electrochemical Equilibria

170. What is the cell reaction for the following voltaic (galvanic) cell?

$$Cu(s) \mid Cu^{2+}(aq) \parallel Fe^{3+}(aq), Fe^{2+}(aq) \mid Pt(s)$$

171. Determine the standard electromotive force for the following galvanic cell reaction.

$$Cu(s) + 2\ Fe^{3+}(aq) \rightarrow 2\ Fe^{2+}(aq) + Cu^{2+}(aq)$$

172. The standard electromotive force ($E°$) for the following galvanic cell reaction is 0.434 V. Determine the value of the equilibrium constant (K) for this process at 25°C.

$$Cu(s) + 2\ Fe^{3+}(aq) \rightarrow 2\ Fe^{2+}(aq) + Cu^{2+}(aq)$$

173. The standard electromotive force for the following galvanic cell reaction is 0.434 V. Write the equilibrium constant (K) expression for this process at 25°C.

$$Cu(s) + 2\ Fe^{3+}(aq) \rightarrow 2\ Fe^{2+}(aq) + Cu^{2+}(aq)$$

174. Determine the cell potential, at 298 K, for the following reaction if the copper ion concentration is 0.100 M, the iron(II) concentration is 0.150 M, and the iron(III) concentration is 0.225 M.

$$Cu(s) + 2\ Fe^{3+}(aq) \rightarrow 2\ Fe^{2+}(aq) + Cu^{2+}(aq)$$

The standard cell potential is $E° = +0.434$ V.

175. The following cell reaction occurs under standard conditions.

$$Cu^{2+}(aq) + Zn(s) \rightarrow Cu(s) + Zn^{2+}(aq)$$

The standard Gibbs free energies of formation for the ions are 65.5 kJ mol^{-1} for Cu^{2+}(aq) and −147.0 kJ mol^{-1} for Zn^{2+}(aq). What is the standard cell potential for this reaction?

176. How much copper will deposit on the cathode if a current of 25.0 A passes through the cell for 1,275 s? The cell reaction is

$$Cu^{2+}(aq) + Zn(s) \rightarrow Cu(s) + Zn^{2+}(aq)$$

177. A Galvanic cell contains half-cells involving the following two half-reactions.

$$Cr_2O_7^{2-}(aq) + 14\ H^+(aq) + 6\ e^- \rightarrow 2\ Cr^{3+} + 7\ H_2O(l) \qquad E° = +1.33\ V$$

$$Fe^{3+}(aq) + e^- \rightarrow Fe^{2+}(aq) \qquad E° = +0.77\ V$$

Assuming the half-cells are under standard conditions, what is the cell potential in volts?

178. The standard Gibbs free energy change for the following half-reaction is $\Delta G° = -65.49$ kJ mol^{-1}. Determine the standard electrode potential (E°) for this half-reaction.

$$Cu^{2+}(aq) + 2\ e^- \rightarrow Cu(s)$$

179. The electrolysis of a solution of copper(II) sulfate led to the deposition of 0.1872 g of copper on the cathode. How much electric charge passed through the solution? The half-reaction was

$$Cu^{2+}(aq) + 2\ e^- \rightarrow Cu(s)$$

180. The cell potential (E) for the following process is 0.6753 V at 298 K.

$$2\ AgCl(s) + Cd(s) + 2.5\ H_2O(l) \rightarrow 2\ Ag(s) + CdCl_2{\bullet}2.5H_2O(s)$$

Determine the change in the Gibbs free energy (ΔG) for this process.

181. The cell potential (E) for the following process is 0.6753 V at 298 K.

$$2\ AgCl(s) + Cd(s) + 2.5\ H_2O(l) \rightarrow 2\ Ag(s) + CdCl_2{\bullet}2.5H_2O(s)$$

The temperature coefficient for this process $\left(\frac{\partial E}{\partial T}\right)_P$ is -6.50×10^{-4} V K^{-1}. What is the value of ΔS?

182. The cell potential (E) for the following process is 0.6753 V at 298 K.

$$2\ AgCl(s) + Cd(s) + 2.5\ H_2O(l) \rightarrow 2\ Ag(s) + CdCl_2{\bullet}2.5H_2O(s)$$

The change in the Gibbs free energy (ΔG) for this process is -1.303×10^5 J, and $\Delta S = -125$ J K^{-1}. What is the value of ΔH for this cell?

183. The solubility of silver chromate is 8.00×10^{-5} M at 298 K. What is the value of the solubility product constant (K_{sp}) at this temperature? The K_{sp} equilibrium is

$$Ag_2CrO_4(s) \leftrightarrows 2\ Ag^+(aq) + CrO_4^{2-}(aq)$$

184. The K_{sp} of silver chromate is 2.05×10^{-12} at 298 K. The solubility of silver chromate in 0.040 M sodium nitrate is 8.84×10^{-5} M, which is slightly greater than the solubility of silver chromate in pure water (8.00×10^{-5} M). What is the value of the mean ionic activity ($\gamma_\pm$) of silver chromate in 0.040 M sodium nitrate?

185. The standard cell potential (E°) at 298 K (T) for the following reaction is 0.0373 V.

$$Fe(s) + Cd^{2+}(aq) \rightarrow Fe^{2+}(aq) + Cd(s)$$

If the activity (a_{Cd}) of the Cd^{2+} is exactly 1, what is the maximum activity (a_{Fe}) of the Fe^{2+} that will have a positive E_{cell}?

186. A galvanic cell has a standard electromotive force (E°) of 0.015 V at 25°C. Assuming the charge number ($|\nu_e|$) for the reaction is unity, determine the value of the equilibrium constant.

187. Calculate γ_+ and γ_- for an 0.00150 m potassium chloride solution (I). Use the Debye–Hückel theory. Assume the Debye–Hückel constant (A) is 0.509 at 25°C.

188. Calculate $\gamma_\pm$ for an 0.00150 m potassium chloride solution (I). Use the Debye–Hückel theory. Assume the Debye–Hückel constant (A) is 0.509 at 25°C.

189. Calculate the activity (a_{KCl}) for an 0.00150 m potassium chloride solution. The value of $\gamma_\pm$ is 0.956 for this solution.

190. Using the Gibbs energy of formation and the enthalpy of formation, determine the standard molar entropy of the bromide ion in an aqueous solution at 298.15 K.

191. The specific conductance (κ) of a cell is 0.00277 mho cm^{-1} and the cell has a resistance (R) of 82.4 Ω. What is the value of the cell constant (k)?

192. Determine the specific conductance, κ, of an 0.0075 M KCl solution with a conductance, L, of 1.49×10^{-3} mho if the cell constant is 115 m^{-1}.

193. Determine the molar conductance (Λ) of an 0.0075 M KCl solution with a specific conductance (κ) of 0.171 mho m^{-1}.

194. The molar conductance at infinite dilution, $\lambda°$, for the potassium ion is 7.35×10^{-3} mho m^2 mol^{-1}. What is the ionic mobility, u, of the potassium ion at infinite dilution?

195. The molar conductance, Λ, of a dilute HCl solution is 4.00×10^{-2} mho m^2 mol^{-1}, and the transport number, t_H, for the hydrogen ion is 0.830 at this concentration. What is the ionic molar conductance, λ_H, for the hydrogen ion in this solution?

196. The K_{sp} of barium sulfate is 1.1×10^{-10}. At 298 K, the ionic conductances of the barium and sulfate ions at infinite dilution are 1.27×10^{-2} mho m^2 mol^{-1} and 1.60×10^{-2} mho m^2 mol^{-1}, respectively. What is the specific conductance, κ, of barium sulfate?

197. What is the limiting diffusion coefficient (D_0) for sodium iodide at 298 K (T)? The ion mobilities (μ) for the sodium ion and iodide ion are 5.20×10^{-4} cm^2 V^{-1} s^{-1} and 7.96×10^{-4} cm^2 V^{-1} s^{-1}, respectively.

198. Determine the ionic strength (I) of a 1.00×10^{-6} m solution of $Cr_2(SO_4)_3$.

199. For a particular cell, the variation of the cell potential with temperature at constant pressure, $\left(\frac{\partial E^\circ}{\partial T}\right)_p$, is -1.37×10^{-3} V K^{-1} at 298 K. What is the entropy change ($\Delta S°$) for the cell reaction if the number of moles of electrons transferred (n) is 2?

200. For a particular cell, the variation of the cell potential with temperature at constant pressure, $\left(\frac{\partial E^\circ}{\partial T}\right)_p$, is -1.37×10^{-3} V K^{-1} at 298 K (T). The standard cell potential ($E°$) for the cell is 1.25 V. What is the enthalpy change ($\Delta H°$) for the cell reaction if the number of moles of electrons transferred (n) is 2?

PART 2

Quantum Mechanics

CHAPTER 8

Quantum Theory

201. What is the frequency (ν) of light with a wavelength (λ) of 375 nm?

202. What is the energy (E) of a photon with a wavelength (λ) of 675 nm?

203. What is the energy (E) of a photon with a frequency (ν) of 7.99×10^{14} s^{-1}?

204. What is the uncertainty in the momentum (Δp_x) of an electron if the uncertainty in its position (Δx) is 75 pm?

205. Determine the uncertainty in the velocity (Δv_x) of an electron ($m = 9.109 \times 10^{-31}$ kg) if the uncertainty in its momentum (Δp_x) is 7.0×10^{-25} kg m s^{-1}.

206. What is the energy (E) for an electron in its ground state ($n = 1$) and in a potential well with a width of 15 pm (a)?

207. The molar mass of carbon-13 (m_1) is 13.00335×10^{-3} kg mol^{-1}, and the molar mass of oxygen-16 (m_2) is 15.99491×10^{-3} kg mol^{-1}. Determine the reduced mass (μ) for $^{13}C^{16}O$.

208. The reduced mass (μ) for $^{13}C^{16}O$ is 1.191×10^{-26} kg and the fundamental vibration is 2122 cm^{-1}. What is the force constant (k) for the vibration?

209. The reduced mass (μ) for $^{13}C^{16}O$ is 1.191×10^{-26} kg, and the equilibrium bond length (R_e) is 113 pm. What is the moment of inertia (I) for this molecule?

210. Assuming the force constant (k) for $^{14}C^{18}O$ is the same as for $^{13}C^{16}O$ ($k = 1.903 \times 10^3$ kg s^{-2}), predict the fundamental vibrational frequency ($\tilde{\nu}$) for $^{14}C^{18}O$. The reduced mass (μ) of $^{14}C^{18}O$ is 1.3078×10^{-26} kg.

211. What is the de Broglie wavelength of an alpha particle traveling at 675 m s^{-1}? The mass of an alpha particle is 6.65×10^{-27} kg.

212. The work function (Φ) for cesium is 1.95 eV. If light with a wavelength (λ) of 525 nm strikes the surface of a sample of cesium metal, what is the kinetic energy (E) of the photoemitted electron?

213. The work function (Φ) for cesium is 1.95 eV. What is the minimum frequency (ν) of light required to cause photoemission of an electron?

214. The work function (Φ) for cesium is 1.95 eV. What is the maximum wavelength (λ) of light required to cause photoemission of an electron?

215. The work function (Φ) for cesium is 1.95 eV. If light with a wavelength (λ) of 525 nm strikes the surface of a sample of cesium metal, the kinetic energy (E) of the photoemitted electron is 6.60×10^{-20} J. What is the velocity (v) of the emitted electron?

216. Electron diffraction is a useful method to study the structures of materials. The process involves high-velocity electrons. These electrons, according to the de Broglie relation, have a short wavelength. Crystal lattices will diffract electrons waves. At what angle (θ) will the first-order (n) diffraction of electrons, with a wavelength (λ) of 0.155 nm, occur in a crystal with an inner planar spacing (d) of 1.25 nm?

217. What is the energy (E) of an electron accelerated by a potential difference (ϕ) of 10^4 V?

218. What is the momentum (p) of a photon with a wavelength (λ) of 675 pm?

219. A 675-pm photon with a momentum (p) of 9.82×10^{-25} kg m s^{-1} strikes a helium atom. What is the velocity (v) of the helium atom after absorbing this photon?

220. Calculate the quantum number (n) for a neon atom ($m = 3.35 \times 10^{-26}$ kg) in a one-dimensional box with an energy (E) of 6.25×10^{-21} J. Assume the length of the box (a) is 1.00×10^{-8} m.

221. The surface temperature (T) of a certain star is 3,250 K. Use the Wien displacement law to calculate the center of the emission distribution of wavelengths (λ_{max}).

222. The peak in the emission distribution of wavelengths (λ_{max}) is 4.000×10^{-7} m. Use the Wien displacement law to calculate the temperature (T) of the star.

223. What is the eigenvalue (E) of the inversion operator on the p-orbital function?

224. Determine the eigenvalue for the function $\psi = ce^{ax}$, where a is a constant. Assume ψ is an eigenfunction of d/dx.

225. Assume that the basis set consists of two orthonormal functions (Ω_1 and Ω_2) with $H_{11} = -5.0$ eV, $H_{22} = -0.50$ eV, and $H_{12} = H_{21} = -3.0$ eV. What is the secular determinant for this system?

CHAPTER 9

Atomic Structure

226. What are the electron configurations of Fe, Fe^{2+}, and Fe^{3+}?

227. The electron configuration of magnesium is [Ne]$3s^2$. What are the quantum numbers for the $3s^2$ electrons?

228. What are the values of L for two electrons in the 3p orbitals?

229. What are the values of S for two electrons in the 3p orbitals?

230. What is the orbital angular momentum (L) for a 4f electron?

231. What are the components of the angular momentum vector in the z direction (L_z) for a 4f electron?

232. The term symbol for a particular energy level is ^3F. What are the values of L and S for this energy level?

233. Determine the atomic term symbol for a p^6 configuration.

234. The excitation of potassium electrons in a burner flame emits light with a frequency (ν) of $7.41 \times 10^{14}\ s^{-1}$. What is the wavelength (λ) of this light?

235. The excitation of potassium electrons in a burner flame emits light with a frequency (ν) of $7.41 \times 10^{14}\ s^{-1}$. What is the energy ($E$) of a photon of this light?

236. Sodium vapor emits radiation with a wavelength (λ) of 5.89×10^{-7} m. What is the energy (E) of a photon of this light?

237. Calculate the Hartree energy (E_h) using the relationship $E_h = \frac{e^2}{4\pi\epsilon_0 a_0}$.

238. Calculate the Hartree energy (E_h) using the relationship $E_h = \frac{\hbar^2}{m_e a_0^2}$.

239. Calculate the Hartree energy (E_h) using the relationship $E_h = \frac{m_e e^4}{(4\pi\epsilon_0)^2 \hbar^2}$.

240. Determine the value of the Bohr radius (a_0).

241. Determine the value of the Bohr magneton (μ_B).

242. What are allowed energies (E) of a 4f electron placed in a magnetic field of 1 tesla (T)?

243. The Rydberg equation allows the calculation of the frequency (ν) of light associated with an electronic transition for a hydrogen-like atom. The Rydberg equation is $\nu = R\left(\frac{1}{n_1^2} - \frac{1}{n_2^2}\right)$, where R is the Rydberg constant (3.29×10^{15} s^{-1}), and n_1 and n_2 are the initial and final energy levels, respectively. For the Balmer series, n_1 is equal to 2. What is the frequency of light in the Balmer series corresponding to the removal of an electron ($n_2 = \infty$)?

244. What is the ionization energy (E) of atomic hydrogen?

245. The ionization energy (E) for a hydrogen atom is 2.18×10^{-16} J. At what temperature (T) is the translational kinetic energy of a hydrogen atom equal to the ionization energy?

246. What is the velocity of an electron in a ground-state hydrogen atom?

247. Determine the de Broglie wavelength (λ) of an electron in a ground-state hydrogen atom. The velocity (v) of the electron is 2.187692×10^6 m s^{-1}.

248. The wavelength of an electron in a ground-state hydrogen atom is 3.324918×10^{-10} m. The electron in a ground-state hydrogen atom is in an orbital with a radius equal to the Bohr radius ($5.2917726 \times 10^{-11}$ m). Compare the circumference of the orbital to the wavelength of the electron.

249. What is the reduced mass (μ) of a hydrogen atom?

250. What is the energy (E) of the third ($n = 3$) Bohr orbit of hydrogen?

251. What is the position of the node in the 2s wave function for a hydrogen atom?

252. The average distance (r) from the nucleus for an electron in a hydrogen atom is 5.29×10^{-11} m. Determine the potential energy (E_p) of the electron at this distance.

253. The diameter of a typical atom is about 1×10^{-10} m. What is the lowest energy ($n = 1$) of an electron in a potential well of this size?

254. What is the product of a wave function and its complex conjugate ($\psi^*\psi$) for $\psi = (\sin\theta - i\cos\theta)$?

CHAPTER 10

Molecular Structure

255. Draw the Lewis structure of all resonance forms of the carbonate ion.

256. Write the molecular orbital designation for N_2.

257. Write the molecular orbital designation for N_2^+.

258. Write the molecular orbital designation for N_2^-.

259. The molecular orbital designation for N_2 is $\sigma_{1s}{}^2\ \sigma_{1s}{}^{*2}\ \sigma_{2s}{}^2\ \sigma_{2s}{}^{*2}\ \pi_{2p}{}^2\ \pi_{2p}{}^2\ \sigma_{2p}{}^2$. What is the bond order?

260. The molecular orbital designation for N_2^+ is $\sigma_g(1s)^2\ \sigma_u{}^*(1s)^2\ \sigma_g(2s)^2\ \sigma_u{}^*(2s)^2\ \pi_u\ (2p)^2\ \pi_u(2p)^2\ \sigma_g(2p)^1$. What is the bond order?

261. The molecular orbital designation for N_2^- is $\sigma_{1s}{}^2\ \sigma_{1s}{}^{*2}\ \sigma_{2s}{}^2\ \sigma_{2s}{}^{*2}\ \pi_{2p}{}^2\ \pi_{2p}{}^2\ \sigma_{2p}{}^2\ \pi_{2p}{}^{*1}$. What is the bond order?

262. How many electrons are involved in the sigma and pi bonding orbitals in pyridine?

263. The dipole moment (μ) of NO is 5.08×10^{-31} C m and the bond length (R) is 1.13×10^{-10} m. What is the fractional charge (q) on the nitrogen and oxygen atoms?

264. The dipole moment (μ) of gaseous LiF is 2.01×10^{-29} C m and the bond length (R) is 1.55×10^{-10} m. Assuming the two atoms have unit charges, the dipole moment should be 2.48×10^{-29} C m. What is the percent ionic character of the bond?

265. The internuclear distance (r) for LiF in the gas phase is 1.55×10^{-10} m. What is the dipole moment (μ) of LiF assuming that the charges are equal in magnitude to the charge in a proton ($Q = 1.602 \times 10^{-19}$ C) and opposite in sign?

266. The chromium(V) ion is an unstable intermediate in oxidation–reduction reactions involving chromium(III) and chromium(VI). This ion has one unpaired electron. What is the contribution of the spin of this electron to the magnetic moment (μ) of this ion?

267. The chromium(V) ion is an unstable intermediate in oxidation–reduction reactions involving chromium(III) and chromium(VI). This ion has one unpaired electron. What is the contribution of the spin of this electron to the molar magnetic susceptibility (x_m) of this ion at 298 K?

268. An oxygen molecule is confined in an 0.500-m potential well. Determine the lowest energy state ($n = 1$) of the system.

269. What is the average quantum number (n) of an oxygen molecule confined in an 0.500-m potential well? Assume the average energy of an oxygen molecule is 1.694×10^{-21} J.

270. The moment of inertia (I) for a carbon dioxide molecule is 6.65×10^{-46} kg m^2. If the energy (E) of the molecule is 2.06×10^{-21} J, what is the value of the rotational quantum number (J)?

271. What is the energy (E_n) of the third quantum level ($n = 3$) for a conjugated system of 16 carbon atoms in a chain? There are eight double bonds in a system that is about 1.9×10^{-9} m in length (a).

CHAPTER 11

Molecular Symmetry

It will help to have a model kit to do some of these problems. Use of gumdrops and toothpicks will work in a pinch.

Numerous flowcharts are available to assign a point group. Choose any of these to assign the point group.

272. What symmetry operations are present in the letter A?

273. It is possible to achieve certain symmetry operations in more than one way. What symmetry operations are unique to a C_8 axis?

274. Show the effect of a σ_{xy} on a point represented by a column vector (x, y, z).

275. Show the effect of a center of inversion (i) on a point represented by a column vector (x, y, z).

276. What is the general matrix representation of a proper axis along the z axis [$C(z)$]?

277. What is the general matrix representation of an improper axis along the z axis [$S(z)$]?

278. Using matrix representations, determine the result of a σ_{xz} followed by a σ_{yz}.

279. The symmetry elements for the group C_{2v} are E, C_2, $\sigma_v(xz)$, and $\sigma_v'(yz)$. Construct a multiplication table for the C_{2v} group.

280. What symmetry elements are in *cis*-1,2-dibromoethene?

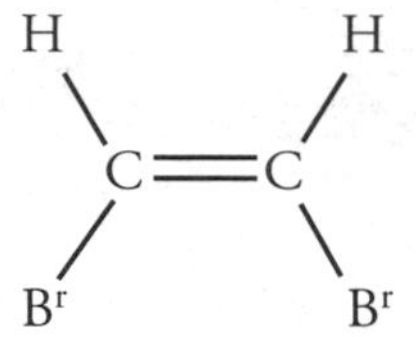

281. Is 1,3,5-triphenyl benzene optically active? The molecule is nonplanar with the phenyl groups rotated out of the plane by equal amounts and in the same direction.

282. Determine the point group of ClF_3.

283. The C_{2v} point group contains the symmetry operations E, C_2, σ_v, and σ_v'. Show that this set indeed forms a group.

284. The water molecule has three vibrational modes. The modes are the symmetric stretch, the asymmetric stretch, and bending (scissoring). What is the point group symmetry of each of these modes?

285. There are three isomers of difluoroethene. The isomers and their point groups are 1,1-difluoroethene (C_{2v}), *cis*-1,2-difluoroethene (C_{2v}), and *trans*-1,2-difluoroethene (C_{2h}). Which isomer(s) does not have a dipole moment?

CHAPTER 12

Rotational and Vibrational Spectra

286. Determine the energy (E) of a photon of infrared radiation with a wavelength (λ) of 5.00×10^{-6} m.

287. Determine the energy (E) per mole of photons of infrared radiation with a wavelength (λ) of 5.00×10^{-6} m.

288. The energy difference between two different vibrational states (ΔE) is 4.21×10^{-20} J. What is the vibrational frequency (ν) relating these two states?

289. Photochemical reactions may require an activation energy (E_a) of 5.5×10^4 J mol^{-1}. What is the wavelength (λ) of a photon with this energy?

290. Photochemical reactions may require an activation energy (E_a) of 5.5×10^4 J mol^{-1}. The wavelength (λ) is 2.2×10^{-6} m. What is the energy in terms of wavenumbers ($\tilde{\nu}$)?

291. Photochemical reactions may require an activation energy (E_a) of 5.5×10^4 J mol^{-1}. The wavelength (λ) is 2.2×10^{-6} m. What is the energy in terms of electronvolts?

292. Determine the wavenumber ($\tilde{\nu}$) that corresponds to the thermal energy (kT) at 298 K (T).

293. How many degrees of freedom are in dinitrogen oxide, N_2O?

294. How many degrees of freedom are in nitrogen dioxide, NO_2?

295. How many normal modes of vibration are there for pyridine, C_5H_5N?

296. The fundamental vibrational frequency ($\overline{\nu}$) for $^{1}H^{35}Cl$ is 2,990 cm^{-1}, and the anharmonicity correction ($x\overline{\nu}$) is 52.1 cm^{-1}. What is the dissociation energy (D) of $^{1}H^{35}Cl$?

297. Determine the reduced mass (μ) of a $^{2}H^{37}Cl$ molecule. The atomic weights of hydrogen-2 and chlorine-37 are 2.0140 and 36.947 g mol^{-1}, respectively.

298. The reduced mass (μ) of the $^{2}H^{37}Cl$ molecule is 3.1715×10^{-24} g, and the bond length (r) is 1.275×10^{-10} m. What is the moment of inertia (I) for a $^{2}H^{37}Cl$ molecule?

299. The moment of inertia (I) for a $^{2}H^{37}Cl$ molecule is 5.156×10^{-47} kg m^2. Determine the wavelengths for the $J = 0$ to $J = 1$ and the $J = 1$ to $J = 2$ transition.

300. Calculate the force constant (k) for a $^{2}H^{37}Cl$ molecule. For this molecule, the reduced mass (μ) is 3.1715×10^{-27} kg, and the fundamental vibration frequency (ν_0) is 6.198×10^{13} s^{-1}.

301. The microwave rotational spectrum of $^{2}H^{37}Cl$ gave ($\overline{B}$) = 1.6277×10^{11} s^{-1}. For this molecule, the reduced mass (μ) is 3.1715×10^{-27} kg. Determine the bond length (r).

302. The spectrum of $^{2}H^{37}Cl$ consists of a series of equally spaced lines, which lead to a moment of inertia (I) of 5.156×10^{-47} kg m^2. Calculate the bond length (R). The reduced mass (μ) of $^{2}H^{37}Cl$ is 3.1715×10^{-27} kg.

303. The moment of inertia (I) for a $^{2}H^{37}Cl$ molecule is 5.156×10^{-47} kg m^2. Determine the wavenumber ($\tilde{\nu}$) for the $J = 0$ to $J = 1$ transition.

304. The spectrum of $D^{35}Cl$ consists of a series of equally spaced lines with ($\Delta\tilde{\nu}$) = 10.89 cm^{-1}. Calculate the moment of inertia (I).

305. The bond angle in a hydrogen sulfide molecule is 92.1°, and the H–S bond lengths (r) are 1.366×10^{-10} m. Where is the center of mass of a hydrogen sulfide molecule?

306. The bond angle in a hydrogen sulfide molecule is 92.1°, and the H–S bond lengths (r) are 1.366 Å. The sulfur atom is at $x = -0.0883$ Å, $y = 0$, and $z = 0$ relative to the center of mass. What are the coordinates of the hydrogen atoms?

307. The bond angle in a hydrogen sulfide molecule is 92.1°, and the H–S bond lengths (r) are 1.366 Å. The sulfur atom is at $x = -0.0883$ Å, $y = 0$, and $z = 0$ relative to the center of mass, and the hydrogen atoms are located at $x = 1.37$ Å, $y = 0.983$ Å, and $z = 0$ and at $x = 1.37$ Å, $y = -0.983$ Å, and $z = 0$. What are the moments of inertia for hydrogen sulfide?

308. The energy (E) of a photon is $E = \hbar c / \lambda$, and the energy of a molecular quantum state, in a Boltzmann distribution, is the energy divided by kT. What is the temperature (T) in which kT is equal to the energy of a photon with a wavelength (λ) equal to 9.95×10^{-7} m?

309. Which of the following species will have a pure microwave absorption spectrum? F_2, HF, CF_4, $CH_3CH_2CH_2CH_3$, $CH_3CHOHCH_3$, NH_3, BF_3, C_6H_5F.

CHAPTER 13

Electronic Spectra

310. The spectroscopic dissociation energy (D) of $^{79}Br_2$ is 3.157×10^{-19} J. What wavelength (λ) is necessary to dissociate a molecule of $^{79}Br_2$ and impart each atom with a kinetic energy of 1.330×10^{-19} J?

311. A laser emits a 5-fs pulse. What is the frequency distribution width?

312. A 5-W laser emits a 5-fs pulse at a rate of 2×10^7 pulses per second with a wavelength of 725 nm. What is the radiant energy in each pulse?

313. A 5-W laser emits pulses with a wavelength of 725 nm. The energy of each pulse is 5×10^{-7} J. Calculate the number of photons per pulse in each pulse.

314. What is the absorbance (A) of a solution of vitamin D_2, which has a percent transmittance (I) of 32% at a wavelength of 264 nm?

315. What is the molar absorption coefficient (ε) of a 1.25×10^{-3} M solution if the observed absorbance (A) in a 1.00-cm cell is 0.49 at 264 nm?

316. A 0.15 M (C) solution of a dye in a 1.0-cm (l) cell transmits 75% (I) of the incident radiation with a wavelength of 455.2 nm. What is the extinction coefficient (ε) for this dye at this wavelength?

317. The extinction coefficient (ε) for a certain dye is 0.83 M^{-1} cm^{-1} for radiation with a wavelength of 455.2 nm. If a solution in a 1.0-cm (l) cell transmits 35% (I) of the incident radiation, what is the concentration (C) of the dye in the solution?

318. The extinction coefficient (ε) for a certain dye is 0.83 M^{-1} cm^{-1} for radiation with a wavelength of 455.2 nm. If a solution in a 1.0-cm (l) cell has a concentration of 0.35 M (C), what percent (I) of the incident radiation is transmitted?

319. The molar absorption coefficient (ε) for a sample is 5.2×10^4 L mol^{-1} cm^{-1}. What is the absorption cross section (σ)?

320. The maximum molar absorption coefficient (ε_{max}) for a sample is 5.2×10^4 L mol^{-1} cm^{-1} at 28,000 cm^{-1}. If the bandwidth at half maximum ($\Delta\tilde{\nu}_{1/2}$) is 3,500 cm^{-1} and the band is Gaussian, what is the integrated absorption coefficient?

321. What is the lowest absorption frequency ($\tilde{\nu}$) for a conjugated system of 16 carbon atoms in a chain? There are eight double bonds (N) in a system that is about 1.9×10^{-9} m in length (a).

322. The work necessary to separate the nuclei to infinite distance (D') is greater than the spectroscopic dissociation energy by the zero point energy. Determine the value of D', in kJ mol^{-1}, for HCl given that D is 4.430 eV and the fundamental vibration frequency (ν_0) is 8.964×10^{13} s^{-1}.

323. Collisions with other molecules can deactivate vibrationally excited states. The deactivation leads to a broadening of the vibrational lines ($\Delta\bar{\nu}$) in the spectra. Calculate the broadening of the vibrational lines if 10^{12} collisions deactivate an excited state molecule each second (Δt).

324. What is the line width ($\Delta\bar{\nu}$) for an electronic excited state if the lifetime (Δt) is 2×10^{-6} s?

325. What is the line width ($\Delta\bar{\nu}$) for an electronic excited state if the lifetime (Δt) is 2×10^{6} s?

326. The first ionization potential for radon gas is 10.746 eV (1.7215×10^{-18} J). If photons with an energy of 4.000×10^{-17} J bombard a sample of radon gas, what will be the kinetic energy of the emitted electrons?

327. The first ionization potential for radon gas is 10.746 eV (1.7215×10^{-18} J). If photons with an energy of 4.000×10^{-17} J bombard a sample of radon gas, the emitted electrons have a kinetic energy (E) of 3.827×10^{-17} J. What is the velocity (v) of the emitted electrons?

328. A sample of xenon gas is bombarded by photons with an energy of 4.000×10^{-18} J. The photoelectron spectrum produced contains electrons traveling at a velocity (v) of 1.00×10^6 m s^{-1}. What was the binding energy of these electrons?

329. The specific rotation ($[\alpha]_D$) for α-D-galactose is +150.7° and the specific rotation of β-D-galactose is +52.8°. If either pure α-D-galactose or pure β-D-galactose is dissolved in water, mutarotation occurs and the resultant equilibrium mixture has a specific rotation of +80.2°. What is the percentage of β-D-galactose in the equilibrium mixture?

CHAPTER 14

Magnetic Resonance Spectra

330. A 500-MHz proton NMR signal is at 3,200 Hz relative to TMS (tetramethylsilane). What is the chemical shift?

331. Calculate the value of the nuclear magneton (μ_N).

332. Calculate the magnetogyric (γ) ratio for hydrogen.

333. The magnetogyric ratio (γ) for hydrogen is $2.675 \times 10^8\ T^{-1}\ s^{-1}$. What magnetic field strength (B) is necessary for hydrogen in a sample to absorb radiation at a frequency (ν) of 250 MHz?

334. The magnetogyric ratio (γ) for hydrogen is $2.675 \times 10^8\ T^{-1}\ s^{-1}$. What is the Larmor frequency (ν_L) of a hydrogen atom in a magnetic field (B) of 5.0 T?

335. The magnetogyric ratio (γ) for fluorine is $2.518 \times 10^8\ T^{-1}\ s^{-1}$. If the magnetic field strength (B) in the NMR is 6.0 T, at what frequency (ν), in megahertz, will the fluorine absorb the radiation?

336. The magnetic transition frequency (ν) for a hydrogen atom in an NMR spectrometer is 250 MHz ($2.5 \times 10^8\ s^{-1}$). What is the corresponding energy (E) in kilojoules per mole?

337. In proton NMR, the hydrogen nuclei can be in one of two states. Calculate the ratio of hydrogen nuclei in the lower state (N_1) to the hydrogen nuclei in the higher state (N_2). Assume that the field strength (B) is 5.9 T at 298 K (T).

338. In proton NMR, the hydrogen nuclei can be in one of two states. Calculate the ratio of hydrogen nuclei in the lower state (N_1) to the hydrogen nuclei in the higher state (N_2). Assume that this is a very-low-temperature experiment where the field strength (B) is 5.9 T at 1.0 K (T).

339. The nuclear spin (I) of boron-11 is 3/2. What are the energies (E) of the nuclear spin states for a boron-11 atom in a field of 6.5 T (B)?

340. The nuclear g factor (g_N) for boron-11 is 1.792 and its nuclear spin (I) is 3/2. At what frequency (ν_{NMR}) will the boron signal appear in an NMR instrument with a magnet rated at 5.5 T (B)?

341. The g value for a radical trapped in a matrix is 2.0088 when the field is aligned along the principal molecular symmetry axis. What magnetic field strength (B) is necessary to observe an ESR (Electron Spin Resonance) signal using a frequency (ν_{ESR}) of 9.42 GHz (9.42×10^9 s^{-1}) from a microwave generator?

342. What magnetic field strength (B) is necessary for an electron in a sample to absorb radiation at a frequency (ν) of 1.0×10^4 MHz?

343. What is the Larmor frequency (ν_L) of an electron in a magnetic field (B) of 5.0 T?

CHAPTER 15

Statistical Mechanics

344. Two containers of equal volume are connected. If there are four molecules in the system, what is the probability (P) of all the molecules being in one of the containers?

345. What is the symmetry number (σ) for $CHCl_3$?

346. What is the symmetry number (σ) for methane?

347. A system contains two identical particles and 50 quantum states. Assuming the particles are localized, how many microstates are there in the system?

348. What is the entropy change ($\Delta S°$) for the cooling of argon gas from 315 K (T_1) to 273 K (T_2)?

349. What is the approximate value of $\Delta S°$ for the following reaction?

$$^{79}Br^{79}Br(g) + {}^{81}Br^{81}Br(g) \rightarrow 2\ {}^{79}Br^{81}Br(g)$$

Assume that the differences in the vibrational energy levels, molar masses, and moments of inertia are negligible.

350. A system has two energy states separated by 3.0×10^{-23} J ($\varepsilon_i - \varepsilon_j$). The higher energy state (i) contains 45% of the particles. What is the temperature (T) of the system?

351. In general, the difference in energies ($\varepsilon_i - \varepsilon_j$) for translational energy states is about 10^{-42} J. What is the population distribution $\left(\frac{N_i}{N_j}\right)$ between the states for $T = 298$ K?

352. In general, the difference in energies ($\varepsilon_i - \varepsilon_j$) for rotational energy states is about 10^{-23} J. What is the population distribution $\left(\frac{N_i}{N_j}\right)$ between the states for $T = 298$ K?

353. In general, the difference in energies ($\varepsilon_i - \varepsilon_j$) for vibrational energy states is about 10^{-20} J. What is the population distribution $\left(\frac{N_i}{N_j}\right)$ between the states for $T = 298$ K?

354. In general, the difference in energies ($\varepsilon_i - \varepsilon_j$) for two energy states is about 1.42×10^{-21} J. The higher energy state (N_i) is a singlet state and the other state is a triplet. What is the population distribution $\left(\frac{N_i}{N_j}\right)$ between the states for $T = 175$ K?

355. The standard molar volume ($\overline{V}$) of an ideal gas at 298 K is 22.79 L mol^{-1}. Assuming that oxygen is an ideal gas, determine the value for the molecular partition function (q_{trans}).

356. Determine the value of the molecular rotational partition function (q_{rot}) for $H^{35}Cl$ gas at 298 K. The moment of inertia (I) for $H^{35}Cl$ is 2.644×10^{-47} kg m^2; assume the symmetry number (σ) is 2.

357. What is the translational contribution to the molar heat capacity at constant pressure $\left(\overline{C}_P^\circ\right)_t$ for argon?

358. What is the translational contribution to the molar entropy ($\overline{S}^\circ$) for argon at 298 K (T) and 1.00 bar (P)? The mass of an argon atom (m) is 6.634×10^{-26} kg.

359. What is the translational contribution to the molar Gibbs free energy $(\overline{G}^\circ)_t$ for argon at 298 K (T) and 1.00 bar (P)? The mass of an argon atom (m) is 6.634×10^{-26} kg.

360. What is the characteristic vibrational temperature (Θ_v) of nitrogen? The vibrational frequency ($\overline{\nu}$) of a nitrogen molecule is 2,358 cm^{-1}.

361. What is the vibrational contribution to the molar heat capacity at constant temperature $\left(\overline{C}_P^\circ\right)$? The characteristic vibrational temperature (Θ_v) of nitrogen is 3,392 K, and T is 298 K.

362. What is the vibrational contribution to the molar entropy $(\overline{S}^\circ)_v$? The characteristic vibrational temperature (Θ_v) of nitrogen is 3,392 K, and T is 298 K.

363. What is the vibrational contribution to the molar enthalpy $(\bar{H}°)_v$? The characteristic vibrational temperature (Θ_v) of nitrogen is 3,392 K, and T is 298 K.

364. What is the vibrational contribution to the molar Gibbs free energy $(\bar{G}°)_v$? The characteristic vibrational temperature (Θ_v) of nitrogen is 3,392 K, and T is 298 K.

365. What is the characteristic rotational temperature (Θ_r) for $^{35}Cl_2$? The moment of inertia (I) for $^{35}Cl_2$ is 1.148×10^{-45} kg m^2.

366. Determine the value of the molecular partition function (q_r) for the rotation of $^{35}Cl_2$ at 2,000 K (T). The characteristic rotational temperature (Θ_r) for $^{35}Cl_2$ is 0.3507 K.

367. What is the rotational contribution to the molar entropy $(\bar{S}°)_r$ for $^{35}Cl_2$ at 298 K (T)? The characteristic rotational temperature (Θ_r) for $^{35}Cl_2$ is 0.3507 K, and the symmetry number (σ) is 2.

368. What is the rotational contribution to the molar enthalpy $(\bar{H}°)_r$ for $^{35}Cl_2$ at 298 K (T)?

369. What is the rotational contribution to the molar Gibbs free energy $(\bar{G}°)_r$ for $^{35}Cl_2$ at 298 K (T)? The characteristic rotational temperature (Θ_r) for $^{35}Cl_2$ is 0.3507 K, and the symmetry number (σ) is 2.

370. What is the absolute molar entropy ($\bar{S}$) of helium gas at 298 K (T) and 1.00 atm? Assume that helium behaves ideally, with a mass (m) of each atom being 6.6465×10^{-27} kg and molar volume ($\bar{V}$) of 0.02445 m^3.

371. The three principal moments of inertia (I_x, I_y, and I_z) for ozone are 7.88×10^{-47} kg m^2, 6.29×10^{-46} kg m^2, and 7.09×10^{-46} kg m^2. What is the value of the molecular rotational partition function (q_{rot}) for ozone at 298 K (T)? The symmetry number (σ) for ozone is 2.

372. The Einstein characteristic temperature (θ_E) for silver is 161 K. What is the value of ($A_T° - E_0°$) for silver at 298 K (T)?

373. The Debye characteristic temperature (θ_D) for silver is 208 K. What is the value of ($A_T° - E_0°$) for silver at 298 K (T)?

CHAPTER 16

Molecular Interactions

374. The iodine–fluorine bond length (r) is 1.91×10^{-10} m in IF. What is the dipole moment (μ) in debyes? Assume the molecule consists of two ions with univalent charges.

375. The dipole moment of IF is 1.948 D (μ_{obs}). The predicted dipole moment for purely ionic IF is 9.17 D ($\mu_{predicted}$). What is the percent ionic character of IF?

376. The electronegativity difference ($EN_F - EN_I$) is 1.32 in IF. What is the percent ionic character of IF?

377. The dipole moment of IF is 1.948 D (μ_{obs}). The predicted dipole moment for purely ionic IF is 9.17 D ($\mu_{predicted}$), which makes the bond 21.2% ionic. What are the net charges at the atomic centers of IF?

378. The bond in ClF is 11% ionic, and the molecule has a dipole moment (μ_{obs}) of 0.888 D. What is the bond length (r) in ClF?

379. A krypton atom approaches to 3.5×10^{-10} m (r) from a univalent positive ion. What is the electric field (E) generated by the ion?

380. The polarizability (α) of krypton is 2.48×10^{-30} m^3. What is the induced dipole moment (μ_{ind}) produced when a krypton atom comes within 3.5×10^{-10} m of a univalent positive ion? The induced field (E) of this univalent ion at this distance is 1.18×10^{10} V m^{-1}.

381. What is the ion-induced dipole energy ($E_{i\text{-}id}$) for the interaction of a krypton atom with a univalent positive ion? Assume the krypton atom and the ion approach to within 3.5×10^{-10} m of each other, which leads to an induced dipole moment (μ_{ind}) of 1.76 D and an electrostatic field (E) of 1.18×10^{10} V m^{-1}.

382. What is the interaction energy ($E_{\text{d-id}}$) for the interaction of a polar molecule with a krypton atom? Assume the atom and the polar molecule approach to within 3.5×10^{-10} m (r) of each other and that the dipole moment (μ) of the molecule is 1.2 D. The polarizability (α) of krypton is 2.48×10^{-30} m^3.

383. The ionization energy (I) of krypton is 2.24×10^{-18} J, the polarizability (α) of krypton is 2.48×10^{-30} m^3, and the van der Waals radius of a krypton atom is 2.02×10^{-10} m. What is the London dispersion interaction energy (E_{disp}) between two krypton atoms in contact?

384. The relative permittivity (ε_r) of carbon disulfide is 2.6, and its density (ρ) is 126.32 kg m^{-3}. What is the polarizability (α) of carbon disulfide?

385. Two molecules of a polar molecule come into contact. When the molecules are in contact, their centers (r) are 3.7×10^{-10} m apart. What is the value of the dipole moment (μ) that gives an interaction energy (E_{dd}) equal to 3.77×10^{-21} J (kT at 273 K)?

PART 3

Kinetics

CHAPTER 17

Kinetic Theory of Gases

386. What is the mean relative speed (v_{rs}) of hydrogen molecules relative to chlorine molecules at 298 K? The masses of the molecules are 3.35×10^{-27} kg for H_2 (m_1) and 1.18×10^{-22} kg for Cl_2 (m_2).

387. What is the most probable speed (v_{mp}) for oxygen gas at 298 K?

388. What is the mean speed (v_{ms}) for oxygen gas at 298 K?

389. What is the root-mean-square speed (v_{rms}) for oxygen gas at 298 K?

390. The root mean square velocity (v) of oxygen gas at 298 K (T) is 482 m s^{-1}. Calculate the fraction (F) of oxygen molecules with velocities within 5 m s^{-1} of this velocity. Assume that F is independent of v in this small interval.

391. The root-mean-square velocity (v) of oxygen gas at 298 K and 1.00 atm is 482 m s^{-1} and the mean free path (λ) is 7.10×10^{-8} m. Calculate the average time (Δt) between collisions.

392. Determine the probability [$f(v_x)$] at 225 m s^{-1} for the x (v_x) component of the velocity of an oxygen molecule at 298 K (T).

393. If the probability [$f(v_x)$] for oxygen gas is 1.03×10^{-3} s m^{-1} at 298 K, what fraction of the molecules has velocities (v) between 225.0 and 225.5 m s^{-1}?

394. The thermal conductivity (κ) for nitrogen at 298 K is 0.0261 J m^{-1} s^{-1} K^{-1}, and the mean speed (v_{ms}) at this temperature is 475 m s^{-1}. What is the collision cross section (d) for nitrogen gas?

395. The viscosity (η) of xenon gas at 273 K is 2.10×10^{-5} kg m^{-1} s^{-1}, and the mean speed (v_{ms}) at this temperature is 210 m s^{-1}. What is the collision cross section (d) for xenon?

396. The viscosity (η) of xenon gas at 273 K (T) is 2.10×10^{-5} kg m^{-1} s^{-1}. What is the collision cross section (d) for xenon? The mass (m) of a xenon atom is 2.18×10^{-25} kg.

397. At 298 K, the mean speed (v_{ms}) of a methane molecule is 628 m s^{-1}, the collision diameter (d) is 4.09×10^{-10} m, and the number density (ρ) is 2.43×10^{25} m^{-3}. What is the collision frequency (z)?

398. At 298 K, the mean speed (v_{ms}) of a methane molecule is 628 m s^{-1}, the collision diameter (d) is 4.09×10^{-10} m, and the number density (ρ) is 2.43×10^{25} m^{-3}. What is the collision density (Z)?

399. The collision diameter (d) of methane is 4.09×10^{-10} m, and the number density (ρ) is 2.43×10^{25} m^{-3} at 1.00 bar and 298 K. What is the mean free path (λ) in meters at 1.00 bar?

400. Assuming methane molecules are hard spheres with a molecular diameter (d) of 4.09×10^{-10} m, calculate the viscosity (η) at 298 K (T) and 1.00 bar. The mass (m) of a methane molecule is 2.66×10^{-26} kg.

401. The collision diameter of methane is 4.09×10^{-10} m. What multiple of the collision diameter is the separation between the molecules at 1.00 atm and 273 K? Assume that the separation is equal to the edge of a cube containing one molecule.

402. The density of intergalactic space is estimated to be as low as one hydrogen atom per cubic meter at 2.7 K (T). What is the pressure (P) in pascals?

403. The density of intergalactic space is estimated to be as low as one hydrogen atom per cubic meter at 2.7 K (T). What is the mean speed (v_{ms}) of the hydrogen atom?

404. The density of intergalactic space is estimated to be as low as one hydrogen atom per cubic meter at 2.7 K (T). Under these conditions, the mean speed (v_{ms}) of a hydrogen atom is 2×10^{2} m s^{-1}. What is the collision frequency (z)? Assume the collision diameter (d) of a hydrogen atom is 1×10^{-10} m.

405. The density of intergalactic space is estimated to be as low as one hydrogen atom per cubic meter at 2.7 K (T). Under these conditions, the mean speed (v_{ms}) of a hydrogen atom is 2×10^2 m s^{-1}. What is the mean free path (λ) in meters at this pressure? Assume the collision diameter (d) of a hydrogen atom is 1×10^{-10} m.

406. At 700.0 K (T), the activation energy for the second-order decomposition of hydrogen iodide gas is 191 kJ mol^{-1}. What is the threshold energy (E_0) for this reaction?

407. At 700.0 K (T), the activation energy for the second-order decomposition of hydrogen iodide gas is 191 kJ mol^{-1}. The rate constant (k) for this reaction is 2.6×10^{-4} M^{-1} s^{-1}. The threshold energy (E_0) is 1.88×10^5 J mol^{-1}. Assuming the orientation factor (P) is equal to one and the collision diameter (σ) is 3.5×10^{-10} m, what is the second rate constant for this reaction as predicted from collision theory?

408. The two different heat capacities for sulfur hexafluoride are $C_p = 97$ J mol^{-1} K^{-1} and $C_v = 85.2$ J mol^{-1} K^{-1}. Use these heat capacities to calculate the speed of sound (v_s) in sulfur hexafluoride at 298 K (T).

409. It is possible to determine the vapor pressure of a solid using a Knudsen cell. In one experiment, the area (A) of the effusion hole was 7.9×10^{-6} m^2, which allowed 2.85×10^{-5} kg (Δw) of aluminum vapor to effuse through in 3,600 s (t). The temperature was 1,460 K. What was the flux (J_N) for the aluminum vapor?

410. It is possible to determine the vapor pressure of a solid using a Knudsen cell. In one experiment, the area of the effusion hole was 7.9×10^{-6} m^2, which allowed 2.85×10^{-5} kg of aluminum vapor to effuse through in 3,600 s. The temperature (T) was 1,460 K. The flux (J_N) for the aluminum vapor was 2.2×10^{22} m^{-2} s^{-1}. What was the vapor pressure (P_{vap}) of aluminum?

CHAPTER 18

The Rates of Chemical Reactions

411. What is the general form of the rate law of an *n*-order reaction for a one-reactant system?

412. What is the general form for the extent of a reaction ($d\xi$)? Assume n_i is the moles of reactant or product and x_i is the coefficient of the reactant or product.

413. What is the general form for the rate of a reaction? Assume n_i is the moles of reactant or product and x_i is the coefficient of the reactant or product.

414. Solid iodine and hydrogen gas are sealed in an 0.500-L container and allowed to react. In one experiment, 0.010 mol of iodine reacted in 0.20 s. What was the rate of conversion for iodine ($d\xi/dt$)?

415. Iodine vapor and hydrogen gas are sealed in an 0.500-L (V) container and allowed to react. In one experiment, 0.010 mol of iodine ($d\xi$) reacted in 0.20 s (dt). The rate of conversion for iodine ($d\xi/dt$) is 0.050 mol I_2 s^{-1}. What is the rate of the reaction with respect to iodine ($d[I_2]/dt$)?

416. Iodine vapor and hydrogen gas are sealed in an 0.500-L (V) container and allowed to react. In one experiment, 0.010 mol of iodine reacted in 0.20 s. The rate of reaction for iodine ($d[I_2]/dt$) is –0.10 mol I_2 L^{-1} s^{-1}. What are the rates of the reaction with respect to hydrogen ($d[H_2]/dt$) and hydrogen iodide ($d[HI]/dt$)? The reaction is

$$H_2(g) + I_2(g) \rightarrow 2\ HI(g)$$

417. The reaction for the Haber–Bosch process for the preparation of ammonia is

$$N_2(g) + 3\ H_2(g) \rightarrow 2\ NH_3(g)$$

How do the rates of reaction for the different substances compare?

418. For the reaction A → 2 B, the rate constant for the formation of B (k_f) is 2.4×10^{-1} s^{-1} at 298 K. Determine the value of for the reverse reaction (k_r) if the equilibrium constant (K_c) for the reaction is 1.8×10^{-3} at the same temperature.

419. What is the second-order rate constant (k) at 298 K (T) for the "simple" collision of two radicals? Assume the collision diameter (d_{12}) is 5.25×10^{-10} m and the reduced mass (μ) is 5.30×10^{-26} kg.

420. The rate constant (k) for a particular first-order reaction is 25.0 s^{-1}. If the initial concentration of single reactant ($[A]_0$) is 1.00 M, what will be the concentration ($[A]_t$) after 0.0125 s (t)?

421. The rate constant (k) for a particular second-order reaction is 25.0 M^{-1} s^{-1}. If the initial concentration of single reactant ($[A]_0$) is 1.00 M, what will be the concentration ($[A]_t$) after 0.0125 s (t)?

422. The rate constant (k) for a particular zero-order reaction is 25.0 M s^{-1}. If the initial concentration of single reactant ($[A]_0$) is 1.00 M, what will be the concentration ($[A]_t$) after 0.0125 s (t)?

423. The rate constant (k) for a particular first-order reaction is 25.0 s^{-1}. If the initial concentration of single reactant ($[A]_0$) is 1.00 M, what is the half-life ($t_{1/2}$)?

424. The rate constant (k) for a particular second-order reaction is 25.0 M^{-1} s^{-1}. If the initial concentration of single reactant ($[A]_0$) is 1.00 M, what is the half-life ($t_{1/2}$)?

425. The rate constant (k) for a particular zero-order reaction is 25.0 M s^{-1}. If the initial concentration of single reactant ($[A]_0$) is 1.00 M, what is the half-life ($t_{1/2}$)?

426. The activation for a particular reaction is 75 kJ mol^{-1}, and the enthalpy change for the reaction is −25 kJ mol^{-1}. What is the activation energy of the reverse reaction?

427. The rate law for the formation of NOCl(g) from NO(g) and Cl_2(g) at 273 K is

$$\text{Rate} = k[\text{NO}]^2\,[\text{Cl}_2]$$

where k is the rate constant (5.7 $M^{-2}\ s^{-1}$) and the square brackets refer to the molar concentrations. What is the initial rate of the reaction if the initial concentration of NO(g) is 0.50 M and the initial concentration of Cl_2(g) is 0.75 M?

428. What is the second-order rate constant (k) for a diffusion-controlled reaction? Assume the reaction radius (R_{12}) is 5.0×10^{-10} m, and the diffusion coefficients for each of the uncharged reacting species (D_1 and D_2) are $4.9 \times 10^{-9}\ m^2\ s^{-1}$.

429. At 273 K (T), the viscosity (η) of chloroform, $CHCl_3$, is 7.00×10^{-4} kg $m^{-1}\ s^{-1}$. What is the rate constant (k) of a diffusion-controlled reaction in chloroform?

430. The reaction A(g) + B(g) → C(g) is known to be first order in both reactants with a rate constant (k) equal to $1.76 \times 10^{10}\ M^{-1}\ s^{-1}$. Assuming the reaction is diffusion controlled and that the diffusion coefficients (D) for both A and B are $2.72 \times 10^{-9}\ m^2\ s^{-1}$, what is the reaction radius (R^*)?

431. The reaction A(g) + B(g) → C(g) is known to be first order in both reactants. At 298 K, the rate (R) of the reaction is 2.75 M s^{-1} when each of the reactant concentrations is 1.25×10^{-5} M. What is the value of the rate constant (k)?

432. The activation energy (E_a) for the reaction A(g) + B(g) → C(g) is 23.7 kJ mol^{-1} at 425 K (T). What is the enthalpy of activation ($\Delta H^\ddagger$) for the reaction?

433. The carbon-14 decay rate for a fossil bone from an Irish elk was 4.00×10^5 disintegrations per gram C per year (4.00×10^5 dis $g^{-1}\ y^{-1}$) in comparison with 8.05×10^6 dis $g^{-1}\ y^{-1}$ for a currently living organism. The radioactive decay constant (k) for carbon-14 is $1.21 \times 10^{-4}\ y^{-1}$. What is the age of the bone?

CHAPTER 19

The Kinetics of Complex Reactions

434. The half-life ($t_{1/2}$) for the radioactive decay of thorium-232 to radium-228 is 1.41×10^{10} y. What is the decay constant (k) for this process?

435. The half-life ($t_{1/2}$) for the radioactive decay of thorium-232 to radium-228 is 1.41×10^{10} y. The half-life ($t_{1/2}$) for the radioactive decay of radium-228 to actinium-228 is 5.75 y. The decay constants are 4.92×10^{-11} y^{-1} for thorium (k_{Th}) and 0.121 y^{-1} for radium (k_{Ra}). Starting with pure thorium-232, what will be the fraction (F) of radium-228 after 3.0 y (t)?

436. The base hydrolysis of ethyl acetate is first order in base (B) and first order in ethyl acetate (A). In a particular experiment, the initial concentration of base (B_0) was 0.00980 M, and the initial concentration of ethyl acetate (A_0) was 0.00486 M. During the experiment, the concentrations of the two reactants and the time were monitored. A plot of $\ln \frac{AB_0}{A_0B}$ versus time (t) was constructed. The plot was linear with a slope of -5.27×10^{-4} s^{-1}. What was the value of the rate constant (k)?

437. Gaseous hydrogen iodide decomposes to the elements when heated. The reaction is second order. The activation energy (E_a) for the reaction is 1.91×10^5 J mol^{-1}, the collision diameter (σ) is 3.5×10^{-10} m, and the molar mass (M) of HI is 127.9 g mol^{-1}. Assume that the orientation factor (ρ) is 1. Calculate the value of the rate constant (k) at 667 K (T).

438. The reversible reaction $H_2(g) + Ar(g) \leftrightarrows 2\,H(g) + Ar(g)$ has a forward rate constant (k_1) of 2.2×10^4 L mol^{-1} s^{-1} and an equilibrium constant (K) of 1.0×10^{-4} at 3,000 K. What is the value of the rate constant for the reverse reaction (k_{-1})?

439. A sample of pure water at 298 K, in a conductivity cell, is suddenly heated by a microwave pulse. The relaxation time (τ) to return to equilibrium is 3.6×10^{-5} s. Determine the rate constant for the forward reaction (k_1) and the rate constant for the reverse reaction (k_{-1}). The ratio of the rate constants (k_1/k_{-1}) is 1.8×10^{-16} M at this temperature. The rates are for the following equilibrium.

$$H_2O(l) \leftrightharpoons H^+(aq) + OH^-(aq)$$

440. A certain reaction has a rate constant (k_1) of 1.07×10^{-3} s^{-1} at 427 K (T_1) and a rate constant (k_2) of 1.08×10^{-4} s^{-1} at 402 K (T_2). What is the activation energy (E_a) for this reaction?

441. Determine the activation energy (E_a) from the data in the following table of temperature and rate constants.

T (K)	427	417	409	407	399
k (s^{-1})	0.00108	0.000410	0.000208	0.00016	0.0000763

442. Many enzyme reactions are diffusion controlled. Assuming this is true, estimate the rate constant (k). Assume the encounter frequencies (D) for the enzyme (E) and substrate (S) are 0.29×10^{-6} cm^2 s^{-1} and 6.73×10^{-6} cm^2 s^{-1}, respectively, the reaction radius (r_{ES}) is 5×10^{-10} m, and that the activation energy (E_a) is 0.

443. The general form of the Arrhenius equation is $k = Ae^{-E_a/RT}$, where E_a is the activation energy, A is the pre-exponential factor, R is the gas constant, and T is the temperature. What is the pre-exponential factor for a reaction with $k = 4.62 \times 10^{-7}$ s^{-1} at 344 K? Assume the activation energy is 129 kJ mol^{-1}.

444. Assuming that the enthalpy of activation ($\Delta H^\ddagger$) is approximately equal to the activation energy (E_a), determine the entropy of activation ($\Delta S^\ddagger$) for a reaction with a pre-exponential factor (A) of 1.79×10^{13} s^{-1} at 344 K (T).

445. A Lineweaver–Burk plot gives a linear graph with the slope equal to 75.5 s and an intercept of 1.18×10^{-2} M^{-1} s. Determine the value of the maximum rate (V_{max}).

446. A Lineweaver–Burk plot gives a linear graph with the slope equal to 75.5 s and the maximum rate (V_{max}) equal to 84.7 M s^{-1}. Determine the value of the Michaelis constant (K_M).

447. An Eadie–Hofstee plot gives a linear graph with the slope equal to -6.52×10^3 M and an intercept of 8.56×10^{-5} M s^{-1}. Determine the value of the maximum rate (V_{max}).

448. An Eadie–Hofstee plot gives a linear graph with the slope equal to -6.52×10^{-3} M and an intercept of 8.56×10^{-5} M s^{-1}. Determine the value of the Michaelis constant (K_M).

449. In enzyme kinetics, the turnover number (k_3) is the number of substrate molecules converted per unit time by a single enzyme molecule. The turnover number for a certain enzyme is 3.7×10^5 s^{-1} at 310 K. The molar mass of this enzyme is 52,000 g mol^{-1}. What is the rate of the reaction if 0.050 g of this enzyme is added to an excess of substrate?

450. In general, there is an assumption that a 10°C increase in the temperature will double the rate of a reaction. Test this assumption using a rate constant (k_2) of 1.0×10^{-3} s^{-1} at 427 K (T_2) to find the rate constant (k_1) at 437 K (T_1). Assume the activation energy (E_a) for this reaction is 1.0×10^5 J mol^{-1}.

451. In a basic solution, hypochlorite ion will oxidize iodide ion to hypoiodite ion with the hypochlorite ion being reduced to chloride ion. The reaction is

$$I^-(aq) + ClO^-(aq) \xrightarrow{[OH]^-} IO^-(aq) + Cl^-(aq)$$

The following data were obtained at a certain temperature.

	Initial Concentration			Initial Rate of
Experiment	$[I^-]$	$[ClO^-]$	$[OH^-]$	IO^- Formation
	(M)	(M)	(M)	(M/s)
1	0.0020	0.010	0.10	1.2×10^{-2}
2	0.0020	0.020	0.10	2.4×10^{-2}
3	0.0020	0.010	0.20	6.0×10^{-3}
4	0.0020	0.020	0.20	1.2×10^{-2}
5	0.0040	0.020	0.20	2.4×10^{-2}

What is the rate law for this reaction?

452. In a basic solution, hypochlorite ion will oxidize iodide ion to hypoiodite ion with the hypochlorite ion reducing to chloride ion. The reaction is

$$I^-(aq) + ClO^-(aq) \xrightarrow{[OH]^-} IO^-(aq) + Cl^-(aq)$$

The rate law is

$$\text{Rate} = k[I^-][ClO^-][OH^-]^{-1}$$

What is the value of the rate constant if $[I^-] = 0.0020$ M, $[ClO^-] = 0.010$ M, $[OH^-] = 0.10$ M, and the initial rate of IO^- formation is 1.2×10^{-2} M s^{-1}?

453. A certain first-order reaction has an activation energy (E_a) of 8.0×10^4 J mol^{-1} and a pre-exponential factor (A) of 3.0×10^{12} s^{-1}. What temperature (T) is necessary for the reaction to have a half-life ($t_{1/2}$) of 1.0 h (3,600 s)?

PART 4

Other Topics

CHAPTER 20

Macromolecules

It may be necessary to convert the units given to the units used in the following problems or to convert the units in the answers from these problems to the units required to answer the problems. There is less consistency in the notation on this topic in physical chemistry than that in the notation on other topics.

454. It is possible to form a condensation polymer from the monomer $H_2N-(CH_2)_3COOH$. Calculate the mole fraction (X) of a polymer consisting of 25 monomer units (i) if the fraction of monomers (p) is 0.90.

455. It is possible to form a condensation polymer from the monomer $H_2N-(CH_2)_3COOH$. Calculate the weight fraction (w) of a polymer consisting of 25 monomer units (i) if the fraction of monomers (p) is 0.90 and the mole fraction (X) is 0.099.

456. An amino acid, H_2NCH_2COOH, undergoes polymerization to form a polymer with a number-average molar mass ($\bar{M}_n$) of 6.30×10^3 g mol^{-1}. What is the extent of reaction (p)?

457. An amino acid, H_2NCH_2COOH, undergoes polymerization to form a polymer with a number-average molar mass ($\bar{M}_n$) of 6.30×10^3 g mol^{-1}. If the extent of the reaction (p) is 0.991, what is the degree of polymerization ($\bar{X}_n$)?

458. An amino acid, H_2NCH_2COOH, undergoes polymerization to form a polymer with a number-average molar mass ($\bar{M}_n$) of 6.30×10^3 g mol^{-1}. If the extent of the reaction (p) is 0.991, what is the mass average molar mass ($\bar{M}_m$)?

459. Determine the root-mean-square end-to-end distance $[(\overline{r}^2)^{1/2}]$ for Teflon $[-(CF_2)_n-]$ using the freely jointed chain model where the molar mass (M) is 2.0×10^5 g mol^{-1}. The carbon–carbon bond length (l) is 156 pm.

460. Determine the root-mean-square end-to-end distance $[(\overline{r}^2)^{1/2}]$ for Teflon $[-(CF_2)_n-]$ using the freely rotating chain model where the molar mass (M) is 2.0×10^5 g mol^{-1}. The carbon–carbon bond length is 156 pm.

461. The intrinsic viscosity (η) of one form of myoglobin is 1,250 cm^3 g^{-1}. The molar mass of this form of myoglobin is 1.50×10^6 g mol^{-1}. What concentration (c) of myoglobin in water is required to give a relative viscosity (η/η_0) of 1.050?

462. Determine the molar mass (M) of a sample of myoglobin in an aqueous solution at 298 K (T), where the density of water (ρ) is 9.968×10^2 kg m^{-3}. For myoglobin, the partial specific volume (ν) is 7.49×10^{-4} kg^{-1} m^3, the diffusion coefficient (D) is 1.25×10^{-10} m^2 s^{-1}, and the sedimentation coefficient (S) is 2.06×10^{-13} s.

463. Starch is a polymer of glucose ($C_6H_{12}O_6$). A solution contains three types of starch (A, B, and C). The molar masses (M) of the three types of starch are A = 1.80×10^4 g mol^{-1}, B = 2.40×10^4 g mol^{-1}, and C = 1.25×10^4 g mol^{-1}. The molar percentages of each form of starch are A = 28%, B = 37%, and C = 35%. Determine the number average molar mass ($\overline{M}_n$) for the solution.

464. It is possible to determine the molecular mass of a large molecule based on diffusion information. Determine the molar mass (M) of serum globulin given that its sedimentation coefficient (S) is 7.1×10^{-13} s, its diffusion coefficient (D) is 4.0×10^{-7} cm^2 s^{-1}, and its partial specific volume ($\tilde{v}$) is 0.75 cm^3 g^{-1} (all values are for aqueous solutions at 293 K). The density of water (ρ) at 293 K (T) is 0.9982 g cm^{-3}.

465. It is possible to determine the molar mass (M) of a sample through the use of the Mark–Houwink equation ($[\eta] = KM^a$). A particular polymer in xylene has an intrinsic viscosity ($[\eta]$) of 78 cm^3 g^{-1}. For this system, at 25°C, the Mark–Houwink constants are $a = 0.67$ and $K = 1.17 \times 10^{-2}$ cm^3 g^{-1}. What is the molar mass of the polymer?

466. The diffusion coefficient (D) for beef insulin in water at 298 K (T) is 1.52×10^{-10} m^2 s^{-1}, and the partial specific volume (ν) is 7.2×10^{-4} kg^{-1} m^3. Determine the sedimentation coefficient (S) of beef insulin. The density of water (ρ) at 25°C is 9.9968×10^2 kg m^{-3}, and the molar mass (M) of beef insulin is 1.20×10^4 g mol^{-1}.

467. The sedimentation coefficient (S) for beef insulin in water at 25°C is 2.06×10^{-13} s, and the partial specific volume (ν) is 7.4×10^{-4} kg^{-1} m^3. The density of water (ρ) at 25°C is 9.9968×10^2 kg m^{-3}, and assume the coefficient of viscosity (η) for water is 0.001005 Pa s at 293 K. What is the molar mass (M) of beef insulin?

468. At 310 K (T), the diffusion constant (D) for hemoglobin in water is 1.06×10^{-10} m^2 s^{-1}. At this temperature, the viscosity (η) of water is 6.915×10^{-4} Pa s. What is the radius (R) of a hemoglobin molecule?

469. The ceiling temperature (T_c) is the temperature where depolymerization begins; thus, it is the highest working temperature for a polymer. What is the ceiling temperature for Teflon? The enthalpy of polymerization ($\Delta H_p°$) for Teflon is −155 kJ mol^{-1}, and the entropy of polymerization ($\Delta S_p°$) is −112 J mol^{-1} K^{-1}.

470. The partial specific volume ($\bar{v}$) for lactalbumin is 0.75 cm^3 g^{-1}, and the diffusion coefficient (D) is 1.06×10^{-6} cm^2 s^{-1}. Determine the maximum molecular weight (M) for lactalbumin. Assume the coefficient of viscosity (η) for water is 0.01005 poise at 293 K (T).

CHAPTER 21

The Solid State

471. The separation between the layers of carbon atoms in graphite is about 3.35×10^{-10} m (d). What is the first-order ($n = 1$) diffraction angle (θ) of x-rays with a wavelength (λ) of 0.15418 nm?

472. Determine the relative radius (r) of the largest ion that can fit into the "hole" formed by four large ions of unit radius (= 1). Assume the four large ions are in contact at the corners of a square.

473. Aluminum is face-centered cubic with a density of 2.70 g cm^{-3}. What is the radius of an aluminum atom?

474. Molybdenum adopts a body-centered cubic lattice. The density of molybdenum is 10.22 g cm^{-3}. What is the radius of a molybdenum atom?

475. A primitive cubic unit cell contains one formula unit per cell. Assuming the unit cell contains one atom with a radius (r) of 1, what is the packing efficiency? The edge of the unit cell (a) is $2r$.

476. A body-centered cubic unit cell contains two formula units per cell. Assuming the unit cell contains two atoms with a radius (r) of 1, what is the packing efficiency? The edge of the unit cell (a) is $\frac{4r}{\sqrt{3}}$.

477. A face-centered cubic unit cell contains four formula units per cell. Assuming the unit cell contains four atoms with a radius (r) of 1, what is the packing efficiency? The edge of the unit cell (a) is $2\sqrt{2}r$.

478. The packing efficiency of a structure is the volume of the contents divided by the volume of the unit cell. The cesium chloride structure is cubic with a unit cell edge (a) of 411.0 pm. The unit cell contains one cesium ion ($r_{Cs} = 174$ pm) and one chloride ion ($r_{Cl} = 181$ pm). What is the packing efficiency of the cesium chloride structure?

479. A sample of a metal has a density (ρ) of 3.1 g cm^{-3}. The metal has a body-centered cubic (2 atoms per unit cell) structure with a cell edge (a) of 4.507×10^{-8} cm. Identify the metal.

480. Lead is face-centered cubic with a density of 11.3 g cm^{-3}. The unit cell edge is 4.96×10^{-8} cm. Determine the value of Avogadro's number (N_A).

481. Rubidium adopts a body-centered cubic unit cell. The metal has a density of 3.1 g cm^{-3}. What is the length of a unit cell edge?

482. Potassium adopts a body-centered cubic lattice with a density of 0.862 g cm^{-3}. What is the lattice constant (a) for potassium?

483. Potassium adopts a body-centered cubic unit cell with a cell edge of 533.3 pm. What is the density of potassium metal in grams per cubic centimeter?

484. One form of iron has a density of 7.87 g cm^{-3}. If the unit cell of this form of iron has a unit cell edge of 361 pm, how many iron atoms are in a unit cell?

485. The mineral spinel ($MgAl_2O_4$) has a density of 3.55 g cm^{-3}. If the unit cell edge of spinel is 644 pm, how many formula units are in a unit cell?

486. Aluminum metal adopts a face-centered cubic lattice ($N = 4$) with a unit cell edge of 4.04×10^{-10} m. What is the Fermi energy (E_F) for silver?

487. Potassium adopts a body-centered cubic lattice with a lattice constant (a) of 5.32×10^{-10} m. What is the conduction electron density for potassium?

488. Potassium adopts a body-centered cubic lattice with a conduction electron density for potassium $\left(\frac{N_A}{V}\right)$ of 1.33×10^{28} electrons m^{-3}. What is the potassium Fermi energy (E_F)?

CHAPTER 22

Processes at Solid Surfaces

489. A 1.0-g sample of a hydrogenation catalyst adsorbs 125 mL (V) of hydrogen gas at 1.00 atm (P) and 298 K (T). What is the surface area (A) of the catalyst? Assume the hydrogen molecules form a monolayer and that each hydrogen molecule covers 1.3×10^{-19} m^2.

490. Nitrogen gas will adsorb on a silica gel surface. At 273 K and 1.00 atm, the volume of nitrogen gas required to form a monolayer on the silica gel is 0.129 L g^{-1}. Assuming each nitrogen molecule occupies 1.62×10^{-19} m^2 of the surface, what is the surface area per gram of gel (A)? At 273 K and 1.00 atm, the molar volume of nitrogen gas is 22.4 L mol^{-1}.

491. A clean metal surface was exposed to ammonia gas for 1 s at 298 K (T). The surface area was 1.00 cm^2, and there were 5.0×10^{15} adsorption sites available per square centimeter. The partial pressure of the ammonia was 2.0×10^{-6} torr (P). What percentage of the sites was occupied after 1 s? Assume that all molecules striking the surface were adsorbed.

492. Oxygen gas will rapidly oxidize a freshly exposed calcium surface to form CaO. A calcium surface with 2.0×10^{15} calcium atoms is exposed to oxygen gas at a partial pressure of 1.2×10^{-5} Pa (P) at 298 K (T). How long will it take the surface to oxidize completely? Assume there is an average of one oxidation per collision.

493. The pressure (P) in an ultrahigh vacuum system is 7.0×10^{-8} Pa. Calculate the number (J_N) of argon atoms striking a square centimeter of the surface each second at 273 K (T).

494. At 298 K (T), a pressure (P) of 3.0×10^{-5} Pa is necessary to half-saturate a silica gel surface with oxygen gas. Assume the enthalpy of adsorption (ΔH_{ads}) is -10.8 kJ mol^{-1} and the sticking coefficient (s^*) is unity. Determine the value of the desorption rate constant (k_d).

495. The following table shows the relationship between the volume (V) (adjusted to 0°C and 1 bar) of methane gas adsorbed per gram of activated charcoal at a series of pressures. Assuming the data fit the Langmuir isotherm, what are the values of the constants?

P (atm)	0.0474	0.0697	0.100	0.134	0.174	0.225	0.283	0.355
V (cm^3 g^{-1})	14.54	18.42	22.85	26.69	30.45	34.35	38.03	41.65

496. Ethane will adsorb on an activated charcoal surface. The adsorption constant (k) for ethane is 7.8×10^{-3} torr^{-1}, and the partial pressure (P) of ethane is 175 torr. What fraction (θ) of the charcoal surface do ethane molecules cover?

497. Silica gel has a surface area of 800 m^2 g^{-1}. How many liters (V) of water vapor at 298 K (T) and 1.0 atm (P) are necessary to coat the surface of 25 g of silica gel completely? Assume that the surface area covered by each water molecule is 1.0×10^{-19} m^2.

498. Calculate the heat of adsorption (ΔH_{ads}) for the adsorption of oxygen gas onto a charcoal surface. The amount of oxygen adsorbed at 195 K (T_1) and 3.20 atm (P_1) is the same as the amount adsorbed at 298 K (T_2) and 32.0 atm (P_2).

499. Calculate the free energy of adsorption (ΔG_{ads}) for the adsorption of oxygen gas onto a charcoal surface. The amount of oxygen adsorbed is at 298 K (T) and 32.0 atm (P).

500. Calculate the entropy of adsorption (ΔS_{ads}) for the adsorption of oxygen gas onto a charcoal surface. The amount of oxygen adsorbed is at 298 K (T) and 32.0 atm (P), where $\Delta H_{ads} = 1.08 \times 10^4$ J mol^{-1} and $\Delta G_{ads} = 8.59 \times 10^3$ J mol^{-1}.

Answers

ANSWERS

Chapter 1: Thermodynamics and Equations of State

1. The SI base units needed in this case are cubic meters, pascals, moles, and kelvins. Therefore, it is necessary to perform a volume conversion and a pressure conversion.

$$R = \left(\frac{0.0820578 \text{ L atm}}{\text{mol K}}\right)\left(\frac{10^{-3} \text{ m}^3}{1 \text{ L}}\right)\left(\frac{101325 \text{ Pa}}{1 \text{ atm}}\right) = 8.31451 \text{ m}^3 \text{ Pa mol}^{-1} \text{ K}^{-1}$$

(Note that this is numerically equal to the value of R in J mol^{-1} K^{-1}.)

2. The volume of the system and the number of moles of gas present remain constant. Therefore, only the P–T relationship is necessary. For each bulb, $\frac{P_1}{T_1} = \frac{P_2}{T_2}$, where the subscripts 1 and 2 indicate the initial and final conditions, respectively. The values are $P_1 = 0.750$ atm, $T_1 = 373$ K, and $T_2 = 273$ K (for one bulb, it remains 373 for the other). The relationship for the system is

$$\frac{P_1}{T_1} + \frac{P_1}{T_1} = \frac{P_2}{T_2} + \frac{P_2}{T_2} \quad \text{or} \quad \frac{P_1}{T_1} + \frac{P_1}{T_1} = \frac{P_2}{T_2} + \frac{P_2}{T_1}$$

which rearranges to

$$2\frac{P_1}{T_1} = \frac{P_2}{T_2} + \frac{P_2}{T_1}$$

Entering values gives

$$2\frac{(0.750 \text{ atm})}{(373 \text{ K})} = \frac{(P_2)}{(273 \text{ K})} + \frac{(P_2)}{(373 \text{ K})}, \quad \text{or} \quad 0.004021 \text{ atm} = (0.003663 + 0.002681)P_2$$

$$P_2 = 0.633 \text{ atm}$$

3. The appropriate relationship is $P_1V_1 = P_2V_2$, where the 1's are the initial conditions and the 2's are the final conditions. In this case, $P_1 = 1.00$ bar, $V_1 = 275$ mL, $V_2 = 75.0$ mL, and P_2 is the unknown final pressure. Rearranging the equation and entering the given values gives

$$P_2 = \frac{(P_1)(V_1)}{(V_2)} = \frac{(1.00 \text{ bar})(275 \text{ mL})}{(75.0 \text{ mL})} = 3.67 \text{ bar}$$

4. This problem requires the ideal gas equation, $PV = nRT$, where P is the pressure (675 torr), V is the volume (1,725 mL), T is the temperature (25°C = 298 K), R is the gas constant (0.08206 L atm mol^{-1} K^{-1}), and n is the number of moles. It is necessary to rearrange this equation before entering the appropriate values and conversions,

$$n = \frac{PV}{RT} = \frac{(675\ \text{torr})(1725\ \text{mL})}{(0.08206\ \text{L atm mol}^{-1}\ \text{K}^{-1})(298\ \text{K})}\left(\frac{1\ \text{atm}}{760\ \text{torr}}\right)\left(\frac{0.001\ \text{L}}{1\ \text{mL}}\right) = 0.0626\ \text{mol}$$

5. This problem utilizes the ideal gas equation rearranged to $n = PV/RT$, with P being 55% of the vapor pressure of the water (23.8 torr), V being the volume of the tank (1,250 L), R being the gas constant (0.08206 L atm mol^{-1} K^{-1}), and T being the temperature (298 K). This problem also needs the molar mass of water (M = 18.02 g mol^{-1}). Using this information,

$$\text{Mass} = \frac{(P)(V)}{(R)(T)}(M) = \frac{\left[23.8\ \text{torr}\left(\frac{55\%}{100\%}\right)\right](1250\ \text{L})}{(0.08206\ \text{L atm mol}^{-1}\ \text{K}^{-1})(298\ \text{K})}\left(\frac{18.02\ \text{g}}{\text{mol}}\right)\left(\frac{1\ \text{atm}}{760\ \text{torr}}\right) = 16\ \text{g}$$

6. To determine the density of a substance, it is necessary to determine the mass and the volume. There are two simplifications to this task. Assume either a fixed volume of gas and determine the mass of the sample or assume a fixed mass of gas and determine the volume of the sample. In this case, assume there is 1.00 mol (n) of CO_2 (44.0 g CO_2) and determine the volume (V) using the ideal gas equation in the form $V = nRT/P$. Entering this information and the gas constant (R),

$$V = \frac{nRT}{P} = \frac{(1.00\ \text{mol})(0.08206\ \text{L atm mol}^{-1}\ \text{K}^{-1})(195\ \text{K})}{(1.10\ \text{atm})} = 14.5\ \text{L}$$

The density of the carbon dioxide is (44.0 g)/(14.5 L) = 3.03 g L^{-1}.

7. The first step in this problem is to determine the number of moles of gas in the original sample (n_1). This will require the ideal gas equation, in the form $n = PV/RT$, and the final conditions. Entering the appropriate values, including the gas constant (R), into the equation gives

$$(n_1 + 0.0100)\text{mol} = \frac{PV}{RT} = \frac{(0.750\ \text{atm})(1.00\ \text{L})}{(0.08206\ \text{L atm mol}^{-1}\ \text{K}^{-1})(298\ \text{K})} = 0.0307\ \text{mol}$$

Therefore, n_1 = (0.0307 – 0.0100) mol = 0.0207 mol. Using the value of n_1 and the ideal gas equation in the form $T = PV/nR$ and entering the appropriate values gives

$$T = \frac{PV}{nR} = \frac{(0.750\ \text{atm})(1.00\ \text{L})}{(0.0207\ \text{mol})(0.08206\ \text{L atm mol}^{-1}\ \text{K}^{-1})} = 442\ \text{K}$$

8. The average molar mass is the grams per mole. One way to determine the required information from the density of an ideal gas is to pick a fixed volume and to determine the mass and the moles in the volume. The simplest volume to pick is 1.00 L (V), which makes the mass of the sample 1.25 g. The moles will come from the ideal gas equation in the form $n = PV/RT$, where R is the gas constant. Entering the given information,

$$\text{Moles} = \frac{(P)(V)}{(R)(T)} = \frac{(1.00\text{ atm})(1.00\text{ L})}{(0.08206\text{ L atm mol}^{-1}\text{ K}^{-1})(298\text{ K})} = 4.09 \times 10^{-2}\text{ mol}$$

The molar mass is $(1.25\text{ g})/(4.09 \times 10^{-2}\text{ mol}) = 30.6\text{ g mol}^{-1}$

9. The molar mass is the grams per mole. The grams are given in the problem (0.3375 g); therefore, it is only necessary to determine the number of moles (n). The moles will come from the ideal gas equation in the form $n = PV/RT$, where R is the gas constant. Entering the given information,

$$\text{Moles} = \frac{(P)(V)}{(R)(T)} = \frac{(0.975\text{ atm})(0.110\text{ L})}{(0.08206\text{ L atm mol}^{-1}\text{ K}^{-1})(372\text{ K})} = 3.51 \times 10^{-3}\text{ mol}$$

The molar mass is $(0.3375\text{ g})/(3.51 \times 10^{-3}\text{ mol}) = 96.2\text{ g mol}^{-1}$

10. The number of molecules is equal to the moles (n) times Avogadro's number (N_A). The moles come from the ideal gas equation in the form $n = PV/RT$, where R is the gas constant. Entering this information,

$$\text{Molecules} = nN_A = \frac{PV}{RT}N_A = \frac{(5.0 \times 10^{-10}\text{ atm})(1.375\text{ L})}{(0.08206\text{ L atm mol}^{-1}\text{ K}^{-1})(298\text{ K})}$$

$$\times \left(\frac{6.022 \times 10^{23}\text{ molecules}}{1\text{ mol}}\right) = 1.7 \times 10^{13}\text{ molecules}$$

11. It is possible to rearrange the ideal gas equation to $n/V = P/RT$, where R is the gas constant and V is the volume (assumed to be 1 L). In this form, the equation will give the concentration directly.

$$\text{M} = \frac{n}{V} = \frac{P}{RT} = \frac{(41.2\text{ torr})}{(0.08206\text{ L atm mol}^{-1}\text{ K}^{-1})(308\text{ K})}\left(\frac{1\text{ atm}}{760\text{ torr}}\right) = 2.14 \times 10^{-3}\text{ M}$$

12. The compressibility factor is equal to PV/nRT. The sample contained $(0.578\text{ g})/(18.02\text{ g mol}^{-1}) = 0.0321\text{ mol } H_2O$ (n). Entering this information and the gas constant (R) into the equation for the compressibility factor gives

$$Z = \frac{PV}{nRT} = \frac{(1.00\text{ atm})(1.00\text{ L})}{(0.0321\text{ mol})(0.08206\text{ L atm mol}^{-1}\text{ K}^{-1})(389\text{ K})} = 0.976$$

13. It is necessary to modify the ideal gas equation to include the compressibility factor. The modified form is $PV = ZnRT$, where R is the gas constant ($0.08206\text{ L atm mol}^{-1}\text{ K}^{-1}$). Rearranging the equation and entering the values gives

$$V = \frac{ZnRT}{P} = \frac{(0.783)(15.0\text{ mol})(0.08206\text{ L atm mol}^{-1}\text{ K}^{-1})(273\text{ K})}{(100\text{ atm})} = 2.63\text{ L}$$

14. The pressure of the system (575.5 torr) is the total pressure (P_T), which, according to Dalton's law, is the sum of the partial pressures of the components. One of the components is hydrogen gas and the other component is water vapor. It is necessary to consult a table to find the vapor pressure of water at 25°C (23.8 torr). The pressure of the hydrogen is the total pressure minus the vapor pressure of water, or [(575.5) – (23.8)] torr = 551.7 torr.

15. To use the van der Waals equation, it is necessary to locate the van der Waals constants in appropriate tables. For chlorine gas, the appropriate constants are $a = 6.49\ \text{L}^2\ \text{atm mol}^{-2}$ and $b = 0.0562\ \text{L mol}^{-1}$. It is necessary to rearrange the van der Waals equation $[(P + an^2/V^2)(V - nb) = nRT]$, and entering the appropriate values and the gas constant (R) gives

$$P = \frac{nRT}{(V-nb)} - \frac{an^2}{V^2} = \frac{(2.00\ \text{mol})(0.08206\ \text{L atm mol}^{-1}\ \text{K}^{-1})(345\ \text{K})}{[(0.500\ \text{L})-(2.00\ \text{mol})(0.0562\ \text{L mol}^{-1})]}$$

$$- \frac{(6.49\ \text{L}^2\ \text{atm mol}^{-2})\ (2.00\ \text{mol})^2}{(0.500\ \text{L})^2} = 42.2\ \text{atm}$$

16. It is possible to determine the molecular diameter from the second van der Waals constant (b). The value of b is $4N_A V$, where N_A is Avogadro's number and V is the molecular volume. The volume is equal to $(4/3)\pi(d/2)^3$, where d is the molecular diameter. These relationships combine to give $b = 4N_A[(4/3)\pi(d/2)^3]$, which will rearrange to give d after entering the appropriate values.

$$\text{Diameter} = d = 2\left(\sqrt[3]{\frac{3b}{16\pi N_A}}\right) = 2\left(\sqrt[3]{\frac{3\ (0.0428\ \text{L mol}^{-1})}{16\ \pi\ (6.022 \times 10^{23}\ \text{mol}^{-1})}\left(\frac{10^{-3}\ \text{m}^3}{1\ \text{L}}\right)}\right)$$

$$= 3.24 \times 10^{-10}\ \text{m}$$

17. The average translational energy for a gas is $(3/2)RT$, where R is the gas constant. Using this relationship,

$$E_{\text{trans}} = (3/2)RT = (3/2)(8.3145\ \text{J mol}^{-1}\ \text{K}^{-1})\ (298\ \text{K}) = 3.72 \times 10^3\ \text{J mol}^{-1}$$

18. The root-mean-square speed for a gas is equal to $\sqrt{\frac{3RT}{M}}$, where M is the molar mass and R is the gas constant. Entering the appropriate values and conversions,

$$v_{\text{rms}} = \sqrt{\frac{3RT}{M}} = \sqrt{\frac{3(8.3145\ \text{J mol}^{-1}\ \text{K}^{-1})(298\ \text{K})}{(4.003\ \text{g mol}^{-1})}\left(\frac{10^3\ \text{g}}{1\ \text{kg}}\right)\left(\frac{\text{kg m}^2/\text{s}^2}{\text{J}}\right)}$$

$$= 1.363 \times 10^3\ \text{m s}^{-1}$$

19. The force is equal to the total mass (m) of the atoms hitting the wall times the speed per second (a). This gives

$$F = ma = \left[(1.00 \text{ mol He})\left(\frac{4.003 \times 10^{-3} \text{ kg}}{\text{mol He}}\right)\right]\left[\frac{1.363 \times 10^{3} \text{ m s}^{-1}}{1 \text{ s}}\right]\left(\frac{\text{N}}{\text{kg m/s}^2}\right)$$

$$= 5.456 \text{ N}$$

20. Based on kinetic molecular theory, the root-mean-square velocity for a gas obeys the relationship $U_{\text{rms}} = \sqrt{\frac{3RT}{M}}$, where R is the gas constant, T is the temperature, and M is the molar mass. This equation rearranges to $T = \frac{MU_{\text{rms}}^2}{3R}$. Entering the values and conversion factors gives

$$T = \frac{MU_{\text{rms}}^2}{3R} = \frac{\left[(4.003 \text{ g mol}^{-1})\left(\frac{1 \text{ kg}}{10^3 \text{ g}}\right)\right](1.1 \times 10^4 \text{ m s}^{-1})^2}{3(8.3145 \text{ J mol}^{-1} \text{ K}^{-1})}\left(\frac{1 \text{ J}}{\text{kg m}^2/\text{s}^2}\right) = 1.9 \times 10^4 \text{ K}$$

21. One form of the Poiseuille equation is $\frac{dV}{dt} = \frac{\left(P_1^2 - P_2^2\right)\pi R^4}{16 \text{ L } \eta P_0}$. In this equation, P_1 is the entering pressure (1.007 bar), P_2 is the exiting pressure (1.000 bar), P_0 is the pressure at which the volume was measured (1.000 bar), L is the length of the tube (1.000 m), η is the viscosity of the gas, R is the radius of the tube (2.000 mm/2), V is the flowing volume (90.00 cm^3), and t is the flow time (100.0 s). Rearranging this equation to solve for the viscosity of the gas gives

$$\eta = \frac{\left(P_1^2 - P_2^2\right)\pi R^4}{16 \text{ L}\left(\frac{dV}{dt}\right)P_0}$$

Entering values and conversion factors gives

$$\eta = \frac{\left(P_1^2 - P_2^2\right)\pi R^4}{16 \text{ L}\left(\frac{dV}{dt}\right)P_0} = \frac{[((1.007)^2 - (1.000)^2) \text{ bar}^2]\ \pi \left[(1.000 \text{ mm})\left(\frac{0.001 \text{ m}}{1 \text{ mm}}\right)\right]^4}{16(1.000 \text{ m})\left[\left(\frac{90.00 \text{ cm}^3}{100.0 \text{ s}}\right)\left(\frac{0.01 \text{ m}}{1 \text{ cm}}\right)^3\right](1.000 \text{ bar})}$$

$$\times \left(\frac{1 \text{ N}/\text{m}^2}{1 \text{ bar}}\right)\left(\frac{1 \text{ kg m}/\text{s}^2}{1 \text{ N}}\right) = 3.065 \times 10^{-9} \text{ kg m}^{-1} \text{ s}^{-1}$$

22. One method to calculate the vapor pressure (P) by Knudsen's method is to use the equation $P = \left(\frac{M_T}{tr^2}\right)\left(\sqrt{\frac{2RT}{\pi M}}\right)$. In this equation, M_T is the mass effused (9.00 mg), t is the elapsed time (960.0 s), r is the radius of the hole (3.20 mm/2), T is the temperature

(1,575 K), R is the gas constant (8.3145 J mol^{-1} K^{-1}), and M is the molar mass of the metal (9.012 g mol^{-1}). Entering the values and conversion factors, and solving by parts, gives

$$P=\left(\frac{M_T}{tr^2}\right)\left(\sqrt{\frac{2RT}{\pi M}}\right)=\left[\frac{(9.00\text{ mg})}{(960.0\text{ s})\,(1.60\text{ mm})^2}\left(\frac{0.001\text{ g}}{1\text{ mg}}\right)\left(\frac{1\text{ mm}}{0.001\text{ m}}\right)^2\left(\frac{1\text{ kg}}{1000\text{ g}}\right)\right]$$

$$\times\left(\frac{1\text{ Pa}}{\text{kg/m s}^2}\right)\left[\sqrt{\frac{2RT}{\pi M}}\right]$$

$$\times\left[\sqrt{\frac{2\,(8.3145\text{ J mol}^{-1}\text{ K}^{-1})(1575\text{ K})}{\pi(9.012\text{ g mol}^{-1})}\left(\frac{1000\text{ g}}{1\text{ kg}}\right)\left(\frac{\text{kg m}^2/\text{s}^2}{\text{J}}\right)}\right]=3.52\text{ Pa}$$

23. The amount of energy is the power (75 W) times the time (1.00 h). Entering these values,

$$E=(75\text{ W})\left(\frac{1\text{ J s}^{-1}}{1\text{ W}}\right)(1.00\text{ h})\left(\frac{3600\text{ s}}{1\text{ h}}\right)=2.7\times10^5\text{ J}$$

24. Assuming no energy is lost to the surroundings, the heat energy transferred from the heater to the block is equal to the power (P) times the time (t) for the heater and equal to the heat capacity times the moles (n) times the temperature change (ΔT) for the aluminum. Solving these relationships for the heat capacity gives

$$\bar{C}_p=\frac{Pt}{n\Delta T}=\frac{(25\text{ W})(15\text{ s})}{(25\text{ g})\,(17\text{ K})}\left(\frac{\text{J s}^{-1}}{\text{W}}\right)\left(\frac{26.98\text{ g}}{\text{mol}}\right)=24\text{ J mol}^{-1}\text{ K}^{-1}$$

25. For an ideal monatomic gas, only translational energy is important. When there is more than one atom present, there are additional contributions covered in later chapters. The relationship for an ideal monatomic gas is $C_p=\frac{5}{2}R$, where R is the gas constant. Entering values into this relationship gives

$$C_p=\frac{5}{2}R=\frac{5}{2}(8.3145\text{ J mol}^{-1}\text{ K}^{-1})=20.786\text{ J mol}^{-1}\text{ K}^{-1}$$

26. For an ideal monatomic gas, only translational energy is important. When there is more than one atom present, there are additional contributions covered in later chapters. The relationship for an ideal monatomic gas is $C_v=\frac{3}{2}R$, where R is the gas constant. Entering values into this relationship gives

$$C_v=\frac{3}{2}R=\frac{3}{2}(8.3145\text{ J mol}^{-1}\text{ K}^{-1})=12.472\text{ J mol}^{-1}\text{ K}^{-1}$$

27. In this problem, it is only necessary to enter the appropriate values into the equation (plus R the gas constant), which when solving by parts gives

$$\bar{C}_p = (a + bT + cT^2)R$$

$$= [(3.245) + (7.108 \times 10^{-4}\ \text{K}^{-1})\ (1{,}500\ \text{K}) + (-4.06 \times 10^{-8}\ \text{K}^{-2})\ (1{,}500\ \text{K})^2]R$$

$$= [4.21985]\ (8.3145\ \text{J mol}^{-1}\ \text{K}^{-1}) = 35.1\ \text{J mol}^{-1}\ \text{K}^{-1}$$

28. The enthalpy change (ΔH) for the reaction is the sum of the energies of the bonds broken minus the sum of the energies of the bonds formed. In this case, a nitrogen–nitrogen triple bond and three hydrogen–hydrogen bonds are broken and six nitrogen–hydrogen bonds form. This gives

$$\Delta H = \{[(941) + 3(436)] - [6(393)]\}\ \text{kJ mol}^{-1} = -109\ \text{kJ mol}^{-1}$$

29. The pressure is the force divided by the area of the column of gallium ($P = F/A$), where A is the area. The force due to the column of gallium is the mass times the acceleration due to gravity ($F = mg$). The mass of the gallium in the column is the height times the area times the density ($m = hA\rho$). Expressing all terms in SI base units will yield the pressure in pascals. (Changing to SI base units may be the long way around, but the process will get to the answer.)

$$P = \frac{F}{A} = \frac{mg}{A} = \frac{(h\cancel{A}\rho)(g)}{\cancel{A}} = h\rho g$$

$$P = (1696.0\ \text{mm})\left(\frac{6.0930\ \text{g}}{\text{mL}}\right)\left(\frac{9.8067\ \text{m}}{\text{s}^2}\right)\left(\frac{10^{-3}\ \text{m}}{\text{mm}}\right)\left(\frac{1\ \text{kg}}{1000\ \text{g}}\right)\left(\frac{1\ \text{mL}}{10^{-3}\ \text{L}}\right)$$

$$\times\left(\frac{1\ \text{L}}{10^{-3}\ \text{m}^3}\right)\left(\frac{1\ \text{Pa}}{1\ \text{kg}/(\text{m s}^2)}\right) = 101{,}340\ \text{Pa}$$

Chapter 2: The First Law of Thermodynamics

30. It is possible to rewrite the relationship $w = -P\Delta V$ as $w = -P_2\ (V_2 - V_1)$, where R is the gas constant. Although it is possible to determine V_1 and V_2 from the information in the problem, conversion to work is not simple. It is possible to modify the last equation using the ideal gas equation to get

$$w = -P_2\left(\frac{nRT}{P_2} - \frac{nRT}{P_1}\right) = -nRT\left(1 - \frac{P_2}{P_1}\right) = -(5.00\ \text{mol})(8.3145\ \text{J mol}^{-1}\ \text{K}^{-1})$$

$$\times\ (325\ \text{K})[1 - (10.0\ \text{bar}/1.00\ \text{bar})] = -1.22 \times 10^5\ \text{J}$$

31. The work (w) is equal to $\phi\Delta Q$, where ϕ is the potential difference and ΔQ is the charge transferred in coulombs. The charge transferred is the number of moles of electrons times the Faraday constant (96,485 C/mole of electrons).

$$w = \phi\Delta Q = (0.25\ \text{V})\left[(2.50\ \text{mol}\ e^-)\left(\frac{96{,}485\ \text{C}}{\text{mol}\ e^-}\right)\right]\left(\frac{1\ \text{J}}{\text{VC}}\right) = 6.0 \times 10^4\ \text{J}$$

32. The work (w) is equal to $\gamma\Delta A$, where γ is the surface tension and ΔA is the change in surface area.

$$w = \gamma\Delta A = \left(\frac{0.072\ \text{N}}{\text{m}}\right)[2(8.0 \times 10^{-5}\ \text{m}^2)]\left(\frac{1\ \text{J}}{\text{N m}}\right) = 1.2 \times 10^{-5}\ \text{J}$$

33. The work (w) is equal to $F\Delta L$, where F is the force and ΔL is the change in length.

$$w = F\Delta L = (1.75\ \text{N})(2.54\ \text{cm})\left(\frac{0.01\ \text{m}}{1\ \text{cm}}\right)\left(\frac{1\ \text{J}}{\text{N m}}\right) = 0.0444\ \text{J}$$

34. Using the equation given, $w_{\text{rev}} = nRT\ln\left(\frac{P_2}{P_1}\right)$, where R is the gas constant, and entering the appropriate values,

$$w_{\text{rev}} = nRT\ln\left(\frac{P_2}{P_1}\right) = (7.00\ \text{mol})(8.3145\ \text{J mol}^{-1}\ \text{K}^{-1})(315\ \text{K})\ln\left(\frac{2.00\ \text{bar}}{10.0\ \text{bar}}\right)$$
$$= -2.95 \times 10^4\ \text{J}$$

35. The relationship needed is $w = \int_{T_1}^{T_2} \bar{C}_V dT$, where the T's are the temperatures and $\bar{C}_V = \frac{3}{2}R$ for an ideal monatomic gas, where R is the gas constant. Solving for the work,

$$w = \int_{T_1}^{T_2} \bar{C}_V dT = \frac{3}{2}R(T_2 - T_1) = \frac{3}{2}(8.3145\ \text{J mol}^{-1}\ \text{K}^{-1})(187.8\ \text{K} - 298.2\ \text{K})$$
$$= -1{,}377\ \text{J mol}^{-1}$$

36. Using the relationship from the problem, $w_{\text{irrev}} = -P_2(V_2 - V_1)$, and the ideal gas equation in the form $V = nRT/P$, where R is the gas constant, gives

$$w_{\text{irrev}} = -P_2(V_2 - V_1) = -P_2\left(\frac{nRT}{P_2} - \frac{nRT}{P_1}\right) = -nRTP_2\left(\frac{1}{P_2} - \frac{1}{P_1}\right)$$
$$= -(7.00\ \text{mol})(8.3145\ \text{J mol}^{-1}\ \text{K}^{-1})(315\ \text{K})(2.00\ \text{bar})\left(\frac{1}{2.00\ \text{bar}} - \frac{1}{10.0\ \text{bar}}\right)$$
$$= -1.47 \times 10^4\ \text{J}$$

37. The determination of the work comes from $w_{\text{rev}} = \int_{V_1}^{V_2} PdV$, with $P = \frac{nRT}{V}$. For an isothermal expansion, nRT is constant; therefore, $w_{\text{rev}} = nRT\int_{V_1}^{V_2}\frac{dV}{V} = nRT\ln\frac{V_2}{V_1}$, where R is the gas constant. From Boyle's law, $P_1V_1 = P_2V_2$, which leads to $\frac{V_2}{V_1} = \frac{P_1}{P_2}$. This leads to

$$w_{\text{rev}} = nRT\ln\frac{P_1}{P_2} = (2.00\ \text{mol})\left(\frac{8.3145\ \text{J}}{\text{mol K}}\right)(298\ \text{K})\ln\frac{1.00\ \text{atm}}{0.200\ \text{atm}} = 7.98 \times 10^3\ \text{J}$$

38. The determination of the work comes from $w = \int_{V_1}^{V_2} P_{ex} dV$, where P_{ex} is the external pressure. Because the external pressure is constant, $w = P_{ex} \int_{V_1}^{V_2} dV = P_{ex}(V_2 - V_1)$. The initial volume ($V_1$) = 5.00 L and V_2 come from Boyle's law, $P_1V_1 = P_2V_2$, which leads to $V_2 = \frac{P_1V_1}{P_2}$. Entering values,

$$V_2 = \frac{P_1V_1}{P_2} = \frac{(15.0 \text{ atm})(5.00 \text{ L})}{(1.00 \text{ atm})} = 75.0 \text{ L}$$

$$w = P_{ex}(V_2 - V_1) = (1.00 \text{ atm})\ (75.0 - 15.0) \text{ L} = 60.0 \text{ L atm}$$

39. The reversible work (w_{rev}) is equal to $-nRT$, where R is the gas constant, which gives

$$w_{rev} = -nRT = -(2.00 \text{ mol})(8.3145 \text{ J mol}^{-1} \text{ K}^{-1})(353 \text{ K}) = -5.87 \times 10^3 \text{ J}$$

40. The relationship is $q_{irrev} = \Delta U - w_{irrev}$. The value of ΔU is zero. Because work is done on the surroundings, the work is negative. Therefore,

$$q_{irrev} = \Delta U - w_{irrev} = 0 - (-1.47 \times 10^4 \text{ J}) = 1.47 \times 10^4 \text{ J}$$

41. The relationship is $q_{rev} = \Delta U - w_{rev}$. The value of ΔU is zero. Because work is done on the surroundings, the work is negative. Therefore,

$$q_{rev} = \Delta U - w_{rev} = 0 - (2.95 \times 10^4 \text{ J}) = -2.95 \times 10^4 \text{ J}$$

42. The enthalpy change is the sum of the heats of formation of the products minus the sum of the heats of formation of the reactants. The values come from tables appearing in various references. Only use values at the given temperature (298 K). The values are $Pb(NO_3)_2$(s) = −451.9 kJ mol^{-1}, PbO(s) = −217.3 kJ mol^{-1}, NO_2(g) = 33.8 kJ mol^{-1}, and O_2(g) = 0.0 kJ mol^{-1}.

$$\Delta H_{rxn}{}^\circ = [2(-217.3 \text{ kJ mol}^{-1}) + 4(33.8 \text{ kJ mol}^{-1}) + (0.0 \text{ kJ mol}^{-1})]$$

$$- [2\ (-451.9 \text{ kJ mol}^{-1})] = 604.4 \text{ kJ mol}^{-1}$$

43. The relationship needed is $P_1\overline{V}_1^\gamma = P_2\overline{V}_2^\gamma$, where the P's are the pressures and the V's are the molar volumes. The value of γ is $\overline{C}_P / \overline{C}_V$, where the C's are the heat capacities at constant pressure and constant volume, respectively. For a monatomic ideal gas, $\overline{C}_P = \frac{5}{2}R$ and $\overline{C}_V = \frac{3}{2}R$; therefore, $\gamma = \frac{5}{3}$. Solving for P_2,

$$P_2 = P_1\left(\frac{\overline{V}_1}{\overline{V}_2}\right)^\gamma = (1.00 \text{ bar})\left(\frac{24.45 \text{ L mol}^{-1}}{48.90 \text{ L mol}^{-1}}\right)^{5/3} = 0.315 \text{ bar}$$

44. The relationship needed is $\frac{T_2}{T_1} = \left(\frac{\overline{V}_1}{\overline{V}_2}\right)^{\gamma-1}$, where the T's are the temperatures and the V's are the molar volumes. The value of γ is $\overline{C}_P / \overline{C}_V$, where the C's are the heat capacities at constant pressure and constant volume, respectively. For a monatomic ideal gas, $\bar{C}_P = \frac{5}{2}R$ and $\bar{C}_V = \frac{3}{2}R$, where R is the gas constant. This leads to $\gamma - 1 = \frac{2}{3}$. Solving for T_2,

$$T_2 = T_1\left(\frac{\bar{V}_1}{\bar{V}_2}\right)^{\gamma-1} = (298.2\text{ K})\left(\frac{24.45\text{ L mol}^{-1}}{48.90\text{ L mol}^{-1}}\right)^{2/3} = 187.8\text{ K}$$

45. The appropriate relationship is $\Delta H_{rxn}{}^\circ = \Delta U_{rxn}{}^\circ + RT\Sigma v_g$, where R is the gas constant. In this problem, $\Delta U_{rxn}{}^\circ = -3{,}515$ kJ mol^{-1}, and the sum of the gases (Σv_g) is (5 – 3) = 2, which leads to

$$\Delta H_{rxn}{}^\circ = \Delta U_{rxn}{}^\circ + RT\sum v_g = -3{,}515\text{ kJ mol}^{-1} + (8.3145\text{ J mol}^{-1})(298.15)(2)\left(\frac{1\text{ kJ}}{1000\text{ J}}\right) = -3{,}510\text{ kJ mol}^{-1}$$

46. The relationship for this calculation is $(C_P - C_V) = \frac{\alpha^2 VT}{\beta}$. Entering the values and the appropriate conversion factors gives

$$(C_P - C_V) = \frac{\alpha^2 VT}{\beta} = \frac{(5.8\times10^{-5}\text{K}^{-1})^2(1.03\times10^{-5}\text{ m}^3\text{ mol}^{-1})(298\text{ K})}{(7.9\times10^{-12}\text{Pa}^{-1})} \times\left(\frac{1\text{ kg}/\text{m s}^2}{\text{Pa}}\right)\left(\frac{1\text{ J}}{\text{kg m}^2/\text{s}^2}\right) = 1.3\text{ J mol}^{-1}\text{ K}^{-1}$$

47. For a nonlinear molecule, the rotational and translational contributions are $3R/2$, and the vibrational contribution is $3R$. R is the gas constant. This leads to

$$C_P = R + \left(\frac{3R}{2}\right)_{\text{trans}} + \left(\frac{3R}{2}\right)_{\text{rot}} + \left(\frac{20\%}{100\%}\right)(3R)_{\text{vib}} = 4.6R$$

$$C_P = 4.6R = 4.6(8.3145\text{ J mol}^{-1}\text{ K}^{-1}) = 38\text{ J mol}^{-1}\text{ K}^{-1}$$

48. For a linear molecule, the rotational contribution is $2R/2$, the translational contribution is $3R/2$, and the vibrational contribution is $4R$. R is the gas constant. This leads to

$$C_P = R + \left(\frac{3R}{2}\right)_{\text{trans}} + \left(\frac{2R}{2}\right)_{\text{rot}} + \left(\frac{20\%}{100\%}\right)(4R)_{\text{vib}} = 4.3R$$

$$C_P = 4.3R = 4.3(8.3145\text{ J mol}^{-1}\text{ K}^{-1}) = 36\text{ J mol}^{-1}\text{ K}^{-1}$$

49. The relationship for the heat required is $\Delta H = \int_{T_1}^{T_2} C_P dT$.

$$\Delta H = \int_{T_1}^{T_2} C_P dT = \int_{298}^{425} (26.9 + 7.0 \times 10^{-3} T + (-8.2 \times 10^{-7}) T^2) dT$$

$$\Delta H = 26.9(425 - 298) + 7.0 \times 10^{-3}(425^2 - 298^2) + (-8.2 \times 10^{-7})(425^3 - 298^3)$$

$$\Delta H = 4.02 \times 10^3 \text{ J mol}^{-1}$$

50. The heat lost by the hot metal is equal to the heat gained by the cold metal. In both cases, $q = mC_p\Delta T$, with q being negative for the hot metal. This leads to

$$-\left[\left(\frac{0.127 \text{ J}}{\text{g°C}}\right)(10.00 \text{ g})(T_f - 75.00)\text{°C}\right] = +\left[\left(\frac{1.024 \text{ J}}{\text{g°C}}\right)(17.00 \text{ g})(T_f - 15.00)\text{°C}\right]$$

$$-[(1.27 \text{ J})(T_f - 75.00)] = +[(17.41 \text{ J})(T_f - 15.00)]$$

$$-[1.27\ T_f - 95.25] = +[17.41\ T_f - 261.1]$$

$$261.1 + 95.25 = (17.41 + 1.27)T_f$$

$$356.4 = (18.68)T_f$$

$$T_f = 356.4/18.68 = 19.1\text{°C}$$

51. This problem requires Hess's law to calculate the enthalpy change for the following reaction (formation)

$$3C(gr) + 4H_2(g) \rightarrow C_3H_8(g)$$

It is necessary to multiply equation (A) by three, to reverse equation (B), and to multiply equation (C) by four. These changes include changes in the energies associated with each reaction and changes in the equations to cancel species appearing on both sides of the reaction arrows. The result is

(A) $3C(gr)$ + ~~$3O_2(g)$~~ → ~~$3CO_2(g)$~~ $\quad \Delta H = 3(-394 \text{ kJ mol}^{-1})$

(B) ~~$3CO_2(g)$~~ + ~~$4H_2O(l)$~~ → $C_3H_8(g)$ + ~~$5O_2(g)$~~ $\quad \Delta H = +2{,}222 \text{ kJ mol}^{-1}$

(C) $4H_2(g)$ + ~~$2O_2(g)$~~ → ~~$4H_2O(l)$~~ $\quad \Delta H = 4(-286 \text{ kJ mol}^{-1})$

Leaving

$$3C(gr) + 4H_2(g) \rightarrow C_3H_8(g)$$

$$\Delta H = 3(-394 \text{ kJ mol}^{-1}) + (2{,}222 \text{ kJ mol}^{-1}) + 4(-286 \text{ kJ mol}^{-1})$$

$$\Delta H = -104 \text{ kJ mol}^{\ 1}$$

52. The enthalpy change for a process at a temperature T_2 is $\Delta H_{T_2} = \Delta H_{T_1} + \int_{T_1}^{T_2} \Delta C_p dT$, assuming an enthalpy change at T_1 is known. Assuming ΔC_P is constant gives

$$\Delta H_{T_2} = \Delta H_{T_1} + \Delta C_p \int_{T_1}^{T_2} dT$$

This becomes

$$\Delta H_{T_2} = -4.90 \text{ kJ mol}^{-1} + [(0.111 - 0.112) \text{ kJ mol}^{-1} \text{ K}^{-1}] (148 - 156) \text{ K}$$

$$\Delta H_{T_2} = -4.89 \text{ kJ mol}^{-1}$$

53. The heat of vaporization is

$$\Delta H_{vap} = \Delta H_f°(\text{gas}) - \Delta H_f°(\text{liquid}) = (-235 \text{ kJ mol}^{-1}) - (-278 \text{ kJ mol}^{-1}) = 43 \text{ kJ mol}^{-1}$$

54. The heat of combustion is $\Delta H_{com} = \sum \Delta H_f°(\text{products}) - \sum \Delta H_f°(\text{products})$.

$$\Delta H_{com} = -2{,}222 \text{ kJ mol}^{-1} = [3(-394 \text{ kJ mol}^{-1}) + 4(-286 \text{ kJ mol}^{-1})]$$

$$- [(\Delta H_f°(\text{propane})) - 5(0)]$$

$$\Delta H_f°(\text{propane}) = [3(-394 \text{ kJ mol}^{-1}) + 4(-286 \text{ kJ mol}^{-1})] + 2{,}222 \text{ kJ mol}^{-1}$$

$$= -104 \text{ kJ mol}^{-1}$$

55. The first law leads to $\Delta E = \Delta H - \Delta(PV)$, where the work is $\Delta n(RT)$. The change in the moles is $\Delta n = 1 - (1/2 + 1/2 + 3/2) = -3/2$ mol. R is the gas constant.

$$\Delta E = \Delta H - \Delta(PV) = \Delta H - \Delta n(RT)$$

$$= -134 \text{ kJ mol}^{-1} - \left(\frac{3}{2}\text{ mol}\right)\left(\frac{8.4145 \text{ J}}{\text{mol K}}\right)(298 \text{ K})\left(\frac{1 \text{ kJ}}{10^3 \text{ J}}\right)$$

$$\Delta E = -138 \text{ kJ mol}^{-1}$$

56. The kinetic energy of an ideal diatomic gas is $\Delta E = \left(\frac{5}{2}\right) R\Delta T$, where R is the gas constant, and, from the first law, $\Delta E = q + w$. Combining these equations gives $\left(\frac{5}{2}\right) R\Delta T$, which rearranges to

$$\Delta T = \left(\frac{2}{5}\right)\left(\frac{(q+w)}{R}\right) = \left(\frac{2}{5}\right)\left(\frac{(75.0+225)\text{J mol}^{-1}}{8.3145 \text{ J mol}^{-1} \text{ K}^{-1}}\right) = 14.4 \text{ K}$$

57. The sample contains 1.00 mol of gas; therefore, the volumes are molar volumes ($\bar{V}$). The relationship is $\bar{C}_v \ln \frac{T_2}{T_1} = -R \ln \frac{\bar{V}_2}{\bar{V}_1}$, where R is the gas constant. Rearranging this equation and entering the values gives

$$\ln T_2 = \ln T_1 - \frac{R \ln \frac{\bar{V}_2}{\bar{V}_1}}{\bar{C}_v} = \ln (298\text{ K}) - \frac{(8.314\text{ J mol}^{-1}\text{ K}^{-1}) \ln \dfrac{22.4\text{ L}}{44.8\text{ L}}}{12.6\text{ J mol}^{-1}\text{ K}^{-1}} = 6.154$$

$$T_2 = 471\text{ K}$$

58. The solution contains $(10.0\text{ g})\left(\frac{1\text{ mol}}{74.5\text{ g}}\right) = 0.134$ mol of solid and $(90.0\text{ g})\left(\frac{1\text{ mol}}{18.0\text{ g}}\right) =$ 5.00 mol of water. The change in the heat capacity, ΔC_P, for the two different temperatures is equal to $\frac{\Delta H}{\Delta T}$, where ΔH is the enthalpy change and ΔT is the temperature change. In addition, $\Delta C_P = \Delta C_P$ (solution) – (moles solid) ΔC_P (solid) – (moles water) ΔC_P (water).

$$\Delta C_P = \frac{\Delta H}{\Delta T} = \frac{(2.93 - 3.24)\text{kJ}}{(25-15)°\text{C}}\left(\frac{1000\text{ J}}{1\text{ kJ}}\right) = -31\text{ J °C}^{-1}$$

$$-31\text{ J °C}^{-1} = \Delta C_P\text{ (solution)} - (0.134\text{ mol})(50.2\text{ J °C}^{-1}\text{ mol}^{-1})$$

$$- (5.00\text{ mol})(75.3\text{ J °C}^{-1}\text{ mol}^{-1})$$

$$\Delta C_P\text{ (solution)} = -31\text{ J °C}^{-1} + (0.134\text{ mol})(50.2\text{ J °C}^{-1}\text{ mol}^{-1})$$

$$+ (5.00\text{ mol})(75.3\text{ J °C}^{-1}\text{ mol}^{-1})$$

$$\Delta C_P\text{ (solution)} = 350\text{ J °C}^{-1}$$

59. The heat of reaction at constant pressure is related to the heat of reaction at constant volume by $q_p = q_v + RT\Delta n$, where R is the gas constant, T is the temperature, and Δn is the change in the number of moles of gas (–4 in this case). Using this information gives

$$q_p = q_v + RT\Delta n = -4.810 \times 10^3\text{ kJ mol}^{-1} + (8.3145\text{ J mol}^{-1}\text{ K}^{-1})(298\text{ K})(-4)(1\text{ kJ}/10^3\text{ J})$$

$$= 4{,}820\text{ kJ mol}^{-1}$$

60. It is necessary to vaporize the carbon, which requires [2 mol C(gr)](718 kJ mol^{-1}) = 1,436 kJ. It is also necessary to atomize the hydrogen, which requires [3 mol H_2(g)] (436 kJ mol^{-1}) = 1,308 kJ. The formation of the ethane requires the formation of one C–C bond and six C–H bonds, which means there is a release of [1 mol C–C)](348 kJ mol^{-1}) + [6 mol C–H)](413 kJ mol^{-1}) = 2,826 kJ. The energy change for the process is

$$\Delta H = 1{,}436\text{ kJ} + 1{,}308\text{ kJ} - 2{,}826\text{ kJ} = -82\text{ kJ mol}^{-1}$$

Chapter 3: The Second Law and the Third Law of Thermodynamics

61. The relationship is $w_{rev} = -nRT \ln\left(\frac{V_2}{V_1}\right)$, where R is the gas constant.

$$w_{rev} = -nRT \ln\left(\frac{V_2}{V_1}\right) = -(1.00\text{ mol})(8.3145\text{ J mol}^{-1})(298.15)\ln\left(\frac{15.00\text{ L}}{5.00\text{ L}}\right)$$

$$= -2.72 \times 10^3\text{ J}$$

62. Under these conditions, there will be no change in internal energy (ΔU). Thus, $\Delta U = q + w = 0$. From this, $q_{sys} = 2.72 \times 10^3$ J and $q_{surr} = -2.72 \times 10^3$ J.

63. In this problem, only half of the energy is available

$$E = \left(\frac{50.0\%}{100\%}\right)(1.4 \times 10^8 \text{ J}) = 7.0 \times 10^7 \text{ J}$$

64. The efficiency is $1 - T_l/T_h$, which gives

$$e = 1 - T_l/T_h = 1 - (273 \text{ K})/(373 \text{ K}) = 0.268$$

65. It is necessary to use the appropriate Gibbs free energy table to determine the values ($\Delta G_f°$) at 298 K for the substances involved. The values, in kilojoules per mole, are −128 for CuO(s), −162 for $CuCl_2$(s), −95 for HCl(g), and −229 for H_2O(g). The relationship is

$$\Delta G° = \sum \Delta G_f°(\text{products}) - \sum \Delta G_f°(\text{reactants})$$

$$= [(-162) + (-229)] \text{ kJ mol}^{-1} - [(-128) + 2(-95)] \text{ kJ mol}^{-1} = -73 \text{ kJ mol}^{-1}$$

66. For this process, $\Delta \bar{S} = \frac{\Delta \bar{H}}{T}$. The overbars indicate molar changes.

$$\Delta \bar{S} = \frac{\Delta \bar{H}}{T} = \frac{(22.9 \text{ kJ mol}^{-1})}{(289 \text{ K})}\left(\frac{1000 \text{ J}}{1 \text{ kJ}}\right) = 79.2 \text{ J mol}^{-1} \text{ K}^{-1}$$

67. It is possible to consider this process as the sum of three reversible steps. The first step is to transfer 1 mol of water from the liquid to saturated vapor (2.121×10^{-5} Pa) at 288 K. The next step is to allow the water vapor to undergo an isothermal expansion from 2.121×10^{-5} Pa to 1.925×10^{-5} Pa. The third step is to transfer 1 mol of water vapor at 1.925×10^{-5} Pa to ice at 298 K. The Gibbs free energy change for the first and third steps is zero because the phases are in equilibrium. The Gibbs free energy change for the second step is $\Delta \bar{G} = RT \ln \frac{P_2}{P_1}$, where R is the gas constant. Entering the appropriate values gives

$$\Delta \bar{G} = RT \ln \frac{P_2}{P_1} = (8.3145 \text{ J mol}^{-1} \text{ K}^{-1})(288 \text{ K}) \ln \frac{(1.925 \times 10^{-5} \text{ Pa})}{(2.121 \times 10^{-5} \text{ Pa})} = -232 \text{ J mol}^{-1}$$

68. The relationship is $\Delta S = nR \ln\left(\frac{V_2}{V_1}\right)$, where R is the gas constant.

$$\Delta S = nR \ln\left(\frac{V_2}{V_1}\right) = (1.00 \text{ mol})(8.3145 \text{ J mol}^{-1}) \ln\left(\frac{15.00 \text{ L}}{5.00 \text{ L}}\right) = 9.13 \text{ J K}^{-1}$$

69. Heat is following out of the surroundings ($q_{surr} = -2.72 \times 10^3$ J), which means there is a decrease in entropy.

$$\Delta S_{\text{surr}} = \frac{q_{\text{surr}}}{T} = \frac{-2.72 \times 10^3 \text{ J}}{298.15 \text{ K}} = -9.12 \text{ J K}^{-1}$$

70. This is a reversible process; therefore, the entropy change (ΔS) is zero.

71. The molar entropy change ($\Delta \bar{S}$) due to the temperature change is $\bar{C}_P \ln\left(\frac{T_2}{T_1}\right)$, and the molar entropy change due to the pressure change is $-R\ln\left(\frac{P_2}{P_1}\right)$. In addition, $\bar{C}_P$ is equal to $\frac{5}{2}R$. In both cases, R is the gas constant.

$$\begin{aligned}\Delta \bar{S} &= \bar{C}_P \ln\left(\frac{T_2}{T_1}\right) - R\ln\left(\frac{P_2}{P_1}\right)\\ &= \frac{5}{2}(8.3145 \text{ J mol}^{-1} \text{ K}^{-1})\ln\left(\frac{175 \text{ K}}{325 \text{ K}}\right) - (8.3145 \text{ J mol}^{-1}\text{K}^{-1})\ln\left(\frac{7.50 \text{ bar}}{1.00 \text{ bar}}\right)\\ &= -29.6 \text{ J mol}^{-1} \text{ K}^{-1}\end{aligned}$$

72. The entropy of mixing (ΔS_{mix}) for ideal gases is $-n_{\text{tot}} R \sum x_i \ln x_i$, where n_{tot} is the total moles, x_i is the mole fraction of each component, and R is the gas constant. In this case, $n_{\text{tot}} = (1.00 + 2.00)$ mol, $x_{\text{He}} = (1.00/3.00)$, and $x_{\text{Ne}} = (2.00/3.00)$.

$$\Delta S_{\text{mix}} = -n_{\text{tot}} R \sum x_i \ln x_i = -(3.00 \text{ mol})(8.3145 \text{ J mol}^{-1} \text{ K}^{-1})$$

$$\times \left[\frac{1.00}{3.00}\ln\frac{1.00}{3.00} + \frac{2.00}{3.00}\ln\frac{2.00}{3.00}\right] = 15.9 \text{ J K}^{-1}$$

73. The formation reaction is $Ca(s) + ½\ O_2(g) \rightarrow CaO(s)$. To determine the entropy change for this reaction, it is necessary to take the products minus the reactants.

$$\Delta S = [39.8 \text{ J mol}^{-1} \text{ K}^{-1}] - [41.4 \text{ J mol}^{-1} \text{ K}^{-1} + ½\,(205.0 \text{ J mol}^{-1} \text{ K}^{-1})]$$

$$= -104.1 \text{ J mol}^{-1} \text{ K}^{-1}$$

74. The total entropy change for the transition is the sum of the changes for the system and the surroundings or $\Delta S_{\text{total}} = \Delta S_{\text{system}} + \Delta S_{\text{surroundings}}$. In this case, $\Delta S_{\text{system}} = \frac{\Delta H}{T}$ and $\Delta S_{\text{surroundings}} = \frac{q}{T}$, where q is the heat transferred (-397 J mol^{-1}). Entering the information into the formulas,

$$\begin{aligned}\Delta S_{\text{total}} = \Delta S_{\text{system}} + \Delta S_{\text{surroundings}} &= \frac{\Delta H_{\text{trans}}}{T_{\text{trans}}} + \frac{q}{T_{\text{bath}}}\\ &= \frac{397 \text{ J mol}^{-1}}{583 \text{ K}}(1.00 \text{ mol}) + \frac{-397 \text{ J mol}^{-1}}{298 \text{ K}}(1.00 \text{ mol})\\ &= 0.681 \text{ J mol}^{-1} - 1.33 \text{ J mol}^{-1} = -0.65 \text{ J mol}^{-1}\end{aligned}$$

75. It is necessary to use the appropriate entropy table to determine the absolute entropy values ($S°$) at 298 K for the substances involved. The values, in J mol^{-1} K^{-1}, are 92 for Cu_2O(s), 33 for Cu(s), 131 for H_2(g), and 189 for H_2O(g). The relationship is

$$\Delta S° = \sum S°(\text{products}) - \sum S°(\text{reactants})$$

$$= [2(33) + (189)]\ \text{J mol}^{-1}\ \text{K}^{-1} - [92 + (131)]\ \text{J mol}^{-1}\ \text{K}^{-1} = 32\ \text{J mol}^{-1}\ \text{K}^{-1}$$

Because the result is positive, the process is spontaneous.

76. The relationship to adjust the entropy change from 298 K to 498 K is $\Delta S_{498}°(\text{reaction}) = \Delta S_{298}°(\text{reaction}) + \int_{298\ K}^{498\ K} \frac{\Delta C_P°}{T} dT$. The value of $\Delta C_P°$ for the reaction is

$$\Delta C_P° = \sum C_P°(\text{products}) - \sum C_P°(\text{reactants})$$

$$= [2(24\ \text{J mol}^{-1}\ \text{K}^{-1}) + (34\ \text{J mol}^{-1}\ \text{K}^{-1})] - [(64\ \text{J mol}^{-1}\ \text{K}^{-1}) + (29\ \text{J mol}^{-1}\ \text{K}^{-1})]$$

$$= -11\ \text{J mol}^{-1}\ \text{K}^{-1}$$

Finishing the problem.

$$\Delta S_{498}°(\text{reaction}) = \Delta S_{298}°(\text{reaction}) + \int_{298\ \text{K}}^{498\ \text{K}} \frac{\Delta C_P°}{T} dT$$

$$= \Delta S_{298}°(\text{reaction}) + \Delta C_P° \ln \frac{498\ \text{K}}{298\ \text{K}}$$

$$= 32\ \text{J mol}^{-1}\ \text{K}^{-1} + (-11\ \text{J mol}^{-1}\ \text{K}^{-1})(0.514) = 26\ \text{J mol}^{-1}\ \text{K}^{-1}$$

77. The definition of the thermal expansion is $\alpha = \frac{1}{V}\left(\frac{\partial V}{\partial T}\right)_P$, and the definition of the entropy for the system is $\Delta S_{\text{system}} = -\int_{P_1}^{P_2} \left(\frac{\partial V}{\partial T}\right)_P dP$. These two equations combine to give $\Delta S_{\text{system}} = -\alpha V \int_{P_1}^{P_2} dP = -\alpha V(P_2 - P_1)$, where V is the volume. Entering values gives

$$\Delta S_{\text{system}} = -(1.16 \times 10^{-5}\ \text{K}^{-1})(1.00\ \text{mol})\left[\frac{(168.93\ \text{kg mol}^{-1})}{(9.32 \times 10^{3}\ \text{kg m}^{-3})}\right]$$

$$\times [(1.0 - 250.0)\text{atm}]\left(\frac{101.325\ \text{J}}{\text{m}^3\ \text{atm}}\right) = 5.30 \times 10^{-3}\ \text{J K}^{-1}$$

78. It is simplest to consider this process as a two-stage process. In one stage, the gas cools to its boiling point, and in the other, the gas condenses to the liquid at the boiling point ($T_{\text{bp}} = 237.8$ K). For the process, $\Delta S_{\text{total}} = \Delta S_{\text{system}} + \Delta S_{\text{surroundings}}$. The calculation of the two entropy contributions utilizes $\Delta S_{\text{system}} = \int_{T_1}^{T_2} \frac{C_P}{T} dT + \frac{-\Delta H_{\text{vap}}}{T_{\text{bp}}}$ and $\Delta S_{\text{surroundings}} = q/T$ with $q = \int_{T_1}^{T_2} C_P dT + \Delta H_{\text{vap}}$. The calculation of the separate entropy contributions are

$$\Delta S_{\text{system}} = \int_{T_1}^{T_2} \frac{C_P}{T} dT + \frac{-\Delta H_{\text{vap}}}{T_{\text{bp}}}$$

$$= \int_{273}^{240} \left[\frac{24.6}{T} + (3.75 \times 10^{-2}) + (-1.38 \times 10^{-6})\, T \right] dT$$

$$+ \frac{-(23.4 \text{ kJ mol}^{-1})}{237.8 \text{ K}} \left(\frac{10^3 \text{ J}}{1 \text{ kJ}} \right)$$

$$= (1.00 \text{ mol } [24.6 \ln \frac{240}{273} + (3.75 \times 10^{-2})$$

$$\times (240 - 273) - (1.38 \times 10^{-6})\,(240^2 - 273)^2] \text{J K}^{-1}) - 98.4 \text{ J K}^{-1} = -103 \text{ J K}^{-1}$$

Solving by parts,

$$\Delta S_{\text{surroundings}} = q/T = \frac{\int_{T_1}^{T_2} C_P dT + \Delta H_{\text{vap}}}{T}$$

$$= n \left\{ \frac{[24.6(240 - 273) + (3.75 \times 10^{-2})(240^2 - 273^2) + (-1.38 \times 10^{-6})\,(240^3 - 273^3)] \text{J mol}^{-1} + \Delta H_{\text{vap}}}{77 \text{ K}} \right\}$$

$$= 1.00 \text{ mol} \left\{ \frac{[-1437.6] \text{J mol}^{-1} + (23.4 \text{ kJ mol}^{-1}) \left(\frac{10^3 \text{ J}}{1 \text{ kJ}} \right)}{77 \text{ K}} \right\} = 285 \text{ J K}^{-1}$$

$$\Delta S_{\text{total}} = \Delta S_{\text{system}} + \Delta S_{\text{surroundings}} = -103 \text{ J K}^{-1} + 285 \text{ J K}^{-1} = 182 \text{ J K}^{-1}$$

79. The increase in entropy is $dS = \frac{C_P dT}{T}$ or $\left(\frac{\partial S}{\partial T}\right)_P = \frac{C_P}{T}$. Integration gives $\int_{S_1}^{S_2} dS = \int_{T_1}^{T_2} \frac{C_P dT}{T}$, which leads to $\Delta S = S_2 - S_1 = \int_0^{75} \frac{C_P dT}{T}$. Entering C_P,

$$\Delta S = S_2 - S_1 = \int_0^{75} \frac{[-0.096\, T + 0.010\, T^2 - 7.9 \times 10^{-5}\, T^3]}{T} dT$$

$$\Delta S = [-0.096(75 - 0) + 0.010\,(75^2 - 0^2) - 7.9 \times 10^{-5}(75^3 - 0^3)] \text{ J mol}^{-1} \text{ K}^{-1}$$

$$= 16 \text{ J mol}^{-1} \text{ K}^{-1}$$

80. The Debye third power law is $C_P = AT^3$, where A is a constant. The change in entropy in going from 0 K (T_1) to 20 K (T_2) is $\Delta S = \int_{T_1}^{T_2} \frac{C_P}{T} dT$, which leads to $\Delta S = \int_{T_1}^{T_2} \frac{AT^3}{T} dT = \int_{T_1}^{T_2} AT^2 dT$. Therefore,

$$\Delta S = \int_{T_1}^{T_2} AT^2 dT = \frac{AT^3}{3} \Big|_0^{20} = \frac{C_P}{3} \Big|_0^{20} = \frac{1}{3}(3.04 \text{ J mol}^{-1} \text{ K}^{-1}) - 0 = 1.01 \text{ J mol}^{-1} \text{ K}^{-1}$$

81. Dinitrogen oxide is a linear molecule, which has two orientations in the solid state. The orientations are NNO NNO and NNO ONN. The zero-point entropy is $k \ln 2^N$, where k is Boltzmann's constant and N is Avogadro's number. This leads to $k \ln 2^N = Nk \ln 2 = R \ln 2$, where R is the gas constant. This gives

$$\text{Zero-point entropy} = R \ln 2 = 8.3145 \text{ J mol}^{-1} \text{ K}^{-1}(\ln 2) = 5.7632 \text{ J mol}^{-1} \text{ K}^{-1}$$

82. Using the relationship $\Delta S_{\text{system}} = \frac{q_{\text{rev}}}{T}$ gives

$$\Delta S_{\text{system}} = \frac{q_{\text{rev}}}{T} = \frac{1000 \text{ J}}{273.15 \text{ K}} = 3.6610 \text{ J K}^{-1}$$

83. The entropy change for a phase transition is the heat of the transition divided by the transition temperature.

$$\Delta S = \frac{\Delta H}{T} = \frac{176 \text{ kJ mol}^{-1}}{1712 \text{ K}}\left(\frac{10^3 \text{ J}}{1 \text{ kJ}}\right) = 103 \text{ J mol}^{-1} \text{ K}^{-1}$$

84. The final temperature of the system is the average of the two initial temperatures (323.15 K). The change in entropy for each block is $nC_p \ln \frac{T_2}{T_1}$, where n is the moles, T_2 is the final temperature (323.15 K), and $T_1 = T_c$ is 273.15 K for the cold block and $T_1 = T_h$ is 373.15 K for the hot block. This becomes

$$\Delta S_{\text{system}} = \Delta S_{\text{cold block}} + \Delta S_{\text{hot block}} = \left[nC_p \ln \frac{T_2}{T_1}\right]_{\text{cold block}} + \left[nC_p \ln \frac{T_2}{T_1}\right]_{\text{hot block}}$$

$$= \left[(2.00 \text{ mol})(25.35 \text{ J mol}^{-1}\text{K}^{-1}) \ln \frac{323.15 \text{ K}}{273.15 \text{ K}}\right]_c$$

$$+ \left[(2.00 \text{ mol})(25.35 \text{ J mol}^{-1}\text{K}^{-1}) \ln \frac{323.15 \text{ K}}{373.15 \text{ K}}\right]_h = 1.23 \text{ J mol}^{-1} \text{ K}^{-1}$$

85. The possible combinations are $^{35}\text{Cl}^{35}\text{Cl}$, $^{35}\text{Cl}^{37}\text{Cl}$, $^{37}\text{Cl}^{35}\text{Cl}$, and $^{37}\text{Cl}^{37}\text{Cl}$. The mole fraction of $^{35}\text{Cl}^{35}\text{Cl}$ is (0.7577)(0.7577) = 0.5741, the mole fraction of $^{35}\text{Cl}^{37}\text{Cl}$ equals the mole fraction of $^{37}\text{Cl}^{35}\text{Cl}$ to give a total of (2)(0.7577)(0.2423) = 0.3672, and the mole fraction of $^{37}\text{Cl}^{37}\text{Cl}$ is (0.2423)(0.2423) = 0.05871, and the $\Delta S_{\text{mix}} = -R \sum x_i \ln x_i$, where x_i is the mole fraction of a component. Combining this information, with R, the gas constant, gives

$$\Delta S_{\text{mix}} = -R \sum x_i \ln x_i$$

$$= -(8.3145 \text{ J mol}^{-1} \text{ K}^{-1})[(0.5741 \ln 0.5741) + (0.3672 \ln 0.3672)$$

$$+ (0.05871 \ln 0.05871)] = 7.092 \text{ J mol}^{-1} \text{ K}^{-1}$$

Chapter 4: Fundamental Equations of Thermodynamics

86. The appropriate relationship is $\Delta\bar{U} = a\left(\frac{1}{\bar{V}_1} - \frac{1}{\bar{V}_2}\right)$. (The value of b is a distracter.) Solving by parts,

$$\Delta\bar{U} = a\left(\frac{1}{\bar{V}_1} - \frac{1}{\bar{V}_2}\right) = \left[(2.22\ \text{L}^2\ \text{bar mol}^{-2})\left(\frac{10^5\ \text{Pa}}{\text{bar}}\right)\left(\frac{10^{-3}\ \text{m}^3}{\text{L}}\right)\left(\frac{(1\ \text{kg})/\text{m s}^2}{\text{Pa}}\right)\right.$$

$$\left.\times\left(\frac{\text{J}}{(\text{kg m}^2/\text{s}^2)}\right)\right]\left(\frac{1}{\bar{V}_1} - \frac{1}{\bar{V}_2}\right)$$

$$= [(222\ \text{J L mol}^{-2})]\left(\frac{1}{2.00\ \text{L mol}^{-1}} - \frac{1}{10.00\ \text{L mol}^{-1}}\right) = 88.8\ \text{J mol}^{-1}$$

87. The work involved is $w = P\Delta\bar{V} = P(\bar{V}_l - \bar{V}_g) \approx -P\bar{V}_g = -RT$, where R is the gas constant. The symbol $\bar{V}$ refers to partial molar volume. This relationship gives

$$w = -RT = -(8.3145\ \text{J mol}^{-1}\ \text{K}^{-1})\ (373\ \text{K}) = -3.10 \times 10^3\ \text{J mol}^{-1}$$

88. The process is not reversible, and both the work (w) and the molar internal energy change ($\Delta\bar{U}$) are equal to zero. The enthalpy relationship is $\Delta\bar{H} = \Delta\bar{U} + \Delta(\text{P}\bar{V})$. The value of $\text{P}\bar{V}$ is constant for an ideal gas.

$$\Delta\bar{H} = \Delta\bar{U} + \Delta(\text{P}\bar{V}) = 0 + 0 = 0$$

89. The process is not reversible, and both the work (w) and the molar internal energy change ($\Delta\bar{U}$) are equal to zero. The Gibbs free energy relationship is $\Delta\bar{G} = \int_{P_1}^{P_2} \bar{V}\,dP$. In the following, R is the gas constant.

$$\Delta\bar{G} = \int_{P_1}^{P_2} \bar{V}\,dP = \int_{7.50}^{2.50} \bar{V}\,dP = RT\ln\frac{P_2}{P_1} = (8.3145\ \text{J mol}^{-1}\ \text{K}^{-1})(315\ \text{K})\ln\frac{2.50\ \text{bar}}{7.50\ \text{bar}}$$

$$= -2.88 \times 10^3\ \text{J mol}^{-1}$$

90. The process is not reversible, and both the work (w) and the molar internal energy change ($\Delta\bar{U}$) are equal to zero. The entropy relationship is $\Delta\bar{S} = \frac{\Delta\bar{H} - \Delta\bar{G}}{T}$.

$$\Delta\bar{S} = \frac{\Delta\bar{H} - \Delta\bar{G}}{T} = \frac{0 - (-2.88 \times 10^3\ \text{J mol}^{-1})}{(315\ \text{K})} = 9.13\ \text{J mol}^{-1}\ \text{K}^{-1}$$

91. The general relationship is $\Delta G_f = \Delta G_f^\circ + \int_{P_1}^{P_2} V\ dP$. Substituting $V = nRT/P$ gives $\Delta G_f = \Delta G_f^\circ + nRT \int_{P_1}^{P_2} d \ln P$, which, in this case, leads to $\Delta G_f = \Delta G_f^\circ + RT \ln\left(\frac{P}{P^\circ}\right)$, where R is the gas constant and P° is standard pressure (1.00 bar).

$$\Delta G_f = \Delta G_f^\circ + RT \ln\left(\frac{P}{P^\circ}\right)$$

$$= 31.8 \text{ kJ mol}^{-1} + \left[(8.3145 \text{ J mol}^{-1} \text{ K}^{-1})(298.15 \text{ K}) \ln\left(\frac{15.0 \text{ bar}}{1.00 \text{ bar}}\right)\right]\left(\frac{1 \text{ kJ}}{1000 \text{ J}}\right)$$

$$= 38.5 \text{ kJ mol}^{-1}$$

92. The general relationship is $\Delta G_f = \Delta G_f^\circ + \int_{P_1}^{P_2} V\ dP$. For liquids and solids, pressure changes lead to only small volume change; therefore, it is possible to consider the volume a constant with this small pressure change. These leads to $\Delta G_f = \Delta G_f^\circ + V(P_2 - P_1)$. The volume is the molar volume of mercury ($\bar{V}$), and P° (= P_1) is standard pressure (1.00 bar). It is necessary to solve this by parts.

$$\Delta G_f = \Delta G_f^\circ + \bar{V}\ (P_2 - P_1)$$

$$= 0.00 \text{ kJ mol}^{-1} + \left[\left(\frac{200.59 \text{ g}}{\text{mol}}\right)\left(\frac{\text{cm}^3}{13.59 \text{ g}}\right)\left(\frac{0.01 \text{ m}}{1 \text{ cm}}\right)^3\right][(15.0 - 1.00)\text{bar}]$$

$$= \left[\left(\frac{1.476 \times 10^{-5} \text{m}^3}{1 \text{ mol}}\right)\right][(15.0 - 1.00)\text{bar}]\left[\left(\frac{10^5 \text{ Pa}}{1 \text{ bar}}\right)\left(\frac{1 \text{ kg/m s}^2}{1 \text{ Pa}}\right)\right.$$

$$\left.\times\left(\frac{1 \text{ J}}{(1 \text{ Kg m}^2/\text{s}^2)}\right)\left(\frac{1 \text{ KJ}}{1000 \text{ J}}\right)\right] = 0.0207 \text{ kJ mol}^{-1}$$

93. The key relationship is $f = P \exp\left[\left(b - \frac{a}{RT}\right)\frac{P}{RT}\right]$, where R is the gas constant. Solving by parts,

$$f = P \exp\left[\left(b - \frac{a}{RT}\right)\frac{P}{RT}\right]$$

$$= (75.0 \text{ bar})\exp\left[\left(\{0.0427 \text{ L mol}^{-1}\} - \frac{(3.54 \text{ L}^2 \text{ bar mol}^{-1})}{(0.083145 \text{ L bar mol}^{-2} \text{ K}^{-1})(273 \text{ K})}\right)\frac{P}{RT}\right]$$

$$= (75.0 \text{ bar})\exp\left[(-0.1133 \text{ L mol}^{-1})\frac{(75.0 \text{ bar})}{(0.083145 \text{ L bar mol}^{-1} \text{ K}^{-1})(273 \text{ K})}\right] = 51.6 \text{ bar}$$

94. The important relationship is $a = e^{\bar{V}(P-P^\circ)/RT}$. Recall, $P^\circ = 1.00$ bar and $R = 0.083145$ L bar mol^{-1} K^{-1}. Do not forget, activities have no units.

$$a = e^{\bar{V}(P-P^\circ)/RT} = e^{[(0.0148 \text{ L mol}^{-1})(75.0\ -1.00)\text{bar}]/[(0.03145 \text{ L bar mol}^{-1}\text{K}^{-1})(298 \text{ K})]} = 1.04$$

95. Use the relationship $\Delta\bar{S} = R\ln\left(\frac{\bar{V}_2 - b}{\bar{V}_1 - b}\right)$, where R is the gas constant.

$$\Delta\bar{S} = R\ln\left(\frac{\bar{V}_2 - b}{\bar{V}_1 - b}\right) = (8.3145\ \text{J mol}^{-1}\ \text{K}^{-1})\ln\left(\frac{10.00\ \text{L mol}^{-1} - 0.0428\ \text{L mol}^{-1}}{2.00\ \text{L mol}^{-1} - 0.0428\ \text{L mol}^{-1}}\right)$$
$$= 13.5\ \text{J mol}^{-1}\ \text{K}^{-1}$$

96. The formation reaction is: Ca(s) + ½ O_2(g) → CaO(s). To determine the standard Gibbs energy for this reaction, it is necessary to use the relationship $\Delta G = \Delta H - T\Delta S$. The values in the table give ΔH and ΔS by taking the products minus the reactants.

$$\Delta H = [-635.5\ \text{kJ mol}^{-1}] - [0] = -635.5\ \text{kJ mol}^{-1}$$
$$\Delta S = [39.8\ \text{J mol}^{-1}\ \text{K}^{-1}] - [41.4\ \text{J mol}^{-1}\ \text{K}^{-1} + ½(205.0\ \text{J mol}^{-1}\ \text{K}^{-1})]$$
$$= -104.1\ \text{J mol}^{-1}\ \text{K}^{-1}$$
$$\Delta G = \Delta H - T\Delta S = (-635.5\ \text{kJ mol}^{-1}) - (298.15\ \text{K})(-104.1\ \text{J mol}^{-1}\ \text{K}^{-1})\left(\frac{1\ \text{kJ}}{1000\ \text{J}}\right)$$
$$= -604.5\ \text{kJ mol}^{-1}$$

97. It is necessary to rearrange the equation $\Delta G° = \Delta H° - T\Delta S°$ to solve for $\Delta S°$. After rearranging, enter the appropriate values.

$$\Delta S° = \frac{\Delta H° - \Delta G°}{T} = \frac{[-78.6 - (-35.5)]\text{kJ}}{298\ \text{K}}\left(\frac{10^3\ \text{J}}{1\ \text{kJ}}\right) = -145\ \text{J K}^{-1}$$

98. It is necessary to enter the appropriate values into the equation $\Delta G° = \Delta H° - T\Delta S°$.

$$\Delta G° = \Delta H° - T\Delta S° = (105.27\ \text{kJ mol}^{-1}) - (1{,}156\ \text{K})(91.06\ \text{J mol}^{-1}\ \text{K}^{-1})(1\ \text{kJ}/10^3\ \text{J})$$
$$= 0.00\ \text{kJ}$$

99. For an ideal gas, the PV dependence of ΔG under isothermal equations is $\Delta G = -nRT\ln(V_2/V_1) = nRT\ln(P_2/P_1)$, where R is the gas constant. Entering the appropriate values gives

$$\Delta G = -nRT\ln\left(\frac{V_2}{V_1}\right) = -(2.00\ \text{mol})(8.3145\ \text{J mol}^{-1}\ \text{K}^{-1})(298\ \text{K})\ln\left(\frac{3.00\ \text{L}}{20.20\ \text{L}}\right) = 9{,}450\ \text{J}$$

100. This is an ideal gas; therefore, $\Delta T = 0$, so $T_1 = T_2$. The expansion against $P_{ext} = 0$ makes $w = 0$, $\Delta U = 0$, and $q = 0$. The relationship to determine ΔS is $\Delta S = \int_{T_1}^{T_2}\frac{C_v}{T}dT + R\ln\frac{V_2}{V_1}$, where R is the gas constant. Assuming the process is reversible, the integral is 0. Entering the values

$$\Delta S = \int_{T_1}^{T_2}\frac{C_v}{T}dT + R\ln\frac{V_2}{V_1} = 0 + (8.3145\ \text{J mol}^{-1}\ \text{K}^{-1})\ln\frac{50.50\ \text{L}}{25.25\ \text{L}} = 5.7632\ \text{J mol}^{-1}\ \text{K}^{-1}$$

101. This is an ideal gas; therefore, $\Delta T = 0$, so $T_1 = T_2$. The expansion against $P_{ext} = 0$ makes $w = 0$, $\Delta U = 0$, and $q = 0$. The equation for the determination of the Helmholtz free energy is $\Delta A = \Delta U - T\Delta S$. Entering the appropriate values gives

$$\Delta A = \Delta U - T\Delta S = 0 - (298.15\text{ K})\ (5.7632\text{ J mol}^{-1}\text{ K}^{-1}) = -1{,}718.3\text{ J mol}^{-1}$$

102. For an ideal gas, the PV dependence of ΔG under isothermal equations is $\Delta G_f = \Delta G_f^\circ - RT\ln (V_2/V_1) = \Delta G_f^\circ + RT\ln (P_2/P_1)$, where R is the gas constant. Entering the appropriate values gives

$$\Delta G = \Delta G_f^\circ + RT\ln\left(\frac{P_2}{P_1}\right)$$

$$= -32.76\text{ kJ mol}^{-1} + (8.3145\text{ J mol}^{-1}\text{ K}^{-1})\left(\frac{1\text{ kJ}}{10^3\text{ J}}\right)(298\text{ K})\ln\left(\frac{7.50\text{ bar}}{1.00\text{ bar}}\right)$$

$$= -27.77\text{ kJ mol}^{-1}$$

103. It is possible to consider this a three-step process. Step 1 is $H_2O(s, P_1) \rightarrow H_2O(g, P_1)$, step 2 is $H_2O(g, P_1) \rightarrow H_2O(g, P_2)$, and step 3 is $H_2O(g, P_2) \rightarrow H_2O(l, P_2)$. It is possible to conduct steps 1 and 3 reversibly under equilibrium conditions; therefore, $\Delta G_1 = \Delta G_3 = 0$. For step 2, the appropriate relationship is $\Delta G_{fus} = -RT\ln (V_2/V_1) = RT \ln (P_2/P_1)$, where R is the gas constant.

$$\Delta G_{fus} = RT\ln\left(\frac{P_2}{P_1}\right) = (8.3145\text{ J mol}^{-1}\text{ K}^{-1})\left(\frac{1\text{ kJ}}{10^3\text{ J}}\right)(263\text{ K})\ln\left(\frac{2.828\times 10^{-3}\text{ atm}}{2.565\times 10^{-3}\text{ atm}}\right)$$

$$= 0.213\text{ kJ mol}^{-1}$$

104. The Gibbs free energy relationship is $\Delta G = \Delta H - T\Delta S$, where T is 298 K, ΔH is -45.8 kJ mol^{-1}, and ΔG is the change in the Gibbs free energy. The change in the Gibbs free energy is $[-419.1\text{ kJ mol}^{-1}] - [-379.4\text{ kJ mol}^{-1}] = -39.7\text{ kJ mol}^{-1}$. Rearranging the Gibbs free energy relationship to find the entropy changes gives

$$\Delta S = \frac{\Delta H - \Delta G}{T} = \frac{([-45.8] - [-39.7])\text{kJ mol}^{-1}}{298\text{ K}}\left(\frac{10^3\text{ J}}{1\text{ kJ}}\right) = -20\text{ J mol}^{-1}$$

105. The appropriate relationship is $\Delta G = nRT\ln (a_2/a_1)$, where R is the gas constant. Entering the values into this relationship gives

$$\Delta G = nRT\ln (a_2/a_1) = \left[(1.00\text{ mol})(8.3145\text{ J mol}^{-1}\text{ K}^{-1})(298\text{ K})\ln\left(\frac{1.27}{4.31}\right)\right]\left(\frac{1\text{ kJ}}{10^3\text{ J}}\right)$$

$$= -3.03\text{ kJ mol}^{-1}$$

106. The activity (a) of an ideal gas is P/bar. The relationship between the Gibbs free energy change and the activity is $\Delta G - \Delta G° = nRT \ln a$, where R is the gas constant. Assume there is 1.00 mol (n) of ideal gas. Entering the values into the last relationship gives

$$\Delta G - \Delta G° = nRT \ln a = 2.482 \text{ kJ mol}^{-1}$$

$$2.482 \text{ kJ mol}^{-1} = \left[(1.00 \text{ mol})(8.3145 \text{ J mol}^{-1} \text{ K}^{-1})(298.15 \text{ K}) \ln\left(\frac{P}{\text{bar}}\right)\right]\left(\frac{1 \text{ kJ}}{10^3 \text{ J}}\right)$$

$$\ln\left(\frac{P}{\text{bar}}\right) = \frac{2.482 \text{ kJ mol}^{-1}}{[(1.00 \text{ mol})(8.3145 \text{ J mol}^{-1} \text{ K}^{-1})(298.15 \text{ K})]\left(\frac{1 \text{ kJ}}{10^3 \text{ J}}\right)} = 1.001223$$

$$P = 2.722 \text{ bar} \approx \text{a}$$

107. The concentrations of the individual ions are $[K^+] = [0.00100 + 2(0.00150)]$ $m = 0.00400$ m, $[Cl^-] = 0.00100$ m, and $[SO_4^{2-}] = 0.00150$ m. The ionic strength of a solution is $I = \frac{1}{2}\sum_i m_i z_i^2$, where the m's are the molal concentrations and the z's are the charges on the ions. Expanding this summation and entering the values gives

$$I = \frac{1}{2}\left[m_{K^+} z_{K^+}^2 + m_{Cl^-} z_{Cl^-}^2 + m_{SO_4^{2-}} z_{SO_4^{2-}}^2\right]$$

$$= \frac{1}{2}[(0.00400 \text{ m})(+1)^2 + (0.00100 \text{ m})(-1)^2 + (0.00150 \text{ m})(-2)^2] = 0.00550 \text{ m}$$

108. According to Debye and Hückel, the relationship is $\log \gamma_i = -z_i^2 A\sqrt{I}$, where γ_i is the activity coefficient, z_i^2 is the ionic charge, A is the Debye–Hückel coefficient, and I is the ionic strength of the solution. Entering the appropriate values,

$$\log \gamma_i = -z_i^2 A\sqrt{I} = -(+1)_{K^+}^2 (0.5116)\sqrt{0.00550} = -0.037941$$

$$\gamma_{K^+} = 0.916$$

109. The change in the internal energy is given by $\Delta\bar{E} = \Delta\bar{H} - P\Delta\bar{V}$, where $P\Delta\bar{V} = w$. Using this relationship and entering the appropriate values gives

$$\Delta\bar{E} = \Delta\bar{H} - P\Delta\bar{V} = (-40.69 \text{ kJ mol}^{-1}) - (-3.10 \text{ kJ mol}^{-1}) = -37.59 \text{ kJ mol}^{-1}$$

110. The change in the molar entropy is $\Delta\bar{S} = \frac{\Delta\bar{H}}{T}$. Using this relationship gives

$$\Delta\bar{S} = \frac{\Delta\bar{H}}{T} = \frac{40.69 \text{ kJ mol}^{-1}}{373 \text{ K}} = 0.109 \text{ kJ mol}^{-1} \text{ K}^{-1}$$

111. It is possible to determine the Gibbs free energy for the fugacities by using $\Delta G = nRT \ln \frac{f_2}{f_1}$, where R is the gas constant. Entering the given values into this equation gives

$$\Delta G = nRT \ln \frac{f_2}{f_1} = (1.00 \text{ mol})(8.3145 \text{ J mol}^{-1} \text{ K}^{-1})(473 \text{ K}) \ln \frac{193 \text{ atm}}{23.9 \text{ atm}}$$
$$= 8.21 \times 10^3 \text{ J mol}^{-1}$$

112. It is possible to use Hess's law to combine the reaction for the standard enthalpy of formation for HBr(aq) and the reverse of the reaction for the standard enthalpy of formation of H^+(aq) (defined as 0 kJ) to get

~~½ H_2(g)~~ + ½ Br_2(l) + ~~aq~~ → ~~H^+(aq)~~ + Br^-(aq) $\quad \Delta H° = -121$ kJ mol^{-1}

~~H^+(aq)~~ + e^-(aq) → ~~½ H_2(g)~~ + ~~aq~~ $\quad \Delta H° = 0$ kJ mol^{-1}

½ Br_2(l) + e^-(aq) → Br^-(aq) $\quad \Delta H° = -121$ kJ mol^{-1}

113. The relationship to determine the heat capacity difference is $(C_p - C_v) = T\bar{V}\alpha^2\kappa^{-1}$. Using the information from the problem gives

$$(C_p - C_v) = T\bar{V}\alpha^2\kappa^{-1} = \frac{(800 \text{ K})(7.26 \times 10^{-6} \text{ m}^3 \text{ mol}^{-1})(6.00 \times 10^{-5} \text{ K}^{-1})^2}{(3.23 \times 10^{-11} \text{kg m s}^{-2})}$$
$$\times \left(\frac{\text{J}}{\text{kg m}^2 / \text{s}^2} \right) = 0.647 \text{ J mol}^{-1} \text{ K}^{-1}$$

Chapter 5: Chemical Equilibria

114. The general expression is $K = \left(\frac{a_{CO_2} a_{N_a}^2}{a_C a_{N_2O}^2} \right)_{eq}$, where the *a*'s are the activities of the species present.

If the pressure is not too high, a_C would be 1 (standard state).

115. The second equilibrium is twice the second; therefore, $K_2 = K_1^2$.

$$K_2 = K_1^2 = (0.335)^2 = 0.112$$

116. The equilibrium constant for the second reaction (K_2) is the reciprocal of the equilibrium constant of the forward reaction.

$$K_2 = 1/K_1 = 1/(0.335) = 2.99$$

117. To determine the standard Gibbs energy of reaction ($\Delta G_{rxn}°$), use the relationship $\Delta G_{rxn}° = -RT \ln K$, where R is the gas constant.

$$\Delta G_{rxn}° = -RT \ln K = -(8.3145 \text{ J mol}^{-1} \text{ K}^{-1})(1000 \text{ K}) \ln(0.335) = 9.09 \times 10^3 \text{ J mol}^{-1}$$

118. The key relationship is $\Delta G_{rxn} = \Delta G_{rxn}{}^\circ + RT \ln Q$, where $Q = \left(\frac{P_{HI}^2}{P_{H_2} P_{I_2}}\right)$, and R is the gas constant. Using this equation

$$\Delta G_{rxn} = \Delta G_{rxn}{}^\circ + RT \ln\left(\frac{P_{HI}^2}{P_{H_2} P_{I_2}}\right)$$

$$= 2.6 \text{ kJ mol}^{-1} + (8.3145 \text{ J mol}^{-1} \text{ K}^{-1})\left(\frac{1 \text{ kJ}}{1000 \text{ J}}\right)(398 \text{ K}) \ln\left(\frac{(0.500)^2}{(2.00)(2.00)}\right)$$

$$= -6.6 \text{ kJ mol}^{-1}$$

Because ΔG_{rxn} is negative, the process will proceed in the forward direction and more hydrogen iodide will form.

119. The key relationship is $\Delta G_{rxn} = \Delta G_{rxn}{}^\circ + RT \ln Q$, where $Q = \left(\frac{P_{HI}^2}{P_{H_2} P_{I_2}}\right)$, where R is the gas constant. Using this equation

$$\Delta G_{rxn} = \Delta G_{rxn}{}^\circ + RT \ln\left(\frac{P_{HI}^2}{P_{H_2} P_{I_2}}\right)$$

$$= 2.6 \text{ kJ mol}^{-1} + (8.3145 \text{ J mol}^{-1} \text{ K}^{-1})\left(\frac{1 \text{ kJ}}{1000 \text{ J}}\right)(398 \text{ K}) \ln\left(\frac{(2.00)^2}{(0.500)(0.500)}\right)$$

$$= 11.8 \text{ kJ mol}^{-1}$$

Because ΔG_{rxn} is positive, the process will proceed in the reverse direction and hydrogen iodide will decompose, not form.

120. M_2 is the molar mass of the equilibrium mixture. M_2 is equal mass of the sample (1.312 g) divided by total moles determined from the ideal gas equation ($n = PV/RT$), where R is the gas constant.

$$M_2 = \frac{m}{\left(\frac{PV}{RT}\right)} = \frac{1.312 \text{ g}}{\left(\frac{(0.8885 \text{ bar})(0.7500 \text{ L})}{(0.083145 \text{ L bar mol}^{-1} \text{ K}^{-1})(298.15 \text{ K})}\right)} = 48.81 \text{ g mol}^{-1}$$

121. It is possible to determine the extent of reaction (ξ) from $\xi = \frac{M_1 - M_2}{M_1}$, where M_1 is the original molar mass ($N_2O_3 = 76.01$ g mol^{-1}) and M_2 is the molar mass of the equilibrium mixture (48.81 g mol^{-1}).

$$\xi = \frac{M_1 - M_2}{M_2} = \frac{(76.01 - 48.81)\text{g mol}^{-1}}{(48.81)\text{g mol}^{-1}} = 0.5573$$

122. It is possible to determine the value of K from the extent of reaction using the partial pressure of the substances involved (P_{NO}, P_{NO_2}, and $P_{N_2O_3}$) and by constructing a table such as

	$N_2O_3(g)$	⇆	$NO(g)$	+	$NO_2(g)$
Initial amounts	1		0		0
Equilibrium amount	$1-\xi$		ξ		ξ
	(Total amount = $1+\xi$)				
Equilibrium mole fraction	$\frac{1-\xi}{1+\xi}$		$\frac{\xi}{1+\xi}$		$\frac{\xi}{1+\xi}$

$$K=\frac{\left(P_{NO}/P^\circ\right)\left(P_{NO_2}/P^\circ\right)}{\left(P_{N_2O_3}/P^\circ\right)}=\frac{\left[\frac{\xi}{1+\xi}\right]\left(P/P^\circ\right)\left[\frac{\xi}{1+\xi}\right]\left(P/P^\circ\right)}{\left[\frac{1-\xi}{1+\xi}\right]\left(P/P^\circ\right)}=\frac{\left[\frac{\xi}{1+\xi}\right]\left(P/P^\circ\right)[\xi]}{[1-\xi]}$$

$$=\frac{[\xi]\left(P/P^\circ\right)}{[1-\xi^2]}=\frac{[0.5573](0.8885)}{[1-(0.5573)^2]}=0.7182$$

123. The important relationship is $\Delta G_{rxn}{}^\circ = -RT\ln K_p$, which requires the calculation of $\Delta G_{rxn}{}^\circ$ from the difference between the products and reactants and where R is the gas constant. The reaction is $N_2O_3(g) \leftrightarrows NO(g) + NO_2(g)$.

$$\Delta G_{rxn}{}^\circ = [86.7\ \text{kJ mol}^{-1} + 51.8\ \text{kJ mol}^{-1}] - [139.3\ \text{kJ mol}^{-1}] = -0.8\ \text{kJ mol}^{-1}$$

$$\ln K_p = -\frac{\Delta G_{rxn}{}^\circ}{RT} = -\frac{-0.8\ \text{kJ mol}^{-1}}{(8.3145\ \text{J mol}^{-1}\ \text{K}^{-1})(298\ \text{K})}\left(\frac{1000\ \text{J}}{1\ \text{kJ}}\right) = 0.3$$

$$K_p = e^{0.3} = 1.3$$

124. The equilibrium is $N_2O_3(g) \leftrightarrows NO(g) + NO_2(g)$.

The relationship between K_p and K_c is $K_p = K_c(RT)^{\Delta n}$, where R is the gas constant (0.08206 L atm mol^{-1} K^{-1}), $T = 298.15\ K$, and Δn is the change in the number of moles (of gas). Rearranging the equation and entering the appropriate values gives

$$K_c = \frac{K_p}{(RT)^{\Delta n}} = \frac{(0.7182)}{[(0.08206)(298.15)]^{(2-1)}} = 0.02935$$

125. The important relationship is $\Delta G_{rxn}° = -RT \ln K$, where R is the gas constant.

$$\ln K = -\frac{\Delta G_{rxn}°}{RT} = -\frac{12.7 \text{ kJ mol}^{-1}}{(8.3145 \text{ J mol}^{-1} \text{ K}^{-1})(298 \text{ K})}\left(\frac{1000 \text{ J}}{1 \text{ kJ}}\right) = -5.126$$

$$K = e^{-5.126} = 5.94 \times 10^{-3}$$

126. There are three species in the system ($N_s = 3$), there is one independent reaction ($R = 1$), and there are three phases ($p = 3$). The number of components (C) comes from $C = N_s - R = 3 - 1 = 2$, and the degrees of freedom (F) comes from $F = C - p + 2 = 2 - 3 + 2 = 1$.

127. There are three species in the system ($N_s = 3$), there is one independent reaction ($R = 1$), and there are three phases ($p = 2$). The number of components (C) comes from $C = N_s - R = 3 - 1 = 2$, and the degrees of freedom (F) comes from $F = C - p + 2 = 2 - 2 + 2 = 2$.

128. To get to equilibrium, the reaction must shift to the right; therefore, some carbon monoxide and sulfur react and some sulfur dioxide forms. To calculate K_p, it is necessary to determine the partial pressures of the gases, which are assumed to be equal to their activities. (The activities of the solids are 1.) If the amount of sulfur dioxide formed is x, then the amount of carbon monoxide reacted is $2x$. From this, the partial pressures are $P_{CO} = (2.000 - 2x)$ atm and $P_{SO_2} = x$ atm. From Dalton's law,

$$P_{total} = P_{CO} + P_{SO_2} = 1.030 \text{ atm} = (2.000 - 2x) \text{ atm} + x \text{ atm} = 2.000 - x$$

$$x = 0.970 \text{ atm}$$

With $x = 0.970$ atm, the equilibrium partial pressures are $P_{CO} = 0.060$ atm and $P_{SO_2} = 0.970$ atm. The K_p expression is $K_p = \frac{P_{SO_2}}{P_{CO}^2}$. Entering the partial pressures into the K_p expression gives

$$K_p = \frac{P_{SO_2}}{P_{CO}^2} = \frac{0.970}{(0.060)^2} = 2.7 \times 10^2$$

129. The total pressure is the sum of the partial pressures of the two gases formed. Because the two gases are formed in equal amounts, the partial pressure of each gas is 0.60 atm. The activities of the solids are unity, so only the gases are important to the calculation of K_p. Assuming the activities of the gases are equal to the partial pressures of the gases gives

$$K_p = P_{SO_2} P_{SO_3} = (0.60)\,(0.60) = 0.36$$

130. As the system moves to equilibrium, equal amounts of the two gases form. Each gas increases in pressure by x atm. Therefore, at equilibrium, the partial pressures are P_{SO_3} = (1.00 + x) atm and $P_{SO_2} = x$ atm. The activities of the solids are unity, and assuming the partial pressures are equal to the activities of the gases, the equilibrium expression is

$$K_p = P_{SO_2} P_{SO_3} = 0.36 = (1.00 + x)(x)$$

This rearranges to the following quadratic form

$$x^2 + x - 0.36 = 0$$

From this, $a = 1$, $b = 1$, and $c = -0.6$.

$$x = \frac{-b \pm \sqrt{b^2 - 4ac}}{2a} = \frac{-1 \pm \sqrt{1^2 - 4(1)(-0.36)}}{2(1)} = 0.28 \text{ or } -1.3$$

The root −1.3 is physically impossible; therefore, 0.28 is the value of x, which leads to

$$P_{SO_3} = (1.00 + x) \text{ atm} = (1.00 + 0.28) \text{ atm} = 1.28 \text{ atm}$$

$$P_{SO_2} = x \text{ atm} = 0.28 \text{ atm}$$

131. The activity coefficient of component A is $\gamma_A = \frac{P_A}{x_A P_A{}^\circ}$, where P_A is the vapor pressure of A in a solution, x_A is the mole fraction of A, and $P_A{}^\circ$ is the vapor pressure of pure A. For bromine, $P_A = 7.90$ torr, $x_A = 0.0600$, and $P_A{}^\circ = 125$ torr. For carbon tetrachloride, $P_A = 33.3$ torr, $x_A = (1.0000 - 0.0600) = 0.9400$, and $P_A{}^\circ = 33.9$ torr. Solving for the two activity coefficients

$$\gamma_{Br_2} = \frac{P_{Br_2}}{x_{Br_2} P_{Br_2}{}^\circ} = \frac{7.90 \text{ torr}}{(0.0600)(125 \text{ torr})} = 1.05$$

$$\gamma_{CCl_4} = \frac{P_{CCl_4}}{x_{CCl_4} P_{CCl_4}{}^\circ} = \frac{33.3 \text{ torr}}{(0.9400)(33.9 \text{ torr})} = 1.04$$

132. The activity for component A is $a_A = \gamma_A x_A$, where a_A is the activity of A, γ_A is the activity coefficient of A, and x_A is the mole fraction of A. For bromine, $\gamma_A = 1.05$ and $x_A = 0.0600$, and for carbon tetrachloride, $\gamma_A = 1.04$ and $x_A = 0.9400 = (1.0000 - 0.0600)$. Solving for the two activities,

$$a_{Br_2} = \gamma_{Br_2} x_{Br_2} = (1.05)(0.0600) = 0.0630$$

$$a_{CCl_4} = \gamma_{CCl_4} x_{CCl_4} = (1.04)(0.9400) = 0.978$$

133. The best starting point is to write the equilibrium expression, $K = \frac{[I]^2}{[I_2]} = 3.76 \times 10^{-5}$. It is also useful to prepare a table of the form (assuming the concentration is equal to the activity).

	$[I_2]$	$[I]$
Initial	0.500	0
Change	$-x$	$2x$
Equilibrium	$0.500 - x$	$2x$

Entering the last line into the equilibrium expression gives

$$K = \frac{[I]^2}{[I_2]} = 3.76 \times 10^{-5} = \frac{[2x]^2}{[0.500 - x]}$$

This becomes $4x^2 + 3.76 \times 10^{-5}x - 1.88 \times 10^{-5} = 0$.

Solving this quadratic equation gives $x = 2.16 \times 10^{-3}$ M; therefore, $[I_2] = (0.500 - x)$ M $= 0.498$; M and $[I] = (2x)$ M $= 4.32 \times 10^{-3}$ M.

134. The general relationship between $\Delta G°$ and K is $\Delta G° = -RT \ln K$, where R is the gas constant. Rearranging and entering the appropriate values

$$\ln K_{sp} = \frac{\Delta G°}{-RT} = \frac{-9.00 \text{ kJ mol}^{-1}}{-(8.3145 \text{ J mol}^{-1}\text{K}^{-1})(298 \text{ K})}\left(\frac{10^3 \text{ J}}{1 \text{ kJ}}\right) = 3.63$$

$$K_{sp} = 37.8$$

135. The general K_{sp} relationship for a 1:1 electrolyte is $K_{sp} = \gamma_{\pm}^2 C^2$, where $\gamma_{\pm}$ is the mean ionic activity coefficient and C is the concentration of the ions. Rearranging and entering the appropriate values,

$$\gamma_{\pm} = \frac{\sqrt{K_{sp}}}{C} = \frac{\sqrt{37.8}}{5.38} = 1.14$$

136. The best starting point is to write the equilibrium expression, $K_p = \frac{P_{CS_2}}{P_{S_2}}$. (Solids do not appear in the expression because their activities are 1.) It is also useful to prepare a table of the form (assuming the partial pressure is equal to the activity).

	$[S_2]$	$[CS_2]$
Initial	0.431	0
Change	$-x$	$+x$
Equilibrium	$0.431 - x$	x

From the equilibrium partial pressure of $S_2(g)$, it is possible to calculate x as $(0.431 - x) = 0.414$ atm. This leads to $x = 0.017$ atm $= P_{CS_2}$. Entering the partial pressures into the equilibrium expression gives

$$K_p = \frac{P_{CS_2}}{P_{S_2}} = \frac{0.017}{0.414} = 0.041$$

137. The relationship between K_p and K_c is $K_p = K_c\,(RT)^{\Delta n}$, where R is the gas constant (0.08206 L atm mol^{-1} K^{-1}), $T = 500$ K, and Δn is the change in the number of moles (of gas). Rearranging the equation and entering the appropriate values gives

$$K_c = \frac{K_p}{(RT)^{\Delta n}} = \frac{(0.041)}{[(0.08206)(500)]^{(1-1)}} = 0.041$$

138. The relationship is $\ln\frac{K_2}{K_1} = \frac{\Delta H°(T_2 - T_1)}{RT_1T_2}$, where R is the gas constant. Rearranging this equation and entering the appropriate values gives

$$\Delta H° = \frac{RT_1T_2\left(\ln\frac{K_2}{K_1}\right)}{(T_2 - T_1)}$$

$$= \frac{(8.3145 \text{ J mol}^{-1}\text{ K}^{-1})(1900\text{ K})(2100\text{ K})\left(\ln\frac{6.86\times 10^{-4}}{2.31\times 10^{-4}}\right)}{(2100 - 1900)\text{K}}\left(\frac{1\text{ kJ}}{10^3\text{ J}}\right) = 181\text{ kJ mol}^{-1}$$

139. The relationship is $\ln\frac{K_2}{K_1} = \frac{\Delta H°(T_2 - T_1)}{RT_1T_2}$, where R is the gas constant. Rearranging this equation and entering the appropriate values gives

$$\ln K_2 = \frac{\Delta H°(T_2 - T_1)}{RT_1T_2} + \ln K_1$$

$$= \frac{(181\text{ kJ mol}^{-1})(2000 - 1900)\text{K}}{(8.3145\text{ J mol}^{-1}\text{ K}^{-1})(1900\text{ K})(2000\text{ K})}\left(\frac{10^3\text{ J}}{1\text{ kJ}}\right) + \ln 2.31\times 10^{-4} = -7.80$$

$$K_e - e^{-7.80} - 4.10\times 10^{-4}$$

Chapter 6: Phase Equilibria

140. The pressure (P) along the bubble point line depends upon the pressure of the pure components and the mole fraction (x) of one of the components. Assigning *n*-pentane as component 1 and using the general equation for the bubble point line

$$P = P_2^* + (P_1^* - P_2^*)x_1 = 0.157\text{ bar} + [(0.573 - 0.157)\text{ bar}]x_1 = 0.157\text{ bar} + 0.416\,x_1$$

(The term x_1 refers to the mole fraction of component 1 in the liquid phase.)

141. The pressure (*P*) along the bubble point line depends upon the pressure of the pure components and the mole fraction (y) of one of the components. Assigning *n*-pentane as component 1 and using the general equation for the dew point line,

$$P = \frac{P_1^* P_2^*}{P_1^* + (P_2^* - P_1^*)y_1} = \frac{(0.573)(0.157)\text{bar}^2}{0.573 \text{ bar} + [(0.157 - 0.573)\text{bar}]y_1}$$

$$= \frac{0.0900 \text{ bar}^2}{0.573 \text{ bar} - [0.416 \text{ bar}]y_1} = \frac{0.0900 \text{ bar}}{0.573 - 0.416\ y_1}$$

(The term y_1 refers to the mole fraction of component 1 in the gas phase.)

142. If x_1 is 0.550, then x_2 must be 0.450 as the sum of the mole fractions is unity. The vapor pressure of a component (P_1 and P_2) is its mole fraction times the pressure of the pure component.

For *n*-pentane: $P_1 = x_1 P_1{}^* = (0.550)(0.573 \text{ bar}) = 0.315$ bar.

For *n*-hexane: $P_2 = x_2 P_2{}^* = (0.450)(0.157 \text{ bar}) = 0.0706$ bar.

143. Using the general equation for the mole fraction of a component in the vapor phase,

$$y_1 = \frac{x_1 P_1^*}{P_2^* + (P_1^* - P_2^*)x_1} = \frac{(0.550)(0.573 \text{ bar})}{0.157 \text{ bar} + [(0.573 - 0.157)\text{bar}]0.550} = 0.817$$

144. The activity (*a*) of a component in a solution is equal to its partial pressure divided by the pressure of the pure component.

For *n*-pentane: $a_1 = \frac{P_1}{P_1^*} = \frac{0.315 \text{ bar}}{0.573} = 0.550$

For *n*-hexane: $a_2 = \frac{P_2}{P_2^*} = \frac{0.0706 \text{ bar}}{0.157 \text{ bar}} = 0.450$

145. The general equation for determining the activity coefficients from the pressures is $\gamma_i = \frac{P_i}{x_i P_i^*}$.

For *n*-pentane: $\gamma_1 = \frac{P_1}{x_1 P_1^*} = \frac{0.295 \text{ bar}}{0.550\ (0.573 \text{ bar})} = 0.936$

For *n*-hexane: $\gamma_2 = \frac{P_2}{x_2 P_2^*} = \frac{0.0606 \text{ bar}}{0.450\ (0.157 \text{ bar})} = 0.858$

146. All the necessary information is in the problem. In other situations, it may be necessary to use one of the references mentioned in Introduction to find the missing values. The important relationship is $\left(\frac{dP}{dT}\right) = \frac{\Delta H_{vap}}{T(\bar{V}_g - \bar{V}_l)}$. This leads to the equation $\left(\frac{dT}{dP}\right) = \frac{T(\bar{V}_g - \bar{V}_l)}{\Delta H_{vap}}$, which satisfies the question.

$$\left(\frac{dT}{dP}\right) = \frac{T(\bar{V}_g - \bar{V}_l)}{\Delta H_{vap}}$$

$$= \frac{(239.82\text{ K})([19.79] - [0.02495])\text{L mol}^{-1}}{(23.33\text{ kJ mol}^{-1})}\left(\frac{1\text{ kJ}}{1000\text{ J}}\right)\left(\frac{10^{-3}\text{ m}^3}{\text{L}}\right)$$

$$\times\left(\frac{\text{J}}{\text{kg m}^2/\text{s}^2}\right)\left(\frac{\text{kg/m s}^2}{\text{Pa}}\right) = 2.032 \times 10^{-4}\text{ K Pa}^{-1}$$

147. The relationship is $\left(\frac{dP}{dT}\right) = \frac{\Delta H_{fus}}{T(\bar{V}_l - \bar{V}_s)}$, where the values appear in the question (or in various references).

$$\left(\frac{dP}{dT}\right) = \frac{\Delta H_{fus}}{T(\bar{V}_l - \bar{V}_s)}$$

$$= \left\{\frac{(5.66\text{ kJ mol}^{-1})}{(195.42\text{ K})[(0.02498) - (0.02082)](\text{L mol}^{-1})}\right\}\left(\frac{1000\text{ J}}{1\text{ kJ}}\right)\left(\frac{1000\text{ L}}{\text{m}^3}\right)$$

$$\times\left(\frac{\text{kg m}^2/\text{s}^2}{\text{J}}\right)\left(\frac{\text{Pa}}{\text{kg/m s}^2}\right) = 6.962 \times 10^6\text{ Pa K}^{-1}$$

148. The equation for determining the freezing point constant is $K_f = \frac{RT_{fus}^2 M}{\Delta H_{fus}^\circ}$, where M is the molar mass of the liquid and R is the gas constant.

$$K_f = \frac{RT_{fus}^2 M}{\Delta H_{fus}^\circ} = \frac{(8.3145\text{ J mol}^{-1}\text{ K}^{-1})(195.42\text{ K})^2(17.031 \times 10^{-3}\text{ kg mol}^{-1})}{(5.66\text{ kJ mol}^{-1})}\left(\frac{1\text{ kJ}}{1000\text{ J}}\right)$$

$$= 0.955\text{ K kg mol}^{-1}$$

149. The key relationship is $(\Delta G_{vap}{}^\circ) = -RT\ln\left(\frac{P}{P^\circ}\right)$, where P is the vapor pressure, P° is 1.00 bar (standard pressure), and R is the gas constant. It is necessary to determine the value of $(\Delta G_{vap}{}^\circ)$ by looking for the standard Gibbs energies of formation (ΔG_f°) for liquid and gaseous hydrazine. The value for the liquid is 149.3 kJ mol^{-1} and for the gas is 159.4 kJ mol^{-1}.

$$\Delta G_{vap}{}^\circ = [159.4\text{ kJ mol}^{-1}] - [149.3\text{ kJ mol}^{-1}] = 10.1\text{ kJ mol}^{-1}$$

Rearranging $\Delta G_{vap}{}^{\circ} = -RT\ln\left(\frac{P}{P^{\circ}}\right)$ gives

$$\ln\left(\frac{P}{P^{\circ}}\right) = \frac{\Delta G_{vap}{}^{\circ}}{-RT} = \frac{10.1 \text{ kJ mol}^{-1}}{-(8.3145 \text{ J mol}^{-1}\text{K}^{-1})(298.15 \text{ K})}\left(\frac{1000 \text{ J}}{1 \text{ kJ}}\right)$$

$$= -4.07428 \text{ (unrounded)}$$

$$\left(\frac{P}{P^{\circ}}\right) = 0.0170$$

$$P = 0.0170 \text{ bar}$$

150. Henry's law constant (K_i) is equal to $\frac{P_i}{x_i}$, where P_i is the partial pressure of oxygen and x_i is the mole fraction of oxygen. The moles of water present in 1 L are $\left(\frac{997.05 \text{ g}}{\text{L}}\right)\left(\frac{1 \text{ mol}}{18.015 \text{ g}}\right) = 55.346 \text{ mol L}^{-1}$. To a first approximation, the moles of oxygen present are negligible when compared to water; therefore, $x_i = \frac{[O_2]}{55.346 \text{ mol L}^{-1}}$, where $[O_2]$ is the concentration of oxygen in moles per liter. Substituting this value of x_i into the Henry's law expression and rearranging gives

$$[O_2] = \frac{P_i(55.346 \text{ mol L}^{-1})}{K_i} = \frac{(1.00 \text{ bar})(55.346 \text{ mol L}^{-1})}{4.40 \times 10^4 \text{ bar}} = 1.26 \times 10^{-3} \text{ mol L}^{-1}$$

151. One form of the osmotic pressure formula is $\Pi = \frac{mRT}{MV}$, where m is the mass of polystyrene (11.0 g), R is the gas constant, T is the temperature (298 K), M is the average molar mass of the polystyrene, and V is the volume of the solution ($1.00 \text{ L} = 1.00 \times 10^{-3} \text{ m}^3$). Rearranging this equation and entering the values gives

$$M = \frac{mRT}{\Pi V} = \frac{(11.0 \text{ g})(8.3145 \text{ J mol}^{-1} \text{ K}^{-1})(298 \text{ K})}{(1018 \text{ Pa})(1.00 \times 10^{-3} \text{ m}^3)}\left(\frac{(1 \text{ kg m}^2/\text{s}^2)}{1 \text{ J}}\right)\left(\frac{1 \text{ Pa}}{1 \text{ kg/m s}^2}\right)$$

$$= 2.68 \times 10^4 \text{ g mol}^{-1}$$

152. The calculation of the osmotic pressure utilizes the relationship $\Pi V = nRT$, where V is the volume, n is the number of moles, and R is the gas constant. Rearranging the equation by dividing by V gives $\Pi = (n/V)RT$ or $\Pi = MRT$, where M is the molarity. The approximate osmotic pressure is

$$\Pi = MRT = (1 \text{ mol L}^{-1})(0.08206 \text{ L atm mol}^{-1} \text{ K}^{-1})(300 \text{ K}) \approx 25 \text{ atm}$$

153. The work necessary is $w = -P\Delta V$, where $P = \Pi$ and the change in volume (ΔV) is approximately $-0.018 \text{ L mol}^{-1}$. ($\Delta V$ is negative because there is a loss of water from the seawater.) This information leads to

$$w = -P\Delta V = -(25 \text{ atm})(-0.018 \text{ L mol}^{-1})(1 \text{ mol})\left(\frac{101 \text{ J}}{\text{L atm}}\right) \approx 45 \text{ J}$$

154. To determine the molar mass of the carbohydrate, it is necessary to know the mass (4.00 g) and the moles of the carbohydrate. The osmotic pressure is related to the concentration of the solution. The relationship is $\Pi V = nRT$, where R is the gas constant. Rearranging this equation to determine the moles (n) of carbohydrate and entering the values gives

$$n = \frac{\Pi V}{RT} = \frac{(0.0132\ \text{atm})(0.275\ \text{L})}{(0.08206\ \text{L atm mol}^{-1}\ \text{K}^{-1})(298\ \text{K})} = 1.48 \times 10^{-4}\ \text{mol carbohydrate}$$

The molar mass is the grams divided by the moles or $(4.00\ \text{g})/(1.48 \times 10^{-4}\ \text{mol}) = 2.70 \times 10^{4}\ \text{g mol}^{-1}$.

155. The general state function for the volume of a solution is $V = n_1(\bar{V}_1) + n_2(\bar{V}_2) + \ldots$, where V is the volume of the solution, the n's are the moles of each of the components, and the $(\bar{V}_n)$ are the molar volumes of the components. For this two-component system,

$$V = \left(n_{H_2O}\right)\left(\bar{V}_{H_2O}\right) + \left(n_{C_2H_5OH}\right)\left(\bar{V}_{C_2H_5OH}\right)$$

$$102.20\ \text{mL} = (1.737\ \text{mol H}_2\text{O})\left(\frac{16.98\ \text{mL H}_2\text{O}}{\text{mol H}_2\text{O}}\right) + (1.263\ \text{mol C}_2\text{H}_5\text{OH})\left(\bar{V}_{C_2H_5OH}\right)$$

$$(1.263\ \text{mol C}_2\text{H}_5\text{OH})\left(\bar{V}_{C_2H_5OH}\right) = 102.20\ \text{mL} - 29.49\ \text{mL} = 72.71\ \text{mL}$$

$$\left(\bar{V}_{C_2H_5OH}\right) = \frac{72.71\ \text{mL}}{(1.263\ \text{mol C}_2\text{H}_5\text{OH})} = 57.57\ \text{mL mol}^{-1}$$

156. According to Raoult's law, the vapor pressure of a solution containing a nonvolatile solute depends only upon the vapor pressure of the solvent. In this case, $P_{\text{solution}} = x_{H_2O} P_{H_2O}{}^{\circ}$, where x_{H_2O} is the mole fraction of water $(1.0000 - 0.0300) = 0.9700$, and $P_{H_2O}{}^{\circ}$ is the vapor pressure of pure water = 42.2 torr. Entering this information into Raoult's law gives

$$P_{\text{solution}} = x_{H_2O} P_{H_2O}{}^{\circ} = (0.9700)(42.2\ \text{torr}) = 40.9\ \text{torr}$$

157. It is possible to solve this problem using one form of the Clapeyron equation. This form is $\frac{dP}{dT} = \frac{\Delta\bar{H}_{\text{vap}}}{T(\bar{V}_g - \bar{V}_l)}$. Entering the appropriate values and conversions gives

$$\frac{dP}{dT} = \frac{\Delta\bar{H}_{\text{vap}}}{T(\bar{V}_g - \bar{V}_l)} = \frac{40.69\ \text{kJ mol}^{-1}}{373\ \text{K}(30.20 - 0.0188)\text{L}}\left(\frac{10^3\ \text{J}}{1\ \text{kJ}}\right)\left(\frac{\text{L atm}}{101.325\ \text{J}}\right)$$
$$= 0.0357\ \text{atm K}^{-1}$$

The answer is the reciprocal of this (28.0 K/atm).

158. This problem requires one form of the Clausius–Clapeyron equation. Using the form $\ln \frac{P_2}{P_1} = \frac{\Delta \bar{H}_{vap}}{R}\left(\frac{1}{T_1} - \frac{1}{T_2}\right)$, where R is the gas constant, T_1 is 399 K, T_2 is 375 K, P_1 is 1.00 atm, and P_2 is the answer. Rearranging and entering the information from the problem into the equation gives

$$\ln P_2 = \frac{\Delta \bar{H}_{vap}}{R}\left(\frac{1}{T_1} - \frac{1}{T_2}\right) + \ln P_1 = \frac{3.498 \times 10^4 \text{ J mol}^{-1}}{8.3145 \text{ J mol}^{-1}\text{ K}^{-1}}\left(\frac{1}{399\text{ K}} - \frac{1}{375\text{ K}}\right) + \ln 1.00 \text{ atm}$$

$$= -0.675$$

$$P_2 = e^{-0.675} = 0.509 \text{ atm}$$

159. Using Raoult's law, $P_{soln} = X_B P^o{}_B + X_T P^o{}_T$, where X_T is the mole fraction of toluene. Substituting $X_T = 1 - X_B$ into the equation gives $P_{soln} = X_B P^o{}_B + (1 - X_B)\, P^o{}_T$, which gives

$$1.00 \text{ atm} = (1.34 \text{ atm})\, X_B + (0.534 \text{ atm})\,(1 - X_B)$$

Solving for X_B gives $X_B = 0.578$.

160. The ratio of the viscosities is the same as the ratio of the product of the densities multiplied by the time. Utilizing this relationship gives

$$\eta_{40} = \frac{\eta_{20}\rho_{40}\Delta t_{40}}{\rho_{20}\Delta t_{20}} = \frac{(1.200 \times 10^{-3} \text{ Pa s})(0.772 \text{ g cm}^{-3})(36.8 \text{ s})}{(0.789 \text{ g cm}^{-3})(53.2 \text{ s})} = 8.12 \times 10^{-4} \text{ Pa s}$$

161. To determine the molar mass of the nonelectrolyte, it is necessary to know the mass (40.0 g) and the moles of the nonelectrolyte. The freezing point relationship for a nonelectrolyte is $\Delta T = K_f m$, where ΔT is the change in the freezing point from the value for the pure solvent, K_f is the freezing point depression constant, and m is the molality of the solution (moles of solute per kilogram of solvent). The value of ΔT is $[0.00 - (-3.50)] = 3.50°C$. Rearranging the freezing point depression relationship to find the molality of the solute gives

$$m = \frac{\Delta T}{K_f} = \frac{3.50°\text{C}}{1.86°\text{C}/m} = 1.88\ m \left(= \frac{1.88 \text{ mol solute}}{\text{kg solvent}}\right)$$

Multiplying the molality of the solution by the kilograms of solvent give the moles of nonelectrolyte.

$$\left(\frac{1.88 \text{ mol solute}}{\text{kg solvent}}\right)(0.100 \text{ kg solvent}) = 0.188 \text{ mol solute}$$

The molar mass is the grams divided by the mole or (40.0 g)/(0.188 mol) = 213 g mol^{-1}.

162. The equation for the boiling point elevation is $\Delta T = iK_b m$. Rearranging this equation and entering the appropriate values gives

$$i = \frac{\Delta T}{K_b m} = \frac{0.60^\circ\text{C}}{\left(0.52\ {}^\circ\text{C}/_\text{m}\right)(0.630\ \text{m})} = 1.8$$

163. The relationship necessary for this problem is $\ln x = \frac{\Delta H_{\text{fus}}}{R}\left(\frac{1}{T^\circ} - \frac{1}{T_\text{m}}\right)$, where R is the gas constant. Rearranging the equation and entering the appropriate values gives

$$\frac{1}{T_\text{m}} = \frac{1}{T^\circ} - \frac{R\ln x}{\Delta H_{\text{fus}}} = \frac{1}{1235\ \text{K}} - \frac{(8.3145\ \text{J mol}^{-1}\ \text{K}^{-1})\ln(0.950)}{11.3\ \text{kJ mol}^{-1}}\left(\frac{1\ \text{kJ}}{10^3\ \text{J}}\right)$$

$$= 8.47 \times 10^{-4}\ \text{K}^{-1}$$

$$T_\text{m} = 1{,}180\ \text{K}$$

164. For both layers, $c = 2$ (water and methylene chloride). In this case, $p = 2$ (there are two layers). Finally, $f = c - p + 2 = 2 - 2 + 2 = 2$.

165. It is necessary to calculate the molar volume ($\bar{V}_{\text{dia}}$ and $\bar{V}_{\text{gr}}$) for each of the two forms

$$\bar{V}_{\text{dia}} = \left(\frac{24.818\ \text{g}}{\text{mol}}\right)\left(\frac{\text{cm}^3}{3.45\ \text{g}}\right)\left(\frac{0.01\ \text{m}}{1\ \text{cm}}\right)^3 = 7.19 \times 10^{-6}\ \text{m}^3\ \text{mol}^{-1}$$

$$\bar{V}_{\text{gr}} = \left(\frac{24.818\ \text{g}}{\text{mol}}\right)\left(\frac{\text{cm}^3}{2.10\ \text{g}}\right)\left(\frac{0.01\ \text{m}}{1\ \text{cm}}\right)^3 = 1.18 \times 10^{-5}\ \text{m}^3\ \text{mol}^{-1}$$

The volume change is $\Delta\bar{V} = (7.19 \times 10^{-6} - 1.18 \times 10^{-5})\ \text{m}^3\ \text{mol}^{-1} = -4.61 \times 10^{-6}\ \text{m}^3\ \text{mol}^{-1}$. Because $\left(\frac{\partial \Delta G}{\partial P}\right)_T = \Delta\bar{V}$, then

$$\int_1^2 d\Delta G = 2.900\ \text{kJ mol}^{-1} = \int_{P_1}^{P_2} \Delta\bar{V}\ dP = \Delta\bar{V}\ (P_2 - P_1)$$

$$P_2 = \left(\frac{\Delta G}{\Delta\bar{V}}\right) + P_1 = \left(\frac{-2.900\ \text{kJ mol}^{-1}}{-4.61 \times 10^{-6}\ \text{m}^3\ \text{mol}^{-1}}\right)\left(\frac{1000\ \text{J}}{1\ \text{kJ}}\right)\left(\frac{(1\ \text{kg m}^2/\text{s}^2)}{1\ \text{J}}\right)$$

$$\times\left(\frac{1\ \text{Pa}}{1\ \text{kg/ms}^2}\right)\left(\frac{1\ \text{bar}}{10^5\ \text{Pa}}\right) + 1.00\ \text{bar} = 6.29 \times 10^3\ \text{bar}$$

166. The work done is $w = -P\Delta V$, which gives

$$w = -P\Delta V = -(1.00\ \text{bar})[(2.06 \times 10^{-5} - 1.62 \times 10^{-5})\text{m}^3]\left(\frac{10^5\ \text{kg/m s}^2}{1\ \text{bar}}\right)\left(\frac{\text{J}}{\text{kg m}^2/\text{s}^2}\right)$$

$$= 0.440\ \text{J}$$

167. The relationship is $\Delta E = q + w$, where w is the heat involved and $q = n\Delta H$. Combining these relationships and entering the appropriate values gives

$$\Delta E = n\Delta H + w = (1.00 \text{ mol})\ (2.238 \times 10^3 \text{ J mol}^{-1}) + 0.440 \text{ J} = 2.238 \times 10^3 \text{ J}$$

168. This is an equilibrium process, so $\Delta S = \frac{\Delta H}{T}$, which leads to

$$\Delta S = \frac{\Delta H}{T} = \frac{(1.00 \text{ mol})(2.238 \times 10^3 \text{ J mol}^{-1})}{286.4 \text{ K}} = 7.81 \text{ J K}^{-1}$$

169. This is an equilibrium process so $\Delta G = 0$.

Chapter 7: Electrochemical Equilibria

170. It is important to understand the cell notation. The vertical bars (|) represent phase boundaries, in this case, the boundary between the solid electrode and the aqueous solutions involved. Before the first vertical bar is the anode, in this case, copper, and after the last vertical bar is the cathode, in this case, platinum. (The anode and the cathode may or may not be part of the cell reaction.) The double vertical bar (||) represents a salt bridge connecting the two half-cells. Everything before the salt bridge is oxidation, and everything after the salt bridge is reduction. The oxidation reaction will involve Fe^{2+} oxidizing to Fe^{3+}, and the reduction will involve the Cu^{2+} reducing to Cu (the platinum is not part of the reaction). The half-reactions are

$$Fe^{3+}(aq) + 1e^- \rightarrow Fe^{2+}(aq)$$

$$Cu(s) \rightarrow Cu^{2+}(aq) + 2e^-$$

These combine to give the following cell reaction.

$$Cu(s) + 2Fe^{3+}(aq) \rightarrow 2Fe^{2+}(aq) + Cu^{2+}(aq)$$

171. To begin, it is necessary to find the appropriate half-reactions with their standard electromotive forces from the appropriate tables. These are

$$Cu^{2+}(aq) + 2e^- \rightarrow Cu(s) \qquad E° = 0.337 \text{ V}$$

$$Fe^{3+}(aq) + 1e^- \rightarrow Fe^{2+}(aq) \qquad E° = 0.771 \text{ V}$$

These are reduction half-reactions, and it is necessary to convert one to an oxidation by reversing the equation (and the sign of the electromotive force). For a galvanic cell, always reverse the half-reaction with the lower electromotive force, in this case, copper. This gives

$$Cu(s) \rightarrow Cu^{2+}(aq) + 2e^- \qquad E° = -0.337 \text{ V}$$

$$Fe^{3+}(aq) + 1e^- \rightarrow Fe^{2+}(aq) \qquad E° = 0.771 \text{ V}$$

The sum of the two electromotive forces is the standard electromotive force = $E° = 0.771$ V − 0.337 V = 0.434 V. Note that the number of electrons does not need to be equal to determine the electromotive force.

172. The relationship between the equilibrium constant and the standard cell potential is $E° = \frac{RT}{|\nu_e|F}\ln K$, where $|\nu_e|$ is the number of electrons transferred (two in this case), F is the Faraday constant (96,485 C mol^{-1}), R is the gas constant (8.3145 J mol^{-1} K^{-1}), and T is the temperature (25°C = 298 K). Rearranging the equation and entering the values gives

$$K = \exp\left[\frac{|\nu_e|FE°}{RT}\right] = \exp\left[\left(\frac{2(96485\ \text{C mol}^{-1})(0.434\ \text{V})}{(8.3145\ \text{J mol}^{-1}\ \text{K}^{-1})(298\ \text{K})}\right)\left(\frac{1\ \text{J}}{1\ \text{C V}}\right)\right] = 4.78 \times 10^{14}$$

173. The equilibrium constant expression can take several forms such as the following where the a's are the activities and the γ's are the activity coefficients.

$$K = \frac{(a(\text{Fe}^{2+}))^2 a(\text{Cu}^{2+})}{(a(\text{Fe}^{3+}))^2} = \frac{[\text{Fe}^{2+}]^2(\gamma(\text{Fe}^{2+}))^2[\text{Cu}^{2+}]\gamma(\text{Cu}^{2+})}{[\text{Fe}^{3+}]^2(\gamma(\text{Fe}^{3+}))^2} = \frac{[\text{Fe}^{2+}]^2[\text{Cu}^{2+}]}{[\text{Fe}^{3+}]^2}$$

The last form assumes the two solutions have the same ionic strength.

174. The concentrations of the ions are not standard (1 M); therefore, this is a nonstandard cell. It is necessary to use the Nernst equation to determine the cell potential (E) for a nonstandard cell. The Nernst equation is $E = E° - \frac{RT}{nF}\ln Q$, where R is the gas constant (8.3145 J mol^{-1} K^{-1}), T is the temperature (298 K), n is the number of electrons transferred (2), F is the Faraday constant (96,485 J mol^{-1} V^{-1}), and Q is the reaction quotient. In this case, the reaction quotient $Q = \frac{[\text{Fe}^{2+}]^2[\text{Cu}^{2+}]}{[\text{Fe}^{3+}]^2}$, the solid copper does not appear in the reaction quotient because the activity of the solid is 1. Entering the values into the Nernst equation,

$$E = E° - \frac{RT}{nF}\ln\frac{[\text{Fe}^{2+}]^2[\text{Cu}^{2+}]}{[\text{Fe}^{3+}]^2}$$

$$= +0.434\ \text{V} - \frac{(8.3145\ \text{J mol}^{-1}\ \text{K}^{-1})(298\ \text{K})}{(2)(96485\ \text{J mol}^{-1}\ \text{V}^{-1})}\ln\frac{[0.150]^2[0.100]}{[0.225]^2}$$

$$= +0.473\ \text{V}$$

175. The standard cell potential ($E°$) comes from $\Delta G° = -nFE°$, where $\Delta G°$ is the change in the Gibbs free energy for the reaction [$\Delta G° = \sum \Delta G_f°(\text{products}) - \sum \Delta G_f°(\text{reactants})$], n is the number of electrons transferred (2), and F is the Faraday constant (96,485 J mol^{-1} V^{-1}). The Gibbs free energies for the ions are in the problem, and the values for the solid metals in their standard states are 0.

$$\Delta G° = \sum \Delta G_f°(\text{products}) - \sum \Delta G_f°(\text{reactants})$$

$$= [-147.0\ \text{kJ mol}^{-1}] - [65.5\ \text{kJ mol}^{-1}] = -212.5\ \text{kJ mol}^{-1}$$

Because the free energy change is negative (spontaneous), the cell potential will be positive (spontaneous). Rearranging the $E°$ equation and entering values gives

$$E° = \frac{\Delta G°}{-nF} = \frac{(-212.5 \text{ kJ mol}^{-1})}{-(2)(96485 \text{ J mol}^{-1} \text{ V}^{-1})}\left(\frac{10^3 \text{ J}}{1 \text{ kJ}}\right) = 1.101 \text{ V}$$

176. The question asks about copper; therefore, only the copper half-reaction [$Cu^{2+}(aq) + 2\ e^- \rightarrow Cu(s)$] is important. An ampere (A) is a coulomb per second. A faraday (F) is 96,485 coulombs per mole of electrons. Combining this information gives

$$\text{Mass Cu} = (25.0 \text{ A})\left(\frac{1 \text{ C/s}}{1 \text{ A}}\right)(1275 \text{ s})\left(\frac{1 \text{ mol e}^-}{96485 \text{ C}}\right)\left(\frac{1 \text{ mol Cu}}{2 \text{ mol e}^-}\right)\left(\frac{63.546 \text{ g Cu}}{1 \text{ mol Cu}}\right) = 10.5 \text{ g Cu}$$

177. Both half-reactions are reduction half-reactions; therefore, it is necessary to reverse one of the two. Reverse the half-reaction with the lower potential. (As this is a galvanic cell, the total voltage must be positive.) Reversing a half-reaction will reverse the sign of its cell potential. Finally, add the two potentials together.

$$E_{cell}° = [+1.33 + (-0.77)] \text{ V} = 0.56 \text{ V}$$

Notice that this calculation does not depend on the number of electrons in the half-reactions.

178. The equation relating the standard electrode potential to the Gibbs free energy is $\Delta G° = -|v_e|\ FE°$, where $|v_e|$ is the number of electrons transferred (two in this case), and F is the Faraday constant (96,485 C mol^{-1}). Rearranging and entering values gives

$$E° = -\frac{\Delta G°}{|v_e|\,F} = -\left(\frac{-65.49 \text{ kJ mol}^{-1}}{2(96485 \text{ C mol}^{-1})}\right)\left(\frac{1000 \text{ J}}{1 \text{ kJ}}\right)\left(\frac{1 \text{ C V}}{1 \text{ J}}\right) = 0.3394 \text{ V}$$

179. The mole of copper deposited is $(0.1872 \text{ g Cu})\left(\frac{1 \text{ mol Cu}}{63.546 \text{ g Cu}}\right) = 2.946 \times 10^{-3}$ mol Cu. Based on the half-reaction, twice this number of moles of electrons (5.892×10^{-3} mol e^-) passed through the cell. The number of moles of electrons and the Faraday constant gives the electric current passing through the solution.

$$\text{Current} = Q = (5.892 \times 10^{-3} \text{ mol e}^-)\left(\frac{96485 \text{ coulombs}}{\text{mol e}^-}\right) = 568.5 \text{ C}$$

180. The relationship between the cell potential and the Gibbs free energy change is $\Delta G = -nFE$, where n is the number of moles of electrons transferred (two in this case) and F is the Faraday constant (96,485 J V^{-1} mol^{-1}). This relationship gives

$$\Delta G = -nFE = -(2 \text{ mol})(96{,}485 \text{ J V}^{-1} \text{ mol}^{-1})(0.6753) = -1.303 \times 10^5 \text{ J}$$

181. The appropriate relationship is $\Delta S = nF\left(\frac{\partial E}{\partial T}\right)_P$, where n is the number of moles of electrons transferred (two in this case) and F is the Faraday constant (96,485 J V^{-1} mol^{-1}). Entering the values into the relationship gives

$$\Delta S = nF\left(\frac{\partial E}{\partial T}\right)_P = (2\ \text{mol})(\ 96485\ \text{J V}^{-1}\ \text{mol}^{-1})(-6.50 \times 10^{-4}\ \text{V K}^{-1}) = -125\ \text{J K}^{-1}$$

182. The relationship $\Delta G = \Delta H - T\Delta S$, where $T = 298$ K, is appropriate. Rearranging and entering the values gives

$$\Delta H = \Delta G + T\Delta S = -1.303 \times 10^5\ \text{J} + (298\ \text{K})(-125\ \text{J K}^{-1}) = -1.676 \times 10^5\ \text{J}$$

183. The concentrations of the species are very low; therefore, it is acceptable to assume that the activities are equal to the molarities. The K_{sp} relationship, in terms of molarities, is $K_{sp} = [Ag^+]^2[CrO_4^{2-}]$. The concentration of the chromate ion is 8.00×10^{-5} M, and the silver ion concentration is twice this value. This leads to

$$K_{sp} = [Ag^+]^2[CrO_4^{2-}] = 2^2(8.00 \times 10^{-5})^3 = 2.05 \times 10^{-12}$$

184. The presence of the sodium nitrate increases the solubility, and therefore it is necessary to adjust the K_{sp} expression from that in pure water ($K_{sp} = [Ag^+]^2[CrO_4^{2-}] = 2^2(8.00 \times 10^{-5})^3 = 2.05 \times 10^{-12}$) to include the mean ionic activity. To make this adjustment, replace the solubility of silver chromate in pure water with the solubility in the sodium nitrate solution. In addition, each concentration is multiplied by the mean ionic activity, and because the concentration is cubed, it is necessary to cube the mean ionic activity. These adjustments change the K_{sp} relationship to

$$K_{sp} = [Ag^+]^2[CrO_4^{2-}] = 2^2(8.84 \times 10^{-5})^3(\gamma_\pm)^3 = 2.05 \times 10^{-12}$$

$$\gamma_\pm = \sqrt[3]{\frac{\text{K}_{sp}}{[\text{Ag}^+]^2[\text{CrO}_4^{2-}]}} = \sqrt[3]{\frac{2.05 \times 10^{-12}}{2^2[8.84 \times 10^{-5}]^3}} = 0.905$$

185. Setting the Nernst equation up in the form $E_{cell} = E° - \frac{RT}{nF}\ln\frac{a_{Fe}}{a_{Cd}}$, where R is the gas constant, F is the Faraday constant, and n is the number of electrons transferred (two). The maximum activity of iron is when $E_{cell} = 0$, which leads to $E° = \frac{RT}{nF}\ln\frac{a_{Fe}}{a_{Cd}}$ and then to $\frac{nFE°}{RT} = \ln\frac{a_{Fe}}{a_{Cd}}$. Using this final relationship and entering the appropriate values gives

$$\ln\frac{a_{Fe}}{a_{Cd}} = \frac{nFE°}{RT} \rightarrow \ln\frac{a_{Fe}}{1} = \frac{2(96485\ \text{J V}^{-1}\ \text{mol}^{-1})(0.0373\ \text{V})}{(8.3145\ \text{J mol}^{-1}\ \text{K}^{-1})(298\ \text{K})} = 2.905$$

$$a_{Fe} = 18.3$$

186. The equation for the equilibrium constant is $K = e^{|\nu_e|FE°/RT}$, where F is the Faraday constant (96,485 C mol^{-1}), $E°$ is the standard electromotive force (0.015 V), R is the gas constant (8.3145 J mol^{-1} K^{-1}), and T is the temperature (25°C = 298 K). Entering the values into the equation

$$K = e^{|\nu_e|FE^\circ/RT} = \exp\left(\frac{(1)(96485\ \text{C mol}^{-1})(0.015\ V)}{(8.3145\ \text{J mol}^{-1}\ \text{K}^{-1})(298\ \text{K})}\left(\frac{1\ \text{J}}{1\ \text{C V}}\right)\right) = 1.8$$

187. The equation from Debye–Hückel theory is $\log \gamma_i = -Az_i^2 I^{1/2}$, where z_i is the ionic charge.

$$\log \gamma_i = -Az_i^2 I^{1/2} = -(0.509)(1)^2(0.00150)^{1/2} = -0.019713 \text{ (unrounded)}$$

$$\gamma_+ = \gamma_- = 10^{-0.019713} = 0.956$$

188. The equation from Debye–Hückel theory is $\log \gamma_i = Az_+z_- I^{1/2}$, where z_i is the ionic charge.

$$\log \gamma_\pm = Az_+z_- I^{1/2} = (0.509)(+1)(-1)(0.00150)^{1/2} = -0.019713 \text{ (unrounded)}$$

$$\gamma_\pm = 10^{-0.019713} = 0.956$$

189. The equation to determine the activity of this solution is $a_{\text{KCl}} = m^2\gamma_\pm^2$.

$$a_{\text{KCl}} = m^2\gamma_\pm^2 = (0.00150)^2(0.956)^2 = 2.06 \times 10^{-6}$$

190. To begin the problem, it is necessary to find the formation energies from the appropriate tables. For the bromide ion, the Gibbs energy of formation (ΔG_f°) is −103.92 kJ mol^{-1} and the enthalpy of formation (ΔH_f°) is −121.55 kJ mol^{-1}, both at 298.15 K (T). Using these values and $\Delta G = \Delta H - T\Delta S$, it is possible to determine the entropy of formation of the bromide ion (the most convenient form would be J mol^{-1} K^{-1}).

$$\Delta \bar{S}_f^\circ = \frac{\Delta H_f^\circ - \Delta G_f^\circ}{T} = \frac{[(-122.55) - (-103.92)]\text{kJ mol}^{-1}}{298.15\ \text{K}}\left(\frac{1000\ \text{J}}{1\ \text{kJ}}\right)$$

$$= -62.49\ \text{J mol}^{-1}\ \text{K}^{-1}$$

The formation reaction is ½ Br_2(l) + e^- → Br^-(aq). This equation requires the value just calculated for $\Delta \bar{S}_f^\circ$ (−62.49 J mol^{-1} K^{-1}), the standard entropy for liquid bromine ($\bar{S}^\circ(Br_2)$ = 152.231 mol^{-1} K^{-1}), and the entropy value for the electron ($\bar{S}^\circ(e^-)$ = 65.342 mol^{-1} K^{-1}).

$$\Delta \bar{S}_f^\circ = \bar{S}^\circ(\text{Br}^-) - ½\,\bar{S}^\circ(\text{Br}_2) - \bar{S}^\circ(\text{e}^-)$$

$$\bar{S}^\circ(\text{Br}^-) = \Delta \bar{S}_f^\circ + ½\,\bar{S}^\circ(\text{Br}_2) + \bar{S}^\circ(\text{e}^-) = [-62.49 + ½(152.231) + 65.342]\ \text{J mol}^{-1}\ \text{K}^{-1}$$

$$= 78.97\ \text{J mol}^{-1}\ \text{K}^{-1}$$

191. The specific conductance is the cell constant divided by the resistance, which rearranges to give the cell constant equal to the specific conductance times the resistance, which is

$$k = \kappa R = (0.00277 \text{ mho cm}^{-1})(82.4 \text{ ohm})\left(\frac{1 \text{ ohm}^{-1}}{1 \text{ mho}}\right) = 0.228 \text{ cm}^{-1}$$

192. The relationship to find the specific conductance is κ = (cell constant) (L). Entering the appropriate values gives

$$\kappa = (\text{cell constant})\ (L) = (115 \text{ m}^{-1})\ (1.49 \times 10^{-3} \text{ mho}) = 0.171 \text{ mho m}^{-1}$$

193. The molar conductance comes from the relationship $\Lambda = \kappa/C$, where C is the concentration of the solution. Entering the appropriate values,

$$\Lambda = \frac{\kappa}{C} = \frac{0.171 \text{ mho m}^{-1}}{0.0075 \dfrac{\text{mol}}{\text{L}}}\left(\frac{10^{-3} \text{ m}^3}{\text{L}}\right) = 0.023 \text{ mho m}^2 \text{ mol}^{-1}$$

194. The relationship is $u = \frac{\lambda°}{ZF}$, where Z is the charge on the cation and F is the Faraday constant. Entering the values into the equation

$$u = \frac{\lambda°}{ZF} = \frac{7.35 \times 10^{-3} \text{ mho m}^2 \text{ mol}^{-1}}{(+1)\left(\dfrac{96485 \text{ C}}{\text{mol}}\right)}\left(\frac{\text{C}}{\text{A s}}\right)\left(\frac{\text{A}/\text{V}}{\text{mho}}\right) = 7.62 \times 10^{-8} \text{ m}^2 \text{ V}^{-1} \text{ s}^{-1}$$

195. The equation for the ionic molar conductance is $\lambda = t\Lambda$. Entering the appropriate values gives

$$\Lambda_{\text{H}} = t_{\text{H}}\, \Lambda = (0.830)\ (4.00 \times 10^{-2} \text{ mho m}^2 \text{ mol}^{-1}) = 3.32 \times 10^{-2} \text{ mho m}^2 \text{ mol}^{-1}$$

196. The equation for the specific conductance is $\kappa = \Lambda^0 C$, where Λ^0 is the ionic conductance of the solution at infinite dilution (the sum of the individual ionic conductance values) and C is the ion concentration. In this case, $\Lambda^0 = (1.27 \times 10^{-2} + 1.60 \times 10^{-2})$ mho m^2 mol^{-1} = 2.87×10^{-2} mho m^2 mol^{-1} and $C = \sqrt{K_{\text{sp}}} = \sqrt{1.1 \times 10^{-10}} = 1.0 \times 10^{-5}$ M. Entering this information into the appropriate equation gives

$$\kappa = \Lambda^0 C = (2.87 \times 10^{-2} \text{ mho m}^2 \text{ mol}^{-1})(1.0 \times 10^{-5} \text{ mol/L})\left(\frac{\text{L}}{10^{-3} \text{ m}^3}\right)$$

$$= 2.87 \times 10^{-4} \text{ mho m}^{-1}$$

197. The equation to determine the limiting diffusion coefficient is $D_0 = \frac{2\mu_1\mu_2 RT}{(\mu_1 + \mu_2)F}$, where R is the gas constant and F is the Faraday constant. Incorporating the values from the problem and the values of the constants gives

$$D_0 = \frac{2\mu_1\mu_2 RT}{(\mu_1+\mu_2)F}$$

$$= \frac{2(5.20\times10^{-4}\ \text{cm}^2\ \text{V}^{-1}\ \text{s}^{-1})(7.96\times10^{-4}\ \text{cm}^2\ \text{V}^{-1}\ \text{s}^{-1})(8.3145\ \text{J mol}^{-1}\ \text{K}^{-1})(298\ \text{K})}{[(5.20+7.96)\times10^{-4}\ \text{cm}^2\ \text{V}^{-1}\ \text{s}^{-1}](96485\ \text{J V}^{-1}\ \text{mol}^{-1})}$$

$$= 1.52\times10^{-5}\ \text{cm}^2\ \text{s}^{-1}$$

198. The general equation to determine the ionic strength of a solution is $I = \frac{1}{2}\sum m_i z_i^2$, where m is the molality of each ion and z is the charge of the ion. Expanding the summation gives

$$I = \frac{1}{2}[(2m)(+3)^2 + (3m)(-2)^2] = 15\ \text{m}$$

In this problem, $m = 1.00\times10^{-6}$ m; therefore, $I = 1.50\times10^{-5}$ m.

199. The relationship to determine the entropy change is $\Delta S° = nF\left(\frac{\partial E°}{\partial T}\right)_p$, where F is the Faraday constant. Using this equation plus the information from the problem gives

$$\Delta S° = nF\left(\frac{\partial E°}{\partial T}\right)_p = (2\ \text{mol})(96{,}485\ \text{C mol}^{-1})(-1.37\times10^{-3}\ \text{V K}^{-1})\left(\frac{\text{J}}{\text{V C}}\right) = -264\ \text{J K}^{-1}$$

200. The relationship to determine the entropy change is $\Delta H° = nF\left[E° - T\left(\frac{\partial E°}{\partial T}\right)_p\right]$, where F is the Faraday constant. Using this equation plus the information from the problem and appropriate conversions gives

$$\Delta H° = -nF\left[E° - T\left(\frac{\partial E°}{\partial T}\right)_p\right]$$

$$= -(2\ \text{mol})(96{,}485\ \text{C mol}^{-1})[1.25\ \text{V} - (298\ \text{K})(-1.37\times10^{-3}\ \text{V K}^{-1})]\left(\frac{\text{J}}{\text{V C}}\right)$$

$$= -3.20\times10^5\ \text{J}$$

Chapter 8: Quantum Theory

201. The relationship between the wavelength and the frequency is $c = \lambda\nu$, where c is the speed of light. Rearranging this relationship and entering the values gives

$$\nu = \frac{c}{\lambda} = \frac{2.9979\times10^8\ \text{m s}^{-1}}{375\ \text{nm}}\left(\frac{1\ \text{nm}}{10^{-9}\ \text{m}}\right) = 7.99\times10^{14}\ \text{s}^{-1}$$

202. The relationship to determine the energy from the wavelength is $E = \frac{hc}{\lambda}$, where h is Planck's constant and c is the speed of light. Entering the values from the problem and a conversion factor gives

$$E = \frac{hc}{\lambda} = \frac{(6.626\times10^{-34}\ \text{J s})(2.9979\times10^8\ \text{m s}^{-1})}{675\ \text{nm}}\left(\frac{1\ \text{nm}}{10^{-9}\ \text{m}}\right) = 2.94\times10^{-19}\ \text{J}$$

203. The key relationship is $E = h\nu$, where h is Planck's constant. This relationship gives

$$E = h\nu = (6.626 \times 10^{-34}\ \text{J s})(7.99 \times 10^{14}\ \text{s}^{-1}) = 5.29 \times 10^{-19}\ \text{J}$$

204. The Heisenberg uncertainty principle in the form $\Delta x \Delta p_x \geq h/4\,\pi$ is the best form for this problem, where h is Planck's constant. Rearranging and entering the appropriate values into the relationship gives

$$\Delta p_x \geq \frac{h}{4\,\pi\,\Delta x} \geq \frac{6.626 \times 10^{-34}\ \text{J s}}{4\,\pi\,(75\ \text{pm})}\left(\frac{1\ \text{pm}}{10^{-12}\ \text{m}}\right)\left(\frac{\text{kg m}^2/\text{s}^2}{\text{J}}\right) \geq 7.0 \times 10^{-25}\ \text{kg m s}^{-1}$$

205. The relationship is $\Delta p_x = m\Delta v_x$, which rearranges to the following

$$\Delta v_x = \frac{\Delta p_x}{m} \geq \frac{7.0 \times 10^{-25}\ \text{kg m s}^{-1}}{9.109 \times 10^{-31}\ \text{kg}} \geq 7.7 \times 10^{5}\ \text{m s}^{-1}$$

206. The formula for the energy of a particle (electron) in a box is $E_n = h^2n^2/8\,ma^2$, where m is the mass of an electron (9.109×10^{-31} kg), and h is Planck's constant. Entering the appropriate values into this formula gives

$$E_1 = \frac{h^2 n^2}{8\,m\,a^2} = \frac{(6.626 \times 10^{-34}\ \text{J s})^2 (1)^2}{8\,(9.109 \times 10^{-31}\ \text{kg})\,(15\ \text{pm})^2}\left(\frac{1\ \text{pm}}{10^{-12}\ \text{m}}\right)^2\left(\frac{\text{kg m}^2/\text{s}^2}{\text{J}}\right) = 2.7 \times 10^{-16}\ \text{J}$$

207. The formula for the reduced mass is $\mu = \frac{m_1 m_2}{m_1 + m_2}$, where the m's are the masses of the two bonded atoms. Entering the appropriate values into this relationship gives

$$\mu = \frac{m_1 m_2}{m_1 + m_2} = \frac{(13.00335 \times 10^{-3}\ \text{kg mol}^{-1})(15.99491 \times 10^{-3}\ \text{kg mol}^{-1})}{[13.00335 + 15.99491] \times 10^{-3}\ \text{kg mol}^{-1}}\left(\frac{\text{mol}}{6.0221415 \times 10^{23}}\right)$$

$$= 1.191007 \times 10^{-26}\ \text{kg}$$

208. This is a harmonic oscillator situation. The equation for the force constant is $k = (2\pi c\tilde{\nu})^2\,\mu$, where c is the speed of light and $\tilde{\nu}$ is the fundamental vibration. Entering the appropriate values gives

$$k = (2\pi c\tilde{\nu})^2\,\mu = [2\pi(2.9979 \times 10^{10}\ \text{cm s}^{-1})(2122\ \text{cm}^{-1})]^2(1.191 \times 10^{-26}\ \text{kg})$$

$$= 1.903 \times 10^{3}\ \text{kg s}^{-2}$$

209. This is a rigid rotor problem. The equation for the moment of inertia is $I = \mu R_e^2$. Entering the appropriate values and conversion gives

$$I = \mu R_e^2 = (1.191 \times 10^{-26}\ \text{kg})(113\ \text{pm})^2\left(\frac{10^{-12}\ \text{m}}{1\ \text{pm}}\right)^2 = 1.52 \times 10^{-46}\ \text{kg m}^2$$

210. This is a harmonic oscillator situation. The equation for the force constant is $k = (2\pi c\tilde{\nu})^2 \mu$, where c is the speed of light and $\tilde{\nu}$ is the fundamental vibration. Rearranging and entering the appropriate values gives

$$\tilde{\nu} = \frac{\sqrt{\frac{k}{\mu}}}{2\pi c} = \frac{\sqrt{\frac{1.903 \times 10^3 \text{ kg s}^{-2}}{1.3078 \times 10^{-26} \text{ kg}}}}{2\pi(2.9979 \times 10^8 \text{ m s}^{-1})}\left(\frac{0.01 \text{ m}}{1 \text{ cm}}\right) = 2{,}025 \text{ cm}^{-1}$$

211. The de Broglie relationship is $\lambda = h/p$, where λ is the wavelength, h is Planck's constant (6.626×10^{-34} J s), and p is the momentum ($p = mv$, where m is the mass and v is the velocity). Entering the appropriate values into the relationship

$$\lambda = \frac{h}{p} = \frac{h}{mv} = \frac{6.626 \times 10^{-34} \text{ J s}}{(6.65 \times 10^{-27} \text{ kg})(675 \text{ m/s})}\left(\frac{\text{kg m}^2/\text{s}^2}{\text{J}}\right) = 1.48 \times 10^{-10} \text{ m}$$

212. The kinetic energy of the electron will be equal to the energy ($E = \frac{hc}{\lambda}$) of the incident radiation minus the work function (energy necessary to escape the surface). In the energy equation, h is Planck's constant and c is the speed of light. The resultant combination is

$$E = \frac{hc}{\lambda} - \Phi = \frac{(6.626 \times 10^{-34} \text{ J s})(2.9979 \times 10^8 \text{ m s}^{-1})}{525 \text{ nm}}\left(\frac{1 \text{ nm}}{10^{-9} \text{ m}}\right)$$

$$- (1.95 \text{ eV})\left(\frac{1.602 \times 10^{-19} \text{ J}}{1 \text{ eV}}\right) = 6.60 \times 10^{-20} \text{ J}$$

213. The minimum frequency is light with energy ($E = h\nu$) equal to the work function. Rearranging the equation and entering the value of Planck's constant (h) gives

$$\nu = \frac{E}{h} = \left(\frac{1.95 \text{ eV}}{6.626 \times 10^{-34} \text{ J s}}\right)\left(\frac{1.602 \times 10^{-19} \text{ J}}{1 \text{ eV}}\right) = 4.71 \times 10^{-14} \text{ s}^{-1}$$

214. The maximum wavelength is light with energy ($E = \frac{hc}{\lambda}$) equal to the work function. Rearranging the equation and entering the values of Planck's constant (h) and the speed of light (c) gives

$$\lambda = \frac{hc}{E} = \frac{(6.626 \times 10^{-34} \text{ J s})(2.9979 \times 10^8 \text{ m s}^{-1})}{(1.95 \text{ eV})}\left(\frac{1 \text{ eV}}{1.602 \times 10^{-19} \text{ J}}\right)$$

$$= 6.36 \times 10^{-7} \text{ m}$$

215. The kinetic energy of the electron is $E = ½mv^2$, where m is the mass of an electron. Rearranging this equation and entering the appropriate values gives

$$v = \sqrt{\frac{E}{m}} = \sqrt{\frac{6.60 \times 10^{-20}\ \text{J}}{9.109 \times 10^{-31}\ \text{kg}}\left(\frac{\text{kg m}^2/\text{s}^2}{\text{J}}\right)} = 2.69 \times 10^5\ \text{m s}^{-1}$$

216. The Bragg equation is useful for the study of diffraction. This equation is $n\lambda = 2d \sin \theta$. Rearranging this equation and entering the appropriate values gives

$$\sin \theta = \frac{n\lambda}{2d} = \frac{(1)(0.155\ \text{nm})}{2(1.25\ \text{nm})} = 0.0620$$

$$\theta = \sin^{-1} \theta = \sin^{-1} (0.0620) = 3.55°$$

217. This is a conversion problem where the energy is the charge (e) on an electron times the potential difference. Using this information gives

$$E = e\phi = (1.602 \times 10^{-19}\ \text{C})(10^4\ \text{V})\left(\frac{\text{J}}{\text{C V}}\right) = 1.602 \times 10^{-15}\ \text{J}$$

218. The momentum of a photon is related to the equation $p = \frac{h}{\lambda}$, where h is Planck's constant. Entering the information from the problem and conversions gives

$$p = \frac{h}{\lambda} = \frac{6.626 \times 10^{-34}\ \text{J s}}{675\ \text{pm}}\left(\frac{\text{kg m}^2/\text{s}^2}{\text{J}}\right)\left(\frac{1\ \text{pm}}{10^{-12}\ \text{m}}\right) = 9.82 \times 10^{-25}\ \text{kg m s}^{-1}$$

219. Because momentum is conserved, the momentum of the helium atom will be the same as the momentum of the photon. The momentum of a particle is equal to the mass (m) of a particle times its velocity. Combining these facts gives

$$v = \frac{p}{m} = \frac{9.82 \times 10^{-25}\ \text{kg m s}^{-1}}{6.647 \times 10^{-27}\ \text{kg}} = 148\ \text{m s}^{-1}$$

220. Beginning with the relationship $E = \frac{h^2n^2}{8\ m\ a^2}$ and solving for n gives $n = \left(\frac{a}{h}\right)\sqrt{8\ mE}$, where h is Planck's constant. Using the rearranged equation gives

$$n = \left(\frac{a}{h}\right)\sqrt{8\ mE} = \left(\frac{1.00 \times 10^{-8}\ \text{m}}{6.626 \times 10^{-34}\ \text{J s}}\right)\left(\frac{\text{J}}{\text{kg m}^2/\text{s}^2}\right)$$

$$\times \sqrt{8\ (3.35 \times 10^{-26}\ \text{kg})(6.25 \times 10^{-21}\ \text{J})\left(\frac{\text{kg m}^2/\text{s}^2}{\text{J}}\right)} = 618$$

221. The Wien displacement law appears in many forms. The form most useful for this problem is $\lambda_{max} = \frac{hc}{4.965\ kT}$, where h is Planck's constant, c is the speed of light, and k is the Boltzmann constant. Entering the appropriate values into this equation gives

$$\lambda_{max} = \frac{hc}{4.965\ kT} = \frac{(6.626 \times 10^{-34}\ \text{J s})(2.9979 \times 10^{8}\ \text{m s}^{-1})}{4.965\ (1.381 \times 10^{-23}\ \text{J K}^{-1})(3250\ \text{K})} = 8.914 \times 10^{-7}\ \text{m}$$

222. The Wien displacement law appears in many forms. The form most useful for this problem is $\lambda_{max} = \frac{hc}{4.965\ kT}$, where h is Planck's constant, c is the speed of light, and k is the Boltzmann constant. Rearranging this equation and entering the appropriate values into this equation gives

$$T = \frac{hc}{4.965\ k\lambda_{max}} = \frac{(6.626 \times 10^{-34}\ \text{J s})(2.9979 \times 10^{8}\ \text{m s}^{-1})}{4.965\ (1.381 \times 10^{-23}\ \text{J K}^{-1})(4.000 \times 10^{-7}\ \text{m})} = 7{,}242\ \text{K}$$

223. The action of inversion on the p-orbital function is $p(x, y, z) \rightarrow -p(-x, -y, -z)$, which means the $E = -1$. This is to be expected as the p-orbitals are ungerade (u).

224. Using $d/dx\ (\psi)$, it is possible to get

$$\frac{d}{dx} ce^{ax} = ace^{ax} = a\psi$$

which makes a the eigenvalue.

225. Because the system is orthonormal, $S_{11} = S_{22} = 1$, and $S_{12} = 0$. Using the general form of the secular determinant and substituting values gives

$$\begin{vmatrix} (H_{11} - ES_{11}) & (H_{12} - ES_{12}) \\ (H_{21} - ES_{12}) & (H_{22} - ES_{22}) \end{vmatrix} = 0 = \begin{vmatrix} (-5.0 - E) & (-3.0) \\ (-3.0) & (-0.50 - E) \end{vmatrix}$$

Chapter 9: Atomic Structure

226. The complete electron configurations are

Fe $1s^2 2s^2 2p^6 3s^2 3p^6 4s^2 3d^6$

Fe^{2+} $1s^2 2s^2 2p^6 3s^2 3p^6 3d^6$

Fe^{3+} $1s^2 2s^2 2p^6 3s^2 3p^6 3d^5$

227. Using the Pauli exclusion principle, the n, l, and m_l quantum numbers are the same for all three electrons. These values are $n = 3$, $l = 0$, and $m_l = 0$. For one of the electrons, m_s is +1/2, and for the other electron, m_s is –1/2.

228. L is the sum of the individual l values. For the p subshell, the possible values of the l quantum number are +1, 0, and –1. The two electrons may be in the same orbital or in different orbitals; therefore, the possible values of L are +2, 0, and –2 if the electrons are in the same orbital and +1, 0, and –1 if they are in different orbitals.

229. S is the sum of the individual m_s values. The possible values of the m_s quantum number are +1/2 or –1/2. The two electrons may have the same values or opposite values; therefore, the possible values are +1, 0, and –1.

230. The relationship for the orbital angular momentum is $L = \sqrt{l(l+1)}\hbar$, where l is the angular momentum quantum number (equal to 3 for a 4f electron) and $\hbar$ is Planck's constant divided by 2π (1.054573×10^{-34} J s). Entering the values into this relationship gives

$$L = \sqrt{l(l+1)}\hbar = \sqrt{3(3+1)}\hbar = \sqrt{12}\hbar$$

231. The components are given by $L_z = m_l\,\hbar$, where m_l is the magnetic quantum number. For a 4f electron, the allowed values of m_l are –3, –2, –1, 0, +1, +2, and +3. Therefore, the components are $-3\,\hbar$, $-2\,\hbar$, $-1\,\hbar$, 0, $+1\,\hbar$, $+2\,\hbar$, and $+3\,\hbar$.

232. The F designation represents L = 3. The superscript (3) is equal to 2 S + 1; therefore, S = 1.

233. In a p^6 configuration, each of the three p-orbitals contains a pair of electrons, one with a +1/2 spin and one with a –1/2 spin. The spin quantum number for the system (S) is the total of the individual spins, which is 0. The angular momentum quantum number for the system (L) is the sum of the individual angular momentum quantum numbers, which is also 0. The total magnetic quantum number (J) is M_L plus M_S or 0 also. The general symbolism for a term symbol is ${}^{2S+1}L_J$. The term symbol for a p^6 configuration is ${}^1S_0$.

234. The relationship is $c = \lambda\nu$, where c is the speed of light. Rearranging and entering the appropriate values gives

$$\lambda = \frac{c}{\nu} = \frac{2.998 \times 10^8 \text{ m s}^{-1}}{7.41 \times 10^{14} \text{ s}^{-1}} = 4.05 \times 10^{-7} \text{ m}$$

235. The appropriate relationship is $E = h\nu$, where h is Planck's constant. Entering the values gives

$$E = h\nu = (6.626 \times 10^{-34} \text{ J s})\,(7.41 \times 10^{14} \text{ s}^{-1}) = 4.91 \times 10^{-19} \text{ J}$$

236. The appropriate relationship is $E = hc/\lambda$, where h is Planck's constant and c is the speed of light. Entering the values gives

$$E = \frac{hc}{\lambda} = \frac{(6.626 \times 10^{-34}\ \text{J s})(2.998 \times 10^{8}\ \text{m s}^{-1})}{5.89 \times 10^{-7}\ \text{m}} = 3.37 \times 10^{-19}\ \text{J}$$

237. One form of the equation to determine the Hartree energy is $E_\text{h} = \frac{e^2}{4\pi\epsilon_0 a_0}$, where e is the charge of a proton ($1.60217733 \times 10^{-19}$ C), ϵ_0 is the permittivity of a vacuum ($8.854187817 \times 10^{-12}\ \text{C}^2\ \text{N}^{-1}\ \text{m}^{-2}$), and a_0 is the Bohr radius ($5.2917726 \times 10^{-11}$ m). Entering these values into the equation gives

$$E_\text{h} = \frac{e^2}{4\pi\epsilon_0 a_0} = \frac{(1.60217733 \times 10^{-19}\ \text{C})^2}{4\pi(8.854187817 \times 10^{-12}\ \text{C}^2\ \text{N}^{-1}\ \text{m}^{-2})(5.2917726 \times 10^{-11}\ \text{m})}$$
$$\times \left(\frac{\text{kg m/s}^2}{\text{N}}\right)\left(\frac{\text{J}}{\text{kg m}^2/\text{s}^2}\right) = 4.3597481 \times 10^{-18}\ \text{J}$$

238. One form of the equation to determine the Hartree energy is $E_\text{h} = \frac{\hbar^2}{m_e a_0^2}$, where $\hbar$ is Planck's constant divided by 2π (1.054573×10^{-34} J s), m_e is the rest mass of an electron ($9.1093897 \times 10^{-31}$ kg), and a_0 is the Bohr radius ($5.2917726 \times 10^{-11}$ m). Entering these values into the equation gives

$$E_\text{h} = \frac{\hbar^2}{m_\text{e} a_0^2} = \frac{(1.054573 \times 10^{-34}\ \text{J s})^2}{(9.1093897 \times 10^{-31}\ \text{kg})(5.2917726 \times 10^{-11}\ \text{m})^2}\left(\frac{\text{kg m}^2/\text{s}^2}{\text{J}}\right)$$
$$= 4.359751 \times 10^{-18}\ \text{J}$$

239. One form of the equation to determine the Hartree energy is $E_\text{h} = \frac{m_e e^4}{(4\pi\epsilon_0)^2\hbar^2}$. In this equation, $\hbar$ is Planck's constant divided by 2π (1.054573×10^{-34} J s), m_e is the rest mass of an electron ($9.1093897 \times 10^{-31}$ kg), e is the charge of a proton ($1.60217733 \times 10^{-19}$ C), and ϵ_0 is the permittivity of a vacuum ($8.854187817 \times 10^{-12}\ \text{C}^2\ \text{N}^{-1}\ \text{m}^{-2}$). Entering these values into the equation gives

$$E_\text{h} = \frac{m_\text{e} e^4}{(4\pi\epsilon_0)^2\hbar^2} = \frac{(9.1093897 \times 10^{-31}\ \text{kg})(1.60217733 \times 10^{-19}\ \text{C})^4}{[4\pi(8.854187817 \times 10^{-12}\ \text{C}^2\ \text{N}^{-1}\ \text{m}^{-2})]^2(1.054573 \times 10^{-34}\ \text{J s})^2}$$
$$\times \left(\frac{\text{J}}{\text{kg m}^2/\text{s}^2}\right)^3\left(\frac{\text{kg m/s}^2}{\text{N}}\right)^2 = 4.359745 \times 10^{-18}\ \text{J}$$

240. One form of the equation to determine the Bohr radius is $a_0 = \frac{h^2\epsilon_0}{\pi m_e e^2}$. In this equation, h is Planck's constant (6.626075×10^{-34} J s), ϵ_0 is the permittivity of a vacuum

($8.854187817 \times 10^{-12}$ $C^2\ N^{-1}\ m^{-2}$), m_e is the rest mass of an electron ($9.1093897 \times 10^{-31}$ kg), and e is the charge of a proton ($1.60217733 \times 10^{-19}$ C). Entering these values into the equation gives

$$a_0 = \frac{h^2\epsilon_0}{\pi m_e e^2} = \frac{(6.6260755 \times 10^{-34}\ \text{J s})^2(8.854187817 \times 10^{-12}\ \text{C}^2\ \text{N}^{-1}\ \text{m}^{-2})}{\pi(9.1093897 \times 10^{-31}\ \text{kg})(1.60217733 \times 10^{-19}\ \text{C})^2}$$

$$\times\left(\frac{\text{N}}{\text{kg m/s}^2}\right)\left(\frac{\text{kg m}^2/\text{s}^2}{\text{J}}\right)^2 = 5.2917726 \times 10^{-11}\ \text{m}$$

241. The relationship to determine the value of the Bohr magneton is $\mu_B = \frac{e\hbar}{2m_e}$, where e is the elementary charge ($1.60217733 \times 10^{-19}$ C), $\hbar$ is Planck's constant divided by 2π (1.054573×10^{-34} J s), and m_e is the rest mass of an electron ($9.1093897 \times 10^{-31}$ kg). Entering the values and appropriate conversions into the relationship gives

$$\mu_B = \frac{e\hbar}{2m_e} = \frac{(1.60217733 \times 10^{-19}\ \text{C})(1.054573 \times 10^{-34}\ \text{J s})}{2(9.1093897 \times 10^{-31}\ \text{kg})}\left(\frac{\text{A s}}{\text{C}}\right)\left(\frac{\text{kg/A s}^2}{\text{T}}\right)$$

$$= 9.274018 \times 10^{-24}\ \text{J T}^{-1}$$

242. The energies come from the relationship $E = -\mu_B B m_l$, where μ_B is the Bohr magneton (9.274×10^{-24} J T^{-1}), B is the magnetic field strength (1 T in this case), and m_l is the magnetic quantum number. For a 4f electron, the allowed values of m_l are −3, −2, −1, 0, +1, +2, and +3. Therefore, the allowed energies are $+3(9.274 \times 10^{-24}$ J), $+2(9.274 \times 10^{-24}$ J), $+1(9.274 \times 10^{-24}$ J), 0, $-1(9.274 \times 10^{-24}$ J), $-2(9.274 \times 10^{-24}$ J), and $-3(9.274 \times 10^{-24}$ J).

243. Entering the values into the Rydberg equation gives

$$\nu = R\left(\frac{1}{n_1^2} - \frac{1}{n_2^2}\right) = (3.29 \times 10^{15}\ \text{s}^{-1})\left(\frac{1}{2^2} - \frac{1}{\infty^2}\right) = 8.22 \times 10^{14}\ \text{s}^{-1}$$

244. The Rydberg equation $\left[\nu = R\left(\frac{1}{n_1^2} - \frac{1}{n_2^2}\right)\right]$ gives the frequency necessary for ionization if $n_1 = 1$ and $n_2 = \infty$. R is the Rydberg constant (3.29×10^{-15} s^{-1}). It is possible to determine the energy from $E = h\nu$, where h is Planck's constant. Combining these two relationships and entering the values gives

$$E = hR\left(\frac{1}{n_1^2} - \frac{1}{n_2^2}\right) = (6.626 \times 10^{-34}\ \text{J s})(3.29 \times 10^{15}\ \text{s}^{-1})\left(\frac{1}{1^2} - \frac{1}{\infty^2}\right)$$

$$= 2.18 \times 10^{-18}\ \text{J}$$

245. One form of the equation to calculate the translational kinetic energy of an atom is $E = \frac{3}{2}kT$, where k is the Boltzmann constant. Rearranging the equation and entering the values gives

$$T = \frac{2E}{3k} = \frac{2\ (2.18 \times 10^{-16}\ \text{J})}{3\ (1.38066 \times 10^{-23}\ \text{J K}^{-1})} = 1.05 \times 10^{7}\ \text{K}$$

246. Using the Bohr theory, the velocity (v) of an electron is $v = \frac{n\hbar}{m_e a_0}$, where $\hbar$ is Planck's constant divided by 2π (1.054573×10^{-34} J s), m_e is the rest mass of an electron ($9.1093897 \times 10^{-31}$ kg), n is the principle (1 for a ground-state hydrogen atom), and a_0 is the Bohr radius ($5.2917726 \times 10^{-11}$ m). Entering the values and appropriate conversions

$$v = \frac{n\hbar}{m_e a_0} = \frac{1(1.054573 \times 10^{-34}\ \text{J s})}{(9.1093897 \times 10^{-31}\ \text{kg})(5.2917726 \times 10^{-11}\ \text{m})}\left(\frac{\text{kg m}^2/\text{s}^2}{\text{J}}\right)$$

$$= 2.187692 \times 10^{6}\ \text{m s}^{-1}$$

247. The de Broglie relationship is $\lambda = \frac{h}{mv}$, where h is Planck's constant and m is the mass. Using the mass of an electron ($9.1093897 \times 10^{-31}$ kg) for m and the other information from the problem gives

$$\lambda = \frac{h}{mv} = \frac{6.6260755 \times 10^{-34}\ \text{J s}}{(9.1093897 \times 10^{-31}\ \text{kg})(2.187692 \times 10^{6}\ \text{m s}^{-1})}\left(\frac{\text{kg m}^2/\text{s}^2}{\text{J}}\right)$$

$$= 3.324918 \times 10^{-10}\ \text{m}$$

248. The equation to determine the circumference is $C = 2\pi r$. This gives

$$C = 2\pi r = 2\pi(5.2917726 \times 10^{-11}\ \text{m}) = 3.306069 \times 10^{-10}\ \text{m}$$

The two values ($3.3249188 \times 10^{-10}$ m and 3.324918×10^{-10} m) are the same.

249. The formula for the reduced mass is $\mu = \frac{m_1 m_2}{m_1 + m_2}$, where the m's are the masses of the particles ($m_1 = m_e = 9.10938 \times 10^{-31}$ kg and $m_2 = m_p = 1.67262 \times 10^{-27}$ kg). Incorporating this information into the formula gives

$$\mu = \frac{m_1 m_2}{m_1 + m_2} = \frac{(9.10938 \times 10^{-31}\ \text{kg})(1.67262 \times 10^{-27}\ \text{kg})}{(9.10938 \times 10^{-31}\ \text{kg}) + (1.67262 \times 10^{-27}\ \text{kg})} = 9.10442 \times 10^{-31}\ \text{kg}$$

250. The relationship to find the energy is $E = -\frac{\mu Z^2 e^4}{2\,\hbar^2 (4\pi\varepsilon_0)^2}\left(\frac{1}{n^2}\right)$. In this equation, $\hbar$ is Planck's constant divided by 2π (1.054573×10^{-34} J s), Z is the atomic number (1 for hydrogen), e is the elementary charge ($1.60217733 \times 10^{-19}$ C), μ is the reduced mass (9.10442×10^{-31} kg), and ε_0 is the permittivity of a vacuum ($8.854187817 \times 10^{-12}$ $C^2\ N^{-1}\ m^{-2}$). Entering these values into the equation gives

$$E = -\frac{\mu Z^2 e^4}{2\,\hbar^2 (4\pi\varepsilon_0)^2}\left(\frac{1}{n^2}\right)$$

$$= -\frac{(9.10442 \times 10^{-31}\ \text{kg})(1)^2(1.60217733 \times 10^{-19}\ \text{C})^4}{2\,(1.054573 \times 10^{-34}\ \text{J s})^2(4\pi(8.854187817 \times 10^{-12}\ \text{C}^2\ \text{N}^{-1}\ \text{m}^{-2}))^2}$$

$$\times\left(\frac{1}{3^2}\right)\left(\frac{\text{kg m/s}^2}{\text{N}}\right)^2\left(\frac{\text{J}}{\text{kg m}^2/\text{s}^2}\right)^3 = -2.42076 \times 10^{-19}\ \text{J}$$

251. The radial wave function for a 2s orbital is $R(r) = \left(\frac{1}{2\sqrt{2}}\right)\left(\frac{Z}{a_0}\right)^{3/2}\left(2 - \frac{r}{a_0}\right)e^{-r/2a_0}$, where Z is the atomic number (1 for hydrogen), a_0 is the Bohr radius, and r is the distance from the nucleus. A node occurs when this function equals 0. This function will equal 0 when $\left(2 - \frac{r}{a_0}\right)$ equals 0, which occurs at $r = 2a_0$.

252. The equation to determine the potential energy is $E_p = \frac{-Ze^2}{4\pi\epsilon_0 r}$, where Z is the nuclear charge, e is the electron charge, and ϵ_0 is the permittivity of a vacuum. Entering the values into the equation gives

$$E_p = \frac{-Ze^2}{4\pi\epsilon_0 r} = \frac{-(1)(1.602 \times 10^{-19}\ \text{C})^2}{4\pi(8.854 \times 10^{-12}\ \text{C}^2\ \text{N}^{-1}\ \text{m}^{-2})(5.29 \times 10^{-11}\ \text{m})}$$

$$\times\left(\frac{\text{kg m/s}^2}{\text{N}}\right)\left(\frac{\text{J}}{\text{kg m}^2/\text{s}^2}\right) = 4.36 \times 10^{-18}\ \text{J}$$

253. One method of determining the energy is $E = \frac{n^2 h^2}{8\,ma^2}$, where h is Planck's constant ($6.6260693 \times 10^{-34}$ J s), m is the mass of the electron (9.10938×10^{-31} kg), and a is the size of the well (1×10^{-10} m). Entering the information into the equation gives

$$\text{E} = \frac{n^2 h^2}{8\,ma^2} = \frac{(1)^2(6.6260693 \times 10^{-34}\ \text{J s})^2}{8\,(9.10938 \times 10^{-31}\ \text{kg})(1 \times 10^{-10}\ \text{m})^2}\left(\frac{\text{kg m}^2/\text{s}^2}{\text{J}}\right) = 6 \times 10^{-18}\ \text{J}$$

254. If $\psi = (\sin\theta - i\cos\theta)$, then $\psi^* = (\sin\theta - i\cos\theta)^*$; therefore,

$$\psi^*\psi = (\sin\theta - i\cos\theta)^*\,(\sin\theta - i\cos\theta) = (\sin\theta - i\cos\theta)\,(\sin\theta + i\cos\theta)$$

$$= (\sin^2\theta - i^2\cos^2\theta) = (\sin^2\theta + \cos^2\theta) = 1$$

Chapter 10: Molecular Structure

255. The forms are

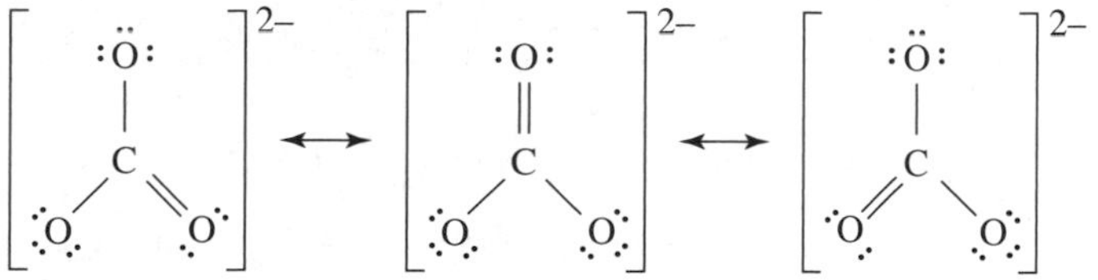

256. There are several variations for writing the molecular orbital designation of molecules and ions. In this case, one option is $\sigma_{1s}{}^2\ \sigma_{1s}{}^{*2}\ \sigma_{2s}{}^2\ \sigma_{2s}{}^{*2}\ \pi_{2p}{}^2\ \pi_{2p}{}^2\ \sigma_{2p}{}^2$.

257. There are several variations for writing the molecular orbital designation of molecules and ions. In this case, one option is $\sigma_g(1s)^2\ \sigma_u{}^*(1s)^2\ \sigma_g(2s)^2\ \sigma_u{}^*(2s)^2\ \pi_u\ (2p)^2\ \pi_u(2p)^2\ \sigma_g(2p)^1$.

258. There are several variations for writing the molecular orbital designation of molecules and ions. In this case, one option is $\sigma_{1s}{}^2\ \sigma_{1s}{}^{*2}\ \sigma_{2s}{}^2\ \sigma_{2s}{}^{*2}\ \pi_{2p}{}^2\ \pi_{2p}{}^2\ \sigma_{2p}{}^2\ \pi_{2p}{}^{*1}$.

259. The bond order (BO) is 0.5 (number of bonding electrons – antibonding electrons). In this case, an asterisk designates the antibonding electrons; therefore, BO = 0.5 (10 – 4) = 3.

260. The bond order (BO) is 0.5 (number of bonding electrons – antibonding electrons). In this case, an asterisk designates the antibonding electrons; therefore, BO = 0.5 (9 – 4) = 2.5.

261. The bond order (BO) is 0.5 (number of bonding electrons – antibonding electrons). In this case, an asterisk designates the antibonding electrons; therefore, BO = 0.5 (10 – 5) = 2.5.

262. The formula of pyridine is C_5H_5N and its structure is analogous to benzene with a nitrogen atom replacing a CH at one corner. In this structure, each C–H bond contains two sigma electrons (10 total). There are four C–C sigma and two C–N sigma bonds in the ring, which require two sigma electrons each (12 total). Thus, there are (10 + 12) = 22 sigma electrons. The resonating pi system gains one pi electron from each atom in the ring to give six pi electrons.

263. The fractional charges are numerical equal and opposite in charge. The dipole moment is equal to *qeR*, where *e* is the unit of electrostatic charge. Rearranging this equation and entering the appropriate values gives

$$q = \frac{\mu}{eR} = \frac{5.08 \times 10^{-31}\ \text{C m}}{(1.602 \times 10^{-19}\ \text{C})(1.13 \times 10^{-10}\ \text{m})} = 0.0281$$

264. It is necessary to compare the two dipole moments. The ratio of the actual to the calculated times 100% will give the percent ionic character. This is

$$\text{Percent ionic character} = \left(\frac{2.01 \times 10^{-29}\ \text{C m}}{2.48 \times 10^{-29}\ \text{C m}}\right) 100\% = 81.0\%$$

265. The relationship to determine the dipole moment is $\mu = Qr$, which is

$$\mu = Qr = (1.602 \times 10^{-19}\ \text{C})\ (1.55 \times 10^{-10}\ \text{m}) = 2.48 \times 10^{-29}\ \text{C m}$$

266. The spin quantum number for the one unpaired electron in this system (s) is ½. The relationships are $\mu = \mu_B\sqrt{s(s+1)} = \mu_B\sqrt{\frac{1}{2}\left(\frac{1}{2}+1\right)} = \mu_B\sqrt{3} = \mu_B\sqrt{3}$, where μ_B is the Bohr magneton (9.274×10^{-24} J T^{-1}) or β. Therefore,

$$\mu = (9.274 \times 10^{-24}\ \text{J T}^{-1})\sqrt{3} = 1.606 \times 10^{-23}\ \text{J T}^{-1}$$

267. The contribution of the electron spin to the molar magnetic susceptibility is $x_m = \frac{4\beta^2 N_A\ s(s+1)}{3kT}$, where β is the Bohr magneton (9.274×10^{-24} J T^{-1}), N_A is Avogadro's number (6.022×10^{23} mol^{-1}), s is the electron spin (1/2), k is the Boltzmann constant (1.3806×10^{-23} J K^{-1}), and T is the temperature (298 K). Entering these values into the equation gives

$$x_m = \frac{4\beta^2 N_A\ s(s+1)}{3kT} = \frac{4(9.274 \times 10^{-24}\ \text{J T}^{-1})^2(6.022 \times 10^{23}\ \text{mol}^{-1})\left[\frac{1}{2}\left(\frac{1}{2}+1\right)\right]}{3(1.3806 \times 10^{-23}\ \text{J K}^{-1})(298\ \text{K})}$$

$$= 1.26 \times 10^{-2}\ \text{mol}^{-1}\ \text{T}^{-2}$$

268. One method of determining the energy is $E = \frac{n^2h^2}{8\ ma^2}$, where h is Planck's constant ($6.6260693 \times 10^{-34}$ J s), m is the mass of the molecule (5.313525×10^{-26} kg), and a is the size of the well (0.500 m). Entering the information into the equation gives

$$E = \frac{n^2h^2}{8ma^2} = \frac{(1)^2(6.6260693 \times 10^{-34}\ \text{J s})^2}{8(5.313525 \times 10^{-26}\ \text{kg})(0.500\ \text{m})^2}\left(\frac{\text{kg m}^2/\text{s}^2}{\text{J}}\right) = 4.13 \times 10^{-42}\ \text{J}$$

269. One method of determining the energy is $E = \frac{n^2h^2}{8\ ma^2}$, where h is Planck's constant ($6.6260693 \times 10^{-34}$ J s), m is the mass of the molecule (5.313525×10^{-26} kg), E is the average energy of the molecule (1.694×10^{-21} J), and a is the size of the well (0.500 m). Rearranging the equation and entering the information into the equation and solving by parts gives

$$n = \sqrt{\frac{8ma^2\ E}{h^2}} = \sqrt{8mE}\left(\frac{a}{h}\right)$$

$$= \sqrt{8mE\left(\frac{\text{kg m}^2/\text{s}^2}{\text{J}}\right)}\left(\frac{0.500\ \text{m}}{6.6260693 \times 10^{-34}\ \text{J s}}\right)\left(\frac{\text{J}}{\text{kg m}^2/\text{s}^2}\right)$$

$$= \sqrt{8(5.313525 \times 10^{-26}\ \text{kg})(1.694 \times 10^{-21}\ \text{J})\left(\frac{\text{kg m}^2/\text{s}^2}{\text{J}}\right)}(7.55\ 10^{32}\ \text{s kg}^{-1}\ \text{m}^{-1})$$

$$= \sqrt{(7.201 \times 10^{-46}\ \text{J kg})\left(\frac{\text{kg m}^2/\text{s}^2}{\text{J}}\right)}(7.55\ 10^{32}\ \text{s kg}^{-1}\ \text{m}^{-1})$$

$$= 2.025 \times 10^{10}$$

270. The relationship necessary for this problem is $E = \frac{J(J+1)\hbar^2}{2\,I}$, where $\hbar$ is Planck's constant divided by 2π (1.054573×10^{-34} J s). Rearranging and entering values gives

$$J(J+1) = \frac{2\,E\,I}{\hbar^2} = \frac{2\,(2.06 \times 10^{-21}\ \text{J})\,(6.65 \times 10^{-46}\ \text{kg m}^2)}{(1.054573 \times 10^{-34}\ \text{J s})^2}\left(\frac{\text{J}}{\text{kg m}^2/\text{s}^2}\right) = 246$$

$$\text{J} \approx 15$$

271. An electron in a conjugated system is free to move throughout the system. Thus, it is a particle in a box with $E_n = \frac{n^2h^2}{8ma^2}$, where h is Planck's constant and m is the mass of an electron. Using this information gives

$$E_n = \frac{n^2h^2}{8\,ma^2} = \frac{(3)^2(6.626 \times 10^{-34}\ \text{J s})^2}{8(9.10939 \times 10^{-31}\ \text{kg})(1.9 \times 10^{-9}\ \text{m})^2}\left(\frac{\text{kg m}^2/\text{s}^2}{\text{J}}\right) = 1.5 \times 10^{-19}\ \text{J}$$

Chapter 11: Molecular Symmetry

272. All species have the identity (E or I). Draw a line that bisects the letter. This line is a C_2 axis. The plane of the paper is a vertical mirror plane (σ_v). A plane perpendicular to the paper (along the C_2 line) is a different vertical mirror plane (σ_v').

273. The possible operations for a C_8 axis are on the first line below, and alternates, where applicable, are below.

C_8^1	C_8^2	C_8^3	C_8^4	C_8^5	C_8^6	C_8^7	$C_8^8 = E$
	C_4^1		C_4^2		C_4^3		$C_4^4 = E$
			C_2^1				$C_2^2 = E$

The unique operations are C_8^1, C_8^3, C_8^5, and C_8^7.

274. The process is $\sigma_{xy}\begin{bmatrix} x \\ y \\ z \end{bmatrix} = \begin{bmatrix} x \\ y \\ -z \end{bmatrix}$.

275. The process is $i\begin{bmatrix} x \\ y \\ z \end{bmatrix} = \begin{bmatrix} -x \\ -y \\ -z \end{bmatrix}$.

276. The matrix representation is $C(z) = \begin{bmatrix} \cos\theta & \sin\theta & 0 \\ -\sin\theta & \cos\theta & 0 \\ 0 & 0 & 1 \end{bmatrix}$.

277. The matrix representation is $S(z) = \begin{bmatrix} \cos\theta & \sin\theta & 0 \\ -\sin\theta & \cos\theta & 0 \\ 0 & 0 & -1 \end{bmatrix}$.

278. The matrix multiplication is $\begin{bmatrix} 1 & 0 & 0 \\ 0 & -1 & 0 \\ 0 & 0 & 1 \end{bmatrix}\begin{bmatrix} -1 & 0 & 0 \\ 0 & 1 & 0 \\ 0 & 0 & 0 \end{bmatrix} = \begin{bmatrix} -1 & 0 & 0 \\ 0 & -1 & 0 \\ 0 & 0 & 0 \end{bmatrix} =$ $C_2(z)$.

279. List the symmetry operations horizontally and vertically then fill the table by multiplying each of the operations of each column by each of the operations of each row.

	E	C_2	$\sigma_v(xz)$	$\sigma_v'(yz)$
E	E	C_2	$\sigma_v(xz)$	$\sigma_v'(yz)$
C_2	C_2	E	$\sigma_v'(yz)$	$\sigma_v(xz)$
$\sigma_v(xz)$	$\sigma_v(xz)$	$\sigma_v'(yz)$	E	C_2
$\sigma_v'(yz)$	$\sigma_v'(yz)$	$\sigma_v(xz)$	C_2	E

280. All species have the identity (E or I). Draw a line that goes halfway between the hydrogen atoms and halfway between the bromine atoms. This line is a C_2 axis. The plane of the paper is a vertical mirror plane (σ_v). A plane perpendicular to the paper (along the C_2 line) is a different vertical mirror plane (σ_v').

281. The symmetry is C_3. The symmetry elements present are E and C_2. Because there is no S operation (or $\sigma = S_1$ or $i = S_2$), the molecule is optically active.

282. The molecule is T-shaped. There is a C_2 ("vertical") and two vertical mirror planes. These describe the C_{2v} point group.

283. It is possible to construct a group multiplication table for these operations. Each operation is listed across the top and down the side. The product of the operation at the side followed by the operation on the top will fill the table as:

	E	C_2	σ_v	σ_v'
E	E	C_2	σ_v	σ_v'
C_2	C_2	E	σ_v'	σ_v
σ_v	σ_v	σ_v'	E	C_2
σ_v'	σ_v'	σ_v	C_2	E

This fulfills all the conditions for a group multiplication table.

284. In both the symmetric stretch and scissoring, there is no loss in symmetry as the mirror plane bisecting the H–O–H bond angle remains; therefore, the symmetry of these two modes is C_{2v}. The asymmetric stretch eliminates the σ_v bisecting the bond angle, and this leads to the elimination of the C_2 axis, which leaves the σ that is the plane of the molecule. A species with only E and σ belongs to the C_s point group.

285. A molecule with a center of inversion (i) will not have a dipole moment. The only one of the three isomers with a center of inversion is *trans*-1,2-difluoroethene; therefore, it is the only one that does not have a dipole moment.

Chapter 12: Rotational and Vibrational Spectra

286. The relationship between energy and wavelength is $E = hc/\lambda$, where h is Planck's constant and c is the speed of light. Using this information, the energy is

$$E = hc/\lambda = \frac{(6.626 \times 10^{-34}\ \text{J s})\,(3.00 \times 10^{8}\ \text{m s}^{-1})}{(5.00 \times 10^{-6}\ \text{m})} = 3.98 \times 10^{-20}\ \text{J}$$

287. The relationship between energy and wavelength is $E = \frac{hcN_A}{\lambda}$, where h is Planck's constant, c is the speed of light, and N_A is Avogadro's number. Using this information, the energy is

$$E = \frac{hcN_A}{\lambda} = \frac{(6.626 \times 10^{-34}\ \text{J s})\,(3.00 \times 10^{8}\ \text{m s}^{-1})(6.022 \times 10^{23}\ \text{mol}^{-1})}{(5.00 \times 10^{-6}\ \text{m})}$$

$$= 2.39 \times 10^{4}\ \text{J mol}^{-1}$$

288. The relationship is $\Delta E = h\nu$, where h is Planck's constant. Rearranging and solving for the frequency gives

$$\nu = \frac{\Delta E}{h} = \frac{4.21 \times 10^{-20}\ \text{J}}{6.626 \times 10^{-34}\ \text{J s}} = 6.35 \times 10^{13}\ \text{s}^{-1}$$

289. The energy (E) of a photon is equal to hc/λ, where h is Planck's constant and c is the speed of light. Using this relationship and entering the appropriate values and conversions (Avogadro's number = N_A) gives

$$\lambda = \frac{hc}{E}N_A = \frac{(6.626 \times 10^{-34}\ \text{J s})(3.00 \times 10^{8}\ \text{m s}^{-1})}{5.5 \times 10^{4}\ \text{J mol}^{-1}}(6.022 \times 10^{23}\ \text{mol}^{-1})$$

$$= 2.2 \times 10^{-6}\ \text{m}$$

290. The wavenumber is the reciprocal of the wavelength; therefore,

$$(\tilde{\nu}) = \frac{1}{\lambda} = \frac{1}{2.2 \times 10^{-6}\ \text{m}}\left(\frac{0.01\ \text{m}}{\text{cm}}\right) = 4.5 \times 10^{3}\ \text{cm}^{-1}$$

291. This is primarily a unit conversion problem, which works as follows.

$$E = \frac{5.5 \times 10^{4}\ \text{J mol}^{-1}}{(6.022 \times 10^{23}\ \text{mol}^{-1})(1.602 \times 10^{-19}\ \text{J eV}^{-1})} = 0.57\ \text{eV}$$

292. The relationship is $hc(\tilde{\nu}) = kT$, where h is Planck's constant, c is the speed of light, and k is the Boltzmann constant. Rearranging and entering the appropriate values gives

$$(\tilde{\nu}) = \frac{kT}{hc} = \frac{(1.381 \times 10^{-23}\ \text{J K}^{-1})(298\ \text{K})}{(6.626 \times 10^{-34}\ \text{J s})(3.00 \times 10^{8}\ \text{m s}^{-1})}\left(\frac{0.01\ \text{m}}{\text{cm}}\right) = 207\ \text{cm}^{-1}$$

293. Dinitrogen oxide is a linear molecule with one of the nitrogen atoms in the center. For a linear molecule, the degrees of freedom are $3N - 5$, where N is the number of atoms. Therefore, there are $3(3) - 5 = 4$ degrees of freedom.

294. Dinitrogen oxide is a bent molecule with the two oxygen atoms bonded to the nitrogen atom. For a nonlinear molecule, the degrees of freedom are $3N - 6$, where N is the number of atoms. Therefore, there are $3(3) - 6 = 3$ degrees of freedom.

295. Pyridine is a nonlinear molecule; therefore, there will be $3N - 6 = 27$ modes. N is the number of atoms present (11).

296. The dissociation energy, from infrared spectral data, is $D = \frac{hc\bar{\nu}}{4x}$, where h is Planck's constant and c is the speed of light. The value of x is $(x\bar{\nu})/(\bar{\nu}) = (52.1\ \text{cm}^{-1})/(2990\ \text{cm}^{-1}) = 0.0174$, which substitutes in the dissociation energy equation to give

$$D = \frac{hc\bar{\nu}}{4x} = \frac{(6.626 \times 10^{-34}\ \text{J s})(2.9979 \times 10^{8}\ \text{m s}^{-1})(2990\ \text{cm}^{-1})}{4(0.0174)}\left(\frac{1\ \text{cm}}{0.01\ \text{m}}\right)$$

$$= 8.53 \times 10^{-19}\ \text{J}$$

297. The formula for the reduced mass of a diatomic molecule is $\mu = \frac{m_1 m_2}{m_1 + m_2}$, where m_1 and m_2 are the masses of the two atoms in the molecule. Using the information from the problem and Avogadro's number gives

$$\mu = \frac{m_1 m_2}{m_1 + m_2} = \frac{(2.0140 \text{ g mol}^{-1})(36.947 \text{ g mol}^{-1})}{(2.0140 + 36.947)\text{g mol}^{-1}}\left(\frac{\text{mol}}{6.0221 \times 10^{23}}\right)$$
$$= 3.1715 \times 10^{-24} \text{ g}$$

298. The relationship to determine the moment of inertia is $I = \mu r^2$. Using this relationship and the information from the problem gives

$$I = \mu r^2 = (3.1715 \times 10^{-24} \text{ g})\,(1.275 \times 10^{-10} \text{ m})^2 = 5.156 \times 10^{-44} \text{ g m}^2$$

299. It is possible to determine the wavelength from the relationship $\lambda = \frac{8\pi^2 Ic}{hJ}$, where I is the moment of inertia, c is the speed of light, h is Planck's constant, and J is the rotational quantum for the higher energy state (either 1 or 2 in this problem). Solving this equation, for $J = 1$ ($J = 0$ to $J = 1$), gives

$$\lambda = \frac{8\pi^2 Ic}{hJ} = \frac{8\pi^2(5.156 \times 10^{-47} \text{ kg m}^2)(2.9979 \times 10^8 \text{ m s}^{-1})}{(6.626 \times 10^{-34} \text{ J s})(1)}\left(\frac{\text{J}}{\text{kg m}^2/\text{s}^2}\right)$$
$$= 1.842 \times 10^{-3} \text{ m}$$

Solving for $J = 2$ ($J = 1$ to $J = 2$), gives

$$\lambda = \frac{8\pi^2 Ic}{hJ} = \frac{8\pi^2(5.156 \times 10^{-47} \text{ kg m}^2)(2.9979 \times 10^8 \text{ m s}^{-1})}{(6.626 \times 10^{-34} \text{ J s})(2)}\left(\frac{\text{J}}{\text{kg m}^2/\text{s}^2}\right)$$
$$= 9.210 \times 10^{-4} \text{ m}$$

300. The relationship to determine the force constant is $k = (2\pi \nu_0)^2 \mu$. Entering the appropriate values into this relationship gives

$$k = (2\pi\nu_0)^2\,\mu = [2\pi(6.198 \times 10^{13} \text{ s}^{-1})]^2\,(3.1715 \times 10^{-27} \text{ kg})\left(\frac{\text{N}}{\text{kg m/s}^2}\right)$$
$$= 4.81 \times 10^2 \text{ N m}^{-1}$$

301. A useful relationship for microwave spectroscopy is $(\bar{B}) = \frac{h}{8\,\pi^2 \mu r^2}$, where h is Planck's constant. This equation rearranges to

$$r = \sqrt{\frac{h}{8\,\pi^2 \mu \bar{B}}} = \sqrt{\frac{6.626 \times 10^{-34} \text{ J s}}{8\,\pi^2(3.1715 \times 10^{-27} \text{ kg})(1.6277 \times 10^{11} \text{ s}^{-1})}\left(\frac{\text{kg m}^2/\text{s}^2}{\text{J}}\right)}$$
$$= 1.275 \times 10^{-10} \text{ m}$$

302. The relationship between the moment of inertia and the bond length for a diatomic molecule is $I = \mu R^2$, which rearranges to

$$R = \sqrt{\frac{I}{\mu}} = \sqrt{\frac{5.156 \times 10^{-47}\ \text{kg m}^2}{3.1715 \times 10^{-27}\ \text{kg}}} = 1.275 \times 10^{-10}\ \text{m}$$

303. It is possible to determine the wavenumber from the relationship $(\bar{\nu}) = \frac{hJ}{4\pi^2 Ic}$, where I is the moment of inertia, c is the speed of light, h is Planck's constant, and J is the rotational quantum for the higher energy state. Solving this equation for $J = 1$ ($J = 0$ to $J = 1$) gives

$$(\bar{\nu}) = \frac{hJ}{4\pi^2 Ic} = \frac{(6.626 \times 10^{-34}\ \text{J s})(1)}{4\pi^2(5.156 \times 10^{-47}\ \text{kg m}^2)(2.9979 \times 10^8\ \text{m s}^{-1})}$$

$$\times \left(\frac{\text{kg m}^2/\text{s}^2}{\text{J}}\right)\left(\frac{0.01\ \text{m}}{\text{cm}}\right) = 10.86\ \text{cm}^{-1}$$

304. It is possible to determine the moment of inertia from the relationship $(\Delta\tilde{\nu}) = \frac{2h}{8\pi^2 Ic}$, where I is the moment of inertia, c is the speed of light, and h is Planck's constant. Solving this equation for I gives

$$I = \frac{2h}{8\pi^2 c(\Delta\tilde{\nu})} = \frac{2(6.626 \times 10^{-34}\ \text{J s})}{8\pi^2(2.9979 \times 10^8\ \text{m s}^{-1})(10.89\ \text{cm}^{-1})}\left(\frac{0.01\ \text{m}}{1\ \text{cm}}\right)\left(\frac{\text{kg m}^2/\text{s}^2}{\text{J}}\right)$$

$$= 5.141 \times 10^{-47}\ \text{kg m}^2$$

305. The symmetry of the molecule simplifies the solution to this problem. Orientate the molecule on the xy plane so the z coordinate of all atoms is 0. Then rotate the molecule so the x axis bisects the bond angle ($\theta = 92.1°/2$) with the sulfur atom at the origin (x and $y = 0$). The displacement of the center in the y direction by one of the hydrogen atoms is offset by the other hydrogen atom; therefore, it is only necessary to determine the displacement in the x direction. The displacement in the x direction (X) is equal to $\frac{\sum_{i=1}^{3} m_i x_i}{M}$, where M is the molecular mass (34.08 amu), m_i is the mass of the individual atoms (only needed for H = 1.01 amu), and x_i is distance from the x axis ($r \cos \theta$). Combining this information gives

$$X = \frac{\sum_{i=1}^{3} m_i x_i}{M} = \frac{2\ (1.01\ \text{amu})(1.366 \times 10^{-10}\ \text{m})\left(\sin\left(\frac{92.1°}{2}\right)\right)}{34.08\ \text{amu}} = 5.83 \times 10^{-12}\ \text{m}$$

306. The symmetry of the molecule simplifies the solution to this problem. Orientate the molecule on the xy plane so the z coordinate of all atoms is 0. Then rotate the molecule so the x axis bisects the bond angle ($\theta = 92.1°/2$) with the sulfur at ($x = -0.0883$ Å, $y = 0$, and $z = 0$). The hydrogen atoms are located at $x = r\cos(92.1°/2) - 0.0883$ Å, $y = \pm r \sin(92.1°/2)$, and $z = 0$, which leads to one H at $x = 1.37$ Å, $y = 0.983$ Å, and $z = 0$, and the other H at $x = 1.37$ Å, $y = -0.983$ Å, and $z = 0$.

307. The general form of the equation to determine the moments of inertia is $I_x = \sum_{i=1}^{N} m_i(y_i^2 + z_i^2)$, where m is the atom mass and the x, y, and z refer to the coordinate axes. The other two moments of inertia come from $I_y = \sum_{i=1}^{N} m_i(x_i^2 + z_i^2)$ and $I_z = \sum_{i=1}^{N} m_i(x_i^2 + y_i^2)$. Using these equations gives

$$I_x = \sum_{i=1}^{N} m_i\left(y_i^2 + z_i^2\right) = m_{\mathrm{H}}(0.983^2 + 0)\text{Å}^2 + m_{\mathrm{H}}(-0.983^2 + 0)\text{Å}^2 + m_{\mathrm{S}}(0)$$

$$= 2(1.01\ \text{amu})\ (0.983^2)\text{Å}^2 = 1.95\ \text{amu Å}^2$$

$$I_y = \sum_{i=1}^{N} m_i\left(x_i^2 + z_i^2\right) = 2m_{\mathrm{H}}(1.37^2 + 0)\text{Å}^2 + m_{\mathrm{S}}(-0.08832 + 0)\text{Å}^2$$

$$= 2(1.01\ \text{amu})(1.37^2)\text{Å}^2 + (32.06\ \text{amu})(-0.0883^2)\text{Å}^2 = 4.04\ \text{amu Å}^2$$

$$I_z = \sum_{i=1}^{N} m_i\left(x_i^2 + y_i^2\right)$$

$$= m_{\mathrm{H}}(1.37^2 + 0.983^2)\text{Å}^2 + m_{\mathrm{H}}(1.37^2 + -0.983^2)\text{Å}^2 + m_{\mathrm{S}}(-0.0883^2 + 0)\text{Å}^2$$

$$= 2(1.01\ \text{amu})(1.37^2 + 0.983^2)\text{Å}^2 + (32.06\ \text{amu})(-0.0883^2)\text{Å}^2 = 5.99\ \text{amu Å}^2$$

308. Combining the information in the problem gives $hc/\lambda = kT$, where h is Planck's constant, c is the speed of light, and k is the Boltzmann constant. Rearranging this relationship and entering the values gives

$$T = \frac{hc}{k\lambda} = \frac{(6.626 \times 10^{-34}\ \text{J s})(3.00 \times 10^{8}\ \text{m s}^{-1})}{(1.381 \times 10^{-23}\ \text{J K}^{-1})(9.95 \times 10^{-7}\ \text{m})} = 1.45 \times 10^{4}\ \text{K}$$

309. To have a pure microwave absorption spectrum, the species must have a permanent dipole moment. The only species with a permanent dipole moment are HF, $CH_3CHOHCH_3$, NH_3, and C_6H_5F.

Chapter 13: Electronic Spectra

310. The total energy necessary is the dissociation energy plus twice the kinetic energy of the atoms. The total energy (E) is 5.817×10^{-19} J. The wavelength comes from the following where h is Planck's constant and c is the speed of light.

$$\lambda = \frac{hc}{E} = \frac{(6.626\times10^{-34}\ \text{J s})(2.9979\times10^{8}\ \text{m s}^{-1})}{5.817\times10^{-19}\ \text{J}} = 3.415 \times 10^{-7}\ \text{m}$$

311. A 5-fs pulse is a 5×10^{-15} s pulse (Δt). The appropriate relationship is $\Delta\nu \geq (2\pi\Delta t)^{-1}$. This relationship leads to

$$\Delta\nu \geq (2\pi\Delta t)^{-1} = [2\pi(5 \times 10^{-15}\ \text{s})]^{-1} = 3 \times 10^{13}\ \text{s}^{-1}$$

312. The energy (E) of each pulse is the energy output of the laser divided by the number of pulses. This is

$$E = \frac{5\text{ W}}{2 \times 10^7\text{ s}^{-1}}\left(\frac{\text{J s}^{-1}}{\text{W}}\right) = 2 \times 10^{-7}\text{ J}$$

313. The energy of a photon with a wavelength (λ) of 725 nm comes from the following where h is Planck's constant and c is the speed of light.

$$E = \frac{hc}{\lambda} = \frac{(6.626 \times 10^{-34}\text{ J s})(2.9979 \times 10^{8}\text{ m s}^{-1})}{725\text{ nm}}\left(\frac{1\text{ nm}}{10^{-9}\text{ m}}\right) = 2.74 \times 10^{-19}\text{ J}$$

The number of photons is the total joules (5×10^{-7} J) divided by the energy per photon (2.74×10^{-19} J) or 2×10^{12} photons.

314. The relationship for determining the absorbance is $A = \log\frac{I_0}{I}$, where I_0 is the reference beam intensity (100%). Entering the values into the equation gives

$$A = \log\frac{I_0}{I} = \log\frac{100\%}{32\%} = 0.49$$

315. The molar absorption coefficient comes from the relationship $\varepsilon = \frac{A}{LC}$, where L is the cell length (1.00 cm in this case) and C is the concentration (1.25×10^{-3} M $= 1.25 \times 10^{-3}$ mol L^{-1}). This information leads to

$$\varepsilon = \frac{A}{LC} = \frac{0.49}{(1.25 \times 10^{-3}\text{ mol L}^{-1})(1.00\text{ cm})} = 390\text{ L mol}^{-1}\text{ cm}^{-1}$$

316. According to Beer's law, $\log\frac{I_0}{I} = \varepsilon Cl$, where I_0 is the intensity of the incident radiation (100%). Solving this relationship for the extinction coefficient gives

$$\varepsilon = \frac{\log\frac{I_0}{I}}{Cl} = \frac{\log\frac{100\%}{75\%}}{(0.15\text{ M})(1.0\text{ cm})} = 0.83\text{ M}^{-1}\text{ cm}^{-1}$$

317. According to Beer's law, $\log\frac{I_0}{I} = \varepsilon Cl$, where I_0 is the intensity of the incident radiation (100%). Solving this relationship for the concentration gives

$$C = \frac{\log\frac{I_0}{I}}{\varepsilon l} = \frac{\log\frac{100\%}{35\%}}{(0.83\text{ M}^{-1}\text{ cm}^{-1})(1.0\text{ cm})} = 0.55\text{ M}$$

318. According to Beer's law, $\log\frac{I_0}{I} = \varepsilon Cl$, where I_0 is the intensity of the incident radiation (100%). Entering the information from the problem into the Beer's law relationship gives

$$\log\frac{\mathrm{I_0}}{\mathrm{I}}\log\frac{\mathrm{I_0}}{\mathrm{I}} = \varepsilon Cl = (0.83\ \mathrm{M^{-1}\ cm^{-1}})(0.35\ \mathrm{M})(1.0\ \mathrm{cm}) = 0.29$$

$$\mathrm{I} = \frac{I_0}{10^{0.29}} = \frac{100\%}{1.95} = 51\%$$

319. The simplified relationship for the determination of the absorption cross section is $\sigma = \frac{2.303\ \varepsilon}{N_A}$, where N_A is Avogadro's number. Using this information gives

$$\sigma = \frac{2.303\varepsilon}{N_A} = \frac{2.303(5.2\times10^4\ \mathrm{L\ mol^{-1}cm^{-1}})}{(6.022\times10^{23}\ \mathrm{mol^{-1}})}\left(\frac{\mathrm{m^3}}{10^3\ \mathrm{L}}\right)\left(\frac{\mathrm{cm}}{0.01\ \mathrm{m}}\right) = 2.0\times10^{-17}\ \mathrm{m^2}$$

320. The integrated absorption coefficient comes from the relationship $\int\varepsilon d\tilde{v} = 1.06\ \varepsilon_{max}\Delta\tilde{v}_{1/2}$. Using this relationship

$$\int\varepsilon d\tilde{v} = 1.06\ \varepsilon_{max}\Delta\tilde{v}_{1/2} = 1.06\ (5.2\times10^4\ \mathrm{L\ mol^{-1}\ cm^{-1}})\ (3{,}500\ \mathrm{cm^{-1}})$$

$$= 1.9\times10^8\ \mathrm{L\ mol^{-1}\ cm^{-2}}$$

321. The equation to determine the absorption frequency is $\tilde{v} = \frac{h\ (N+1)}{8\ c\ m_e a^2}$, where h is Planck's constant, c is the speed of light, and m_e is the mass of an electron. Using this equation leads to

$$\tilde{v} = \frac{h(N+1)}{8cm_e a^2} = \frac{(6.63\times10^{-34}\ \mathrm{J\ s})\ (8+1)}{8(3.00\times10^8\ m\ \mathrm{s^{-1}})\ (9.109\times10^{-31}\ \mathrm{kg})(1.9\times10^{-9}\ m)^2}$$

$$\times\left(\frac{\mathrm{Kg}\ m^2/\mathrm{s}^2}{\mathrm{J}}\right)\left(\frac{0.01\ m}{1\ \mathrm{cm}}\right) = 7.6\times10^3\ \mathrm{cm^{-1}}$$

322. The zero point energy is given by $(1/2)h\nu_0$, where h is Planck's constant. The relationship between D and D' is $D' = D + (1/2)h\nu_0$. Using this relationship and the appropriate conversions,

$$D' = D + (1/2)h\nu_0$$

$$= (4.430\ \mathrm{eV})\left(\frac{96.36\ \mathrm{kJ\ mol^{-1}}}{\mathrm{eV}}\right) + \frac{1}{2}(6.626\times10^{-34}\ \mathrm{J\ s})(8.964\times10^{13}\ \mathrm{s^{-1}})$$

$$\times\left(\frac{1\ \mathrm{kJ}}{10^3\ \mathrm{J}}\right)(6.022\times10^{23}\ \mathrm{mol^{-1}}) = 444.8\ \mathrm{kJ\ mol^{-1}}$$

323. The appropriate relationship, where c is the speed of light, is $\Delta\bar{\nu} \geq (2\pi c\Delta t)^{-1}$. This relationship leads to

$$\Delta\bar{\nu} \geq (2\pi c\Delta t)^{-1} = \left[2\pi(2.9979 \times 10^{10} \text{ cm s}^{-1})\left(\frac{s}{10^{12}}\right)\right]^{-1} = 5 \text{ cm}^{-1}$$

324. The appropriate relationship, where c is the speed of light, is $\Delta\bar{\nu} \geq (2\pi c\Delta t)^{-1}$. This relationship leads to

$$\Delta\bar{\nu} \geq (2\pi c\Delta t)\text{–}1 = [2\pi(2.9979 \times 10^{10} \text{ cm s}^{-1})(2 \times 10^{-6} \text{ s})]^{-1} = 3 \times 10^{-6} \text{ cm}^{-1}$$

325. The appropriate relationship, where c is the speed of light, is $\Delta\bar{\nu} \geq (2\pi c\Delta t)^{-1}$. This relationship leads to

$$\Delta\bar{\nu} \geq (2\pi c\Delta t)^{-1} = [2\pi(2.9979 \times 10^{10} \text{ cm s}^{-1})(2 \times 10^{6} \text{ s})]^{-1} = 3 \times 10^{-18} \text{ cm}^{-1}$$

326. The kinetic energy of the emitted electrons is the energy of the photons (4.000×10^{-17} J) minus the ionization potential (1.7215×10^{-18} J) or 3.827×10^{-17} J.

327. The kinetic energy is equal to $\frac{1}{2}mv^2$, where m is the mass of an electron. Rearranging this relationship to determine the velocity of the electrons gives

$$v = \sqrt{\frac{2E}{m}} = \sqrt{\frac{2(3.827 \times 10^{-17} \text{ J})}{9.10938 \times 10^{-31} \text{ kg}}\left(\frac{\text{kg } m^2/s^2}{\text{J}}\right)} = 9.166 \times 10^{6} \text{ m s}^{-1}$$

328. The binding energy of these electrons is the difference between the energy available (4.000×10^{-18} J) and the kinetic energy (E) of the electrons ($E = \frac{1}{2}mv^2$). Using the mass of the electron as m leads to

$$E = \frac{1}{2}mv^2 = \frac{1}{2}(9.10938 \times 10^{-31} \text{ kg})(1.00 \times 10^{6} \ m \text{ s}^{-1})^2\left(\frac{\text{J}}{\text{kg } m^2/s^2}\right) = 4.55 \times 10^{-19} \text{ J}$$

The binding energy is (4.000×10^{-18} J) – (4.55×10^{-19} J) = 3.545×10^{-18} J

329. Using the fraction (f) of the different forms gives the relationships $f_\alpha + f_\beta = 1$ and $[\alpha]_{\text{mixture}} = f_\alpha[\alpha]_\alpha + f_\beta[\alpha]_\beta$. Setting $f_\alpha = 1 - f_\beta$ and substituting gives $[\alpha]_{\text{mixture}} = (1 - f_\beta)[\alpha]_\alpha + f_\beta[\alpha]_\beta$. Solving for f_β gives

$$f_\beta = \frac{[\alpha]_{\text{mixture}} - [\alpha]_\alpha}{[\alpha]_\beta - [\alpha]_\alpha} = \frac{80.2° - 150.7°}{52.8° - 150.7°} = 0.720 \text{ or } 72.0\%$$

Chapter 14: Magnetic Resonance Spectra

330. The ratio of the signal to NMR frequency gives the chemical (normally expressed as ppm). In this case, the chemical shift (δ) is

$$\delta = \frac{3200\ \text{Hz}}{500\ \text{MHz}}\left(\frac{1\ \text{MHz}}{10^6\ \text{Hz}}\right)\left(\frac{10^6\ \text{ppm}}{1}\right) = 6.40\ \text{ppm}$$

331. The definition of the nuclear magneton is $\mu_N = \frac{e\hbar}{2\,m_p}$, where $\hbar$ is Planck's constant divided by 2π (1.054573×10^{-34} J s), m_p is the rest mass of a proton (1.672623×10^{-27} kg), and e is the charge on a proton (1.602177×10^{-19} C). Using this information gives

$$\mu_N = \frac{e\hbar}{2m_p} = \frac{(1.602177 \times 10^{-19}\ \text{C})(1.054573 \times 10^{-34}\ \text{J s})}{2(1.672623 \times 10^{-27}\ \text{kg})}\left(\frac{\text{A s}}{\text{C}}\right)\left(\frac{\text{kg s}^{-2}\text{A}^{-1}}{\text{T}}\right)$$

$$= 5.050787 \times 10^{-27}\ \text{J T}^{-1}$$

332. The equation to determine the magnetogyric ratio for hydrogen is $\gamma = \frac{g_N\mu_N}{\hbar}$, where g_N is the nuclear g factor (5.585 for hydrogen), $\hbar$ is Planck's constant divided by 2π, and μ_N is the nuclear magneton (5.050787×10^{-27} J T^{-1}). This relationship leads to

$$\gamma = \frac{g_N\mu_N}{\hbar} = \frac{(5.585)(5.050787 \times 10^{-27}\ \text{J T}^{-1})}{1.054573 \times 10^{-34}\ \text{J s}} = 2.675 \times 10^8\ \text{T}^{-1}\ \text{s}^{-1}$$

333. The field strength for the NMR spectrometer will be $B = \frac{2\pi\nu}{\gamma}$. Therefore, the field strength will be

$$B = \frac{2\pi\nu}{\gamma} = \frac{2\pi(250\ \text{MHz})}{(2.675 \times 10^8\ \text{T}^{-1}\text{s}^{-1})}\left(\frac{10^6\ \text{Hz}}{1\ \text{MHz}}\right)\left(\frac{\text{s}^{-1}}{\text{Hz}}\right) = 5.9\ \text{T}$$

334. The relationship to determine the Larmor frequency is $\nu_L = \frac{\gamma B}{2\,\pi}$. Using this relationship gives

$$\nu_L = \frac{\gamma B}{2\pi} = \frac{(2.675 \times 10^8\ \text{T}^{-1}\ \text{s}^{-1})(5.0\ \text{T})}{2\pi} = 2.1 \times 10^8\ \text{s}^{-1}$$

335. The relationship between the field strength for the NMR spectrometer at the absorption frequency is $B = \frac{2\pi\nu}{\gamma}$. Rearranging this equation and entering the appropriate values gives

$$\nu = \frac{B\gamma}{2\pi} = \frac{(6.0\ T)(2.518 \times 10^8\ \text{T}^{-1}\ \text{s}^{-1})}{2\pi}\left(\frac{\text{Hz}}{\text{s}^{-1}}\right)\left(\frac{1\ \text{MHz}}{10^6\ \text{Hz}}\right) = 240\ \text{MHz}$$

336. The relationship $E = h\nu$, where h is Planck's constant, allows the calculation of the energy. Using this equation and Avogadro's number leads to the energy.

$$E = h\nu = (6.626 \times 10^{-34}\ \text{Js})(2.5 \times 10^{8}\ \text{s}^{-1})\left(\frac{6.022 \times 10^{23}}{\text{mol}}\right)\left(\frac{1\ \text{kJ}}{10^{3}\ \text{J}}\right)$$

$$= 1.1 \times 10^{-4}\ \text{kJ mol}^{-1}$$

337. An approximation of this ratio comes from $\frac{N_1}{N_2} = 1 + \frac{g_N \mu_N B}{kT}$, where k is the Boltzmann constant (1.381×10^{-23} J K^{-1}), g_N is the nuclear g factor (5.585 for hydrogen), and μ_N is the Bohr magneton (9.274×10^{-24} J T^{-1}). Substituting the values into the equation gives

$$\frac{N_1}{N_2} = 1 + \frac{g_N \mu_N B}{kT} = 1 + \frac{(5.585)(9.274 \times 10^{-24}\ \text{JT}^{-1})(5.9\ \text{T})}{(1.381 \times 10^{-23}\ \text{JK}^{-1})(298\ \text{K})} = 1 + 0.074 \approx 1$$

338. An approximation of this ratio comes from $\frac{N_1}{N_2} = 1 + \frac{g_N \mu_N B}{kT}$, where k is the Boltzmann constant (1.381×10^{-23} J K^{-1}), g_N is the nuclear g factor (5.585 for hydrogen), and μ_N is the Bohr magneton (9.274×10^{-24} J T^{-1}). Substituting the values into the equation gives

$$\frac{N_1}{N_2} = 1 + \frac{g_N \mu_N B}{kT} = 1 + \frac{(5.585)(9.274 \times 10^{-24}\ \text{JT}^{-1})(5.9\ \text{T})}{(1.381 \times 10^{-23}\ \text{JK}^{-1})(1.0\ \text{K})} = 1 + 22 = 23$$

339. The relationship to find the energies is $E = -\mu_N g_N m_I B$, where μ_N is the nuclear magneton, g_N is the nuclear g factor (2.171), and m_I is the spin-state (3/2, 1/2, –1/2, or –3/2). For $m_I = 3/2$, this relationship gives

$$E = -\mu_N g_N m_I B = -(5.0508 \times 10^{-27}\ \text{JT}^{-1})(2.171)\left(\frac{3}{2}\right)(6.5\ \text{T}) = -1.1 \times 10^{-25}\ \text{J}$$

The other values are -3.6×10^{-26} J for $m_I = 1/2$, 3.6×10^{-26} J for $m_I = -1/2$, and 1.1×10^{-25} J for $m_I = -3/2$.

340. The frequency depends upon the identity of the nucleus and the field strength. The relationship to determine the frequency is $\nu_{NMR} = \frac{|g_N| \mu_N B}{h}$, where h is Planck's constant and μ_N is the nuclear magneton. Combing the given information with this equation gives

$$\nu_{NMR} = \frac{|g_N| \mu_N B}{h} = \frac{|1.792|(5.05078 \times 10^{-27}\ \text{J T}^{-1})(5.5\ \text{T})}{6.626 \times 10^{-34}\ \text{J s}}$$

$$= 7.8 \times 10^{7}\ \text{s}^{-1}\ (78\ \text{MHz})$$

341. The general relationship to determine an ESR signal is $\nu_{ESR} = \frac{g \mu_B B}{h}$, where h is Planck's constant and μ_B is the Bohr magneton. Rearranging this equation and entering the appropriate values gives

$$B = \frac{h\nu_{ESR}}{g\mu_B} = \frac{(6.626 \times 10^{-34}\ \text{J s})(9.42 \times 10^9\ \text{s}^{-1})}{2.0088\ (9.274 \times 10^{-24}\ \text{J T}^{-1})} = 0.335\ \text{T}$$

342. The field strength for the ESR spectrometer will be $B = \frac{h\nu}{g_e\mu_B}$, where h is Planck's constant (6.626×10^{-34} J s), g_e is the g factor (2.0023 for a free electron), and μ_B is the Bohr magneton (9.274×10^{-24} J T^{-1}). The field strength will be

$$B = \frac{h\nu}{g_e\mu_B} = \frac{(6.626 \times 10^{-34}\ \text{Js})(1.0 \times 10^4\ \text{MHz})}{2.0023(9.274 \times 10^{-24}\ \text{J T}^{-1})}\left(\frac{10^6\ \text{Hz}}{1\ \text{MHz}}\right)\left(\frac{\text{s}^{-1}}{\text{Hz}}\right) = 0.31\ \text{T}$$

343. The relationship is $\nu_L = \frac{Bg_e\mu_N}{h}$, where μ_N is the Bohr magneton (9.274×10^{-24} J T^{-1}), g_e is the g factor (2.0023 for a free electron), and h is Planck's constant. This relationship gives

$$\nu_L = \frac{Bg_e\mu_N}{h} = \frac{(5.0\ \text{T})(2.0023)(9.274 \times 10^{-24}\ \text{J T}^{-1})}{6.626 \times 10^{-34}\ \text{Js}} = 1.4 \times 10^{11}\ \text{s}^{-1}$$

Chapter 15: Statistical Mechanics

344. There are two containers; therefore, the probability of one molecule being in a particular container is ½. For more molecules, the general formula for the probability is $P = (1/2)^N$, where N is the number of molecules. Entering the values into the formula gives

$$P = (1/2)^N = (1/2)^4 = 0.0625$$

345. The molecule is tetrahedral with the C–H bond being a C_3 axis. Each C_3 generates an asymmetry number of 3; therefore, the symmetry number is 3.

346. The molecule is tetrahedral with each C–H bond being a C_3 axis. Each C_3 generates an asymmetry number of 3; therefore, the symmetry number is 12.

347. In a localized system, each particle could be in any of the quantum states, which gives $50 \times 50 = 2{,}500$ microstates.

348. Because argon is a monatomic species, the only contribution to the entropy is from the translation of the atoms. The translational entropy contribution is $\Delta S° = R\left(\frac{5}{2} + \ln\left(\frac{(2\pi mkT)^{3/2}V°}{h^3L}\right)\right)$, where R is the gas constant, T is the temperature, m is the molar mass, k is Boltzmann's constant, h is Planck's constant, and $V°$ is the standard molar volume. This is one form of the Sakur–Tetrode equation. Because most of the terms are the same, the difference in the entropies at the two different temperatures simplifies to $\Delta S° = \frac{5}{2} R \ln \frac{T_2}{T_1}$. Using this final form of the equation gives

$$\Delta S° = \frac{5}{2} R \ln \frac{T_2}{T_1} = \frac{5}{2} (8.3145 \text{ J mol}^{-1} \text{ K}^{-1}) \ln \frac{273 \text{ K}}{315 \text{ K}} = -2.97 \text{ J mol}^{-1} \text{ K}^{-1}$$

349. Because many of the factors are negligible, the major contribution to $\Delta S°$ will be from the symmetry term (σ), which is 2 for $^{79}Br^{79}Br$ and $^{81}Br^{81}Br$ and 1 for $^{79}Br^{81}Br$. Combining this with $\Delta S° = \sum S°(\text{products}) - \sum S°(\text{reactants})$ and $\Delta S° = -R \ln \sigma$ gives

$$\Delta S° = (2 \text{ mol})[-R \ln \sigma(^{79}\text{Br}^{81}\text{Br})] - (1 \text{ mol}) [-R \ln \sigma(^{79}\text{Br}^{79}\text{Br})]$$

$$- (1 \text{ mol}) [-R \ln \sigma(^{81}\text{Br}^{81}\text{Br})]$$

$$= (2 \text{ mol}) [-(8.3145 \text{ J mol}^{-1} \text{ K}^{-1}) \ln 1] - (1 \text{ mol}) [-(8.3145 \text{ J mol}^{-1} \text{ K}^{-1}) \ln 2]$$

$$- (1 \text{ mol}) [-(8.3145 \text{ J mol}^{-1} \text{ K}^{-1}) \ln 2] = 11.526 \text{ J mol}^{-1} \text{ K}^{-1}$$

350. This is a special case of the Boltzmann distribution law, which is $\frac{N_i}{N_j} = \left(\frac{g_i}{g_j}\right) e^{-(\varepsilon_i - \varepsilon_j)/kT}$, where the *N*'s are the occupancies of the different energy levels (ε) (45% and 55%), the *g*'s are the statistical weights (1 in this case), *k* is the Boltzmann constant, and *T* is the temperature. Entering the appropriate values gives

$$\frac{N_i}{N_j} = \left(\frac{g_i}{g_j}\right) e^{-(\varepsilon_i - \varepsilon_j)/kT}$$

$$\frac{45}{55} = \left(\frac{1}{1}\right) e^{-[(3.0 \times 10^{-23} - 0)\text{J}]/(1.381 \times 10^{-23} \text{ J K}^{-1})T}$$

$$T = 11 \text{ K}$$

351. This is an example of the Boltzmann distribution law, which is $\frac{N_i}{N_j} = \left(\frac{g_i}{g_j}\right) e^{-(\varepsilon_i - \varepsilon_j)/kT}$, where the *N*'s are the occupancies of the different energy levels (ε), the *g*'s are the statistical weights (1 in this case), *k* is the Boltzmann constant, and *T* is the temperature. Entering the appropriate values gives

$$\frac{N_i}{N_j} = \left(\frac{g_i}{g_j}\right) e^{-(\varepsilon_i - \varepsilon_j)/kT} = \left(\frac{1}{1}\right) e^{-(10^{-42} \text{ J})/[(1.381 \times 10^{-23} \text{ J K}^{-1})(298 \text{ K})]} = 1$$

There is even distribution over all states.

352. This is an example of the Boltzmann distribution law, which is $\frac{N_i}{N_j} = \left(\frac{g_i}{g_j}\right)e^{-(\varepsilon_i - \varepsilon_j)/kT}$, where the N's are the occupancies of the different energy levels (ε), the g's are the statistical weights (1 in this case), k is the Boltzmann constant, and T is the temperature. Entering the appropriate values gives

$$\frac{N_i}{N_j} = \left(\frac{g_i}{g_j}\right)e^{-(\varepsilon_i - \varepsilon_j)/kT} = \left(\frac{1}{1}\right)e^{-(10^{-23}\text{ J})/[(1.381\times10^{-23}\text{ J K}^{-1})(298\text{ K})]} = 0.998$$

353. This is an example of the Boltzmann distribution law, which is $\frac{N_i}{N_j} = \left(\frac{g_i}{g_j}\right)e^{-(\varepsilon_i - \varepsilon_j)/kT}$, where the N's are the occupancies of the different energy levels (ε), the g's are the statistical weights (1 in this case), k is the Boltzmann constant, and T is the temperature. Entering the appropriate values gives

$$\frac{N_i}{N_j} = \left(\frac{g_i}{g_j}\right)e^{-(\varepsilon_i - \varepsilon_j)/kT} = \left(\frac{1}{1}\right)e^{-(10^{-20}\text{ J})/[(1.381\times10^{-23}\text{ J K}^{-1})(298\text{ K})]} = 0.0880$$

354. This is an example of the Boltzmann distribution law, which is $\frac{N_i}{N_j} = \left(\frac{g_i}{g_j}\right)e^{-(\varepsilon_i - \varepsilon_j)/kT}$, where the N's are the occupancies of the different energy levels (ε), the g's are the statistical weights (1 for the singlet and 3 for the triplet), k is the Boltzmann constant, and T is the temperature. Entering the appropriate values gives

$$\frac{N_i}{N_j} = \left(\frac{g_i}{g_j}\right)e^{-(\varepsilon_i - \varepsilon_j)/kT} = \left(\frac{1}{3}\right)e^{-(1.42\times10^{-21}\text{ J})/[(1.381\times10^{-23}\text{ J K}^{-1})(175\text{ K})]} = 0.185$$

355. One form of the molecular partition function for an ideal gas is $q_{\text{trans}} = \sqrt[3]{(2\pi mkT)^2}\left(\frac{V}{h^3}\right)$, where m is the mass of an oxygen molecule (5.3136×10^{-26} kg), k is Boltzmann's constant (1.381×10^{-23} J K^{-1}), T is the temperature, and h is Planck's constant (6.626×10^{-34} J s). Entering the values into the equation, and solving by parts, gives

$$q_{\text{trans}} = \sqrt[2]{(2\pi mkT)^3}\left(\frac{V}{h^3}\right)$$

$$= \sqrt[2]{\left[2\pi(5.3136\times10^{-26}\text{ kg})(1.381\times10^{-23}\text{ J K}^{-1})(298\text{ K})\left(\frac{\text{kg m}^2/\text{s}^2}{\text{J}}\right)\right]^3}\left(\frac{V}{h^3}\right)$$

$$= \sqrt[2]{[1.3740\times10^{-45}\text{ kg}^2\text{m}^2/\text{s}^2]^3}\left(\frac{22.79\text{ L}}{(6.626\times10^{-34}\text{ J s})^3}\right)\left(\frac{\text{J}}{\text{kg m}^2/\text{s}^2}\right)^3\left(\frac{10^{-3}\text{ m}^3}{\text{L}}\right)$$

$$= 3.99\times10^{30}$$

356. For a diatomic molecule, the molecular rotational partition function comes from $q_{\text{rot}} = \frac{8\pi^2 IkT}{h^2\sigma}$, where k is the Boltzmann constant, T is the temperature, and h is Planck's constant. The calculation of the molecular rotational partition function is

$$q_{\text{rot}} = \frac{8\pi^2 IkT}{h^2\sigma}$$

$$= \frac{8\pi^2(2.644 \times 10^{-47}\,\text{kg m}^2)(1.381 \times 10^{-23}\ \text{J K}^{-1})(298\ \text{K})}{(6.626 \times 10^{-34}\ \text{J s})^2(2)}\left(\frac{\text{J}}{\text{kg m}^2/\text{s}^2}\right) = 9.78$$

357. The relationship for a monatomic species is simply $(\bar{C}_P^\circ)_t = \frac{5}{2}R = \frac{5}{2}(8.3145\ \text{J mol}^{-1}) = 20.786\ \text{J mol}^{-1}$.

358. The relationship is $(\bar{S}^\circ)_t = Nk\ln\left[\left(\frac{2\pi mkT}{h^2}\right)^{3/2}\left(\frac{kTe^{5/2}}{P}\right)\right]$. In this equation, N is Avogadro's number, k is the Boltzmann constant, and h is Planck's constant. Solving this relationship by parts gives the following

$$(\bar{S}^\circ)_t = Nk\ln\left[\left(\frac{2\pi mkT}{h^2}\right)^{3/2}\left(\frac{kT\ e^{5/2}}{P}\right)\right]$$

$$= Nk\ln\left[\left(\frac{2\pi(m)(k)(T)}{(h)^2}\right)^{3/2}\left(\frac{(1.381 \times 10^{-23}\,\text{J K}^{-1})(298\ \text{K})e^{5/2}}{(1.00\ \text{bar})}\right.\right.$$

$$\left.\left.\times\left(\frac{\text{bar}}{10^5\,\text{kg/m s}^2}\right)\left(\frac{\text{kg m}^2/\text{s}^2}{\text{J}}\right)\right)\right]$$

$$= Nk\ln\left[\left(\frac{2\pi(6.634 \times 10^{-26}\,\text{kg})(1.381 \times 10^{-23}\,\text{J K}^{-1})(298\ \text{K})}{(6.626 \times 10^{-34}\ \text{J s})^2}\left(\frac{\text{J}}{\text{kg m}^2/\text{s}^2}\right)\right)^{3/2}\right.$$

$$\left.\times (5.0136 \times 10^{-25}\,\text{m})\right]$$

$$= Nk\ln\left[(3.907 \times 10^{21}\,\text{m}^{-1})^{3/2}(5.0136 \times 10^{-25}\ \text{m})\right]$$

$$= \left[(6.022 \times 10^{23}\,\text{mol}^{-1})(1.381 \times 10^{-23}\,\text{J K}^{-1})\right]\ln[1.224 \times 10^8] = 154.8\ \text{J mol}^{-1}\ \text{K}^{-1}$$

359. The relationship is $(\bar{G}°)_t = -NkT \ln\left[\left(\frac{2\pi mkT}{h^2}\right)^{3/2}\left(\frac{kT}{P}\right)\right]$. In this equation, N is Avogadro's number, k is the Boltzmann constant, and h is Planck's constant. Solving this relationship by parts gives the following

$$(\bar{G}°)_t = -NkT \ln\left[\left(\frac{2\pi mkT}{h^2}\right)^{3/2}\left(\frac{kT}{P}\right)\right]$$

$$= -[NkT]\ln\left[\left(\frac{2\pi(m)(k)(T)}{(h)^2}\right)^{3/2}\left(\frac{(1.381 \times 10^{-23}\,\text{J K}^{-1})(298\text{ K})}{(1.00\text{ bar})}\right)\right.$$

$$\left.\times\left(\frac{\text{bar}}{10^5\,\text{kg/m s}^2}\right)\left(\frac{\text{kg m}^2/\text{s}^2}{\text{J}}\right)\right]$$

$$= -[NkT]\ln\left[\left(\frac{2\pi(6.634 \times 10^{-26}\,\text{kg})(1.381 \times 10^{-23}\,\text{J K}^{-1})(298\text{ K})}{(6.626 \times 10^{-34}\text{ J s})^2}\right.\right.$$

$$\left.\left.\times\left(\frac{\text{J}}{\text{kg m}^2/\text{s}^2}\right)\right)^{3/2}(4.115 \times 10^{-26}\text{ m})\right]$$

$$= -[NkT]\ln\left[(3.907 \times 10^{21}\,\text{m}^{-1})^{3/2}(4.115 \times 10^{-26}\text{ m})\right]$$

$$= -[(6.022 \times 10^{23}\,\text{mol}^{-1})(1.381 \times 10^{-23}\,\text{J K}^{-1})(298\text{ K})]\ln[1.005 \times 10^7]$$

$$= -3.995 \times 10^4\text{ J mol}^{-1}$$

360. The relationship to determine the characteristic vibrational temperature is $\Theta_v = \frac{hc\bar{v}}{k}$, where h is Planck's constant, c is the speed of light, and k is the Boltzmann constant. Entering these values into the equation gives

$$\Theta_v = \frac{hc\bar{v}}{k} = \frac{(6.626 \times 10^{-34}\text{ J s})(2.9979 \times 10^8\text{ m s}^{-1})(2{,}358\text{ cm}^{-1})}{(1.381 \times 10^{-23}\,\text{J K}^{-1})}\left(\frac{1\text{ cm}}{0.01\text{ m}}\right)$$

$$= 3{,}392\text{ K}$$

361. The relationship is $(\bar{C}_P^{\circ})_v = R\left(\frac{\Theta_v}{T}\right)^2\left[\frac{e^{\Theta_v/T}}{(e^{\Theta_v/T} - 1)^2}\right]$, where R is the gas constant.

Entering the values gives

$$\left(\bar{C}_P^{\circ}\right)_v = R\left(\frac{\Theta_v}{T}\right)^2\left[\frac{e^{\Theta_v/T}}{(e^{\Theta_v/T} - 1)^2}\right]$$

$$= (8.3145\text{ J mol}^{-1}\text{ K}^{-1})\left(\frac{3{,}392\text{ K}}{298\text{ K}}\right)^2\left[\frac{e^{3{,}392\text{ K}/298\text{ K}}}{(e^{3{,}392\text{ K}/298\text{ K}} - 1)^2}\right] = 0.0123\text{ J mol}^{-1}\text{ K}^{-1}$$

362. The relationship is $(\bar{S}^\circ)_v = R\left[\frac{\Theta_v/T}{e^{\Theta_v/T}-1} - \ln(1-e^{-\Theta_v/T})\right]$, where R is the gas constant. Entering the values gives

$$(\bar{S}^\circ)_v = R\left[\frac{\Theta_v/T}{e^{\Theta_v/T}-1} - \ln(1-e^{-\Theta_v/T})\right]$$

$$= (8.3145 \text{ J mol}^{-1}\text{ K}^{-1})\left[\frac{3{,}392 \text{ K}/298 \text{ K}}{(e^{3{,}392 \text{ K}/298 \text{ K}})-1} - \ln(1-e^{-3{,}392 \text{ K}/298 \text{ K}})\right]$$

$$= 0.00117 \text{ J mol}^{-1}\text{ K}^{-1}$$

363. The relationship is $(\bar{H}^\circ)_v = RT\left[\frac{\Theta_v/T}{e^{\Theta_v/T}-1}\right]$, where R is the gas constant. Entering the values gives

$$(\bar{H}^\circ)_v = RT\left[\frac{\Theta_v/T}{e^{\Theta_v/T}-1}\right] = (8.3145 \text{ J mol}^{-1}\text{ K}^{-1})(298 \text{ K})\left[\frac{3{,}392 \text{ K}/298 \text{ K}}{e^{3{,}392 \text{ K}/298 \text{ K}}-1}\right]$$

$$= 0.321 \text{ J mol}^{-1}$$

364. The relationship is $(\bar{G}^\circ)_v = RT\ln(1-e^{-\Theta_v/T})$, where R is the gas constant. Entering the values gives

$$(\bar{G}^\circ)_v = RT\ln(1-e^{-\Theta_v/T}) = (8.3145 \text{ J mol}^{-1}\text{ K}^{-1})(298 \text{ K})\ln(1-e^{-3{,}392 \text{ K}/298 \text{ K}})$$

$$= -0.0282 \text{ J mol}^{-1}$$

365. The relationship to determine the characteristic rotational temperature is $\Theta_r = \frac{h^2}{8\pi^2 Ik}$, where k is the Boltzmann constant and h is Planck's constant. Entering the appropriate values into the equation gives

$$\Theta_r = \frac{h^2}{8\pi^2 Ik} = \frac{(6.626\times10^{-34}\text{ J s})^2}{8\pi^2(1.148\times10^{-45}\text{ kg m}^2)(1.381\times10^{-23}\text{ J K}^{-1})}\left(\frac{\text{kg m}^2/\text{s}^2}{\text{J}}\right)$$

$$= 0.3507 \text{ K}$$

366. The equation to determine the molecular partition function for rotation is $q_r = \frac{T}{\sigma\,\Theta_r}$, where σ is the symmetry number (2 in this case). Using this equation and entering the values gives

$$q_r = \frac{T}{\sigma\,\Theta_r} = \frac{2{,}000 \text{ K}}{2\,(0.3507 \text{ K})} = 2{,}851$$

367. The entropy relationship is $(\bar{S}^\circ)_r = R\ln\left(\frac{e\,T}{\sigma\,\Theta_r}\right)$, where R is the gas constant. Entering the values gives

$$(\bar{S}^\circ)_r = R\ln\left(\frac{eT}{\sigma\Theta_r}\right) = (8.3145 \text{ J mol}^{-1}\text{ K}^{-1})\ln\left(\frac{e(298 \text{ K})}{2(0.3507 \text{ K})}\right) = 58.6 \text{ J mol}^{-1}\text{ K}^{-1}$$

368. The relationship to determine the enthalpy is $(\bar{H}°)_r = RT$, where R is the gas constant. This becomes

$$(\bar{H}°)_r = RT = (8.3145 \text{ J mol}^{-1} \text{ K}^{-1})(298 \text{ K}) = 2.48 \times 10^3 \text{ J mol}^{-1}$$

369. The rotational contribution to the Gibbs free energy comes from $(\bar{G}°)_r = -RT \ln\left(\frac{T}{\sigma\, \Theta_r}\right)$, where R is the gas constant. This equation gives

$$(\bar{G}°)_r = -RT \ln\left(\frac{T}{\sigma\, \Theta_r}\right) = -(8.3145 \text{ J mol}^{-1}\text{K}^{-1})(298 \text{ K})\ln\left(\frac{298 \text{ K}}{2\ (0.3507 \text{ K})}\right)$$
$$= -1.50 \times 10^4 \text{ J mol}^{-1}$$

370. The relationship is $\bar{S} = \frac{5}{2}R + R\ln\frac{(2\,\pi mkT)^{3/2}\bar{V}}{N_A h^3}$, where R is the gas constant, k is the Boltzmann constant, N_A is Avogadro's number, and h is Planck's constant. Entering the values into the equation and solving by parts gives

$$\bar{S} = \frac{5}{2}R + R\ln\frac{(2\pi mkT)^{3/2}\bar{V}}{N_A h^3} = \frac{5}{2}(8.3145 \text{ J mol}^{-1} \text{ K}^{-1}) + (R)\ln\frac{\left[2\,\pi(m)(k)(T)\right]^{3/2}(\bar{V})}{(N_A)(h)^3}$$

$$= (20.786 \text{ J mol}^{-1} \text{ K}^{-1})$$

$$+ (R)\ln\frac{\left[2\pi(6.6465 \times 10^{-27} \text{ kg})(1.38066 \times 10^{-23} \text{ J K}^{-1})(298 \text{ K})\left(\frac{\text{kg m}^2/\text{s}^2}{\text{J}}\right)\right]^{3/2}(\bar{V})}{(6.6022 \times 10^{23} \text{ mol}^{-1})(6.626 \times 10^{-34} \text{ J s})^3}$$

$$= (20.786 \text{ J mol}^{-1} \text{ K}^{-1}) + (8.3145 \text{ J mol}^{-1} \text{ K}^{-1})$$

$$\times \ln\frac{\left[(1.7182 \times 10^{-46})(\text{kg}^2 \text{ m}^2/\text{s}^2)\right]^{3/2}(0.02445 \text{ m}^3)}{(1.7518 \times 10^{-76} \text{ J}^3 \text{ s}^3 \text{ mol}^{-1})}$$

$$= (20.786 \text{ J mol}^{-1} \text{ K}^{-1}) + (8.3145 \text{ J mol}^{-1} \text{ K}^{-1})\ln\frac{2.2522 \times 10^{-69} \text{ kg}^3 \text{ m}^3 \text{ s}^{-3}(0.02445 \text{ m}^3)}{(1.7518 \times 10^{-76} \text{ J}^3 \text{ s}^3 \text{ mol}^{-1})}$$

$$- (20.786 \text{ J mol}^{-1} \text{ K}^{-1}) + (8.3145 \text{ J mol}^{-1} \text{ K}^{-1})$$

$$\times \ln\frac{5.5066 \times 10^{-71} \text{ kg}^3 \text{ m}^6 \text{ s}^{-3}}{(1.7518 \times 10^{-76} \text{ J}^3 \text{ s}^3 \text{ mol}^{-1})}\left(\frac{\text{J}}{\text{kg m}^2/\text{s}^2}\right)^3$$
$$= 126 \text{ J mol}^{-1} \text{ K}^{-1}$$

371. The equation to determine the molecular rotational partition function is $q_{\text{rot}} = \frac{8\,\pi^2\left(\sqrt{8\pi^3 I_x I_y I_z}\right)\left(\sqrt{(kT)^3}\right)}{h^3\sigma}$, where k is the Boltzmann constant and h is Planck's constant.

The product of the three moments of inertia ($I_xI_yI_z$) is 3.51×10^{-137} kg^{3}m^6. Entering the given values into this relationship, and solving by parts, gives

$$q_{\text{rot}} = \frac{8\pi^2\left(\sqrt{8\pi^3 I_x I_y I_z}\right)\left(\sqrt{(kT)^3}\right)}{h^3\sigma}$$

$$= \frac{8\pi^2\left(\sqrt{8\pi^3 (I_x)(I_y)(I_z)}\right)\left(\sqrt{[(1.38066\times10^{-23}\ \text{J K}^{-1})(298)]^3}\right)}{(6.626\times10^{-34}\ \text{J s})^3(2)}$$

$$= \left(\sqrt{8\pi^3(3.51\times10^{-137}\ \text{kg}^3\ \text{m}^6)\left(\frac{\text{J}}{\text{kg m}^2/\text{s}^2}\right)^3}\right)(3.5802\times10^{70}\ \text{J}^{-3/2}\ \text{s}^{-3})$$

$$= (9.3364\times10^{-68}\ \text{J}^{3/2}\ \text{s}^3)(3.5802\times10^{70}\ \text{J}^{-3/2}\ \text{s}^{-3}) = 3343$$

372. For a monatomic crystal, $(A_T° - E_0°) = 3RT\ln\left(1 - e^{-\theta_E/T}\right)$, where R is the gas constant. This relationship gives

$$(A_T° - E_0°) = 3RT\ln\left(1 - e^{-\theta_E/T}\right)$$

$$= 3(8.3145\ \text{J mol}^{-1}\ \text{K}^{-1})(298\ \text{K})\ln(1 - e^{-161\ \text{K}/298\ \text{K}}) = -6{,}490\ \text{J mol}^{-1}$$

373. For a monatomic crystal, $(A_T° - E_0°) = -3RT\vartheta(\theta_D)$, where R is the gas constant and $\vartheta(\theta_D)$ is the Debye–Helmholtz energy function (0.90) for silver. This relationship gives

$$(A_T° - E_0°) = -3RT\vartheta(\theta_D) = -3(8.3145\ \text{J mol}^{-1}\ \text{K}^{-1})(298\ \text{K})(0.90) = -6{,}700\ \text{J mol}^{-1}$$

Chapter 16: Molecular Interactions

374. The dipole moment for two univalent charges is the charge ($q = 1.6022 \times 10^{-19}$ C) times the distance between the charges. A conversion is necessary to convert to debyes. Using this information gives

$$\mu = qr = (1.6022\times10^{-19}\ \text{C})(1.91\times10^{-10}\ \text{m})\left(\frac{1\ \text{D}}{3.335641\times10^{-30}\ \text{C m}}\right) = 9.17\ \text{D}$$

375. The percent ionic character is the ratio of observed to predicted. This gives

$$\%\ \text{Ionic Character} = \frac{\mu_{\text{obs}}}{\mu_{\text{predicted}}}\times100\% = \frac{1.948\ \text{D}}{9.17\ \text{D}}\times100\% = 21.2\%$$

376. The percent ionic character is equal to $16(\text{EN}_\text{F} - \text{EN}_\text{I}) + 3.5(\text{EN}_\text{F} - \text{EN}_\text{I})^2$. This gives

$$\%\ \text{Ionic Character} = 16(\text{EN}_\text{F} - \text{EN}_\text{I}) + 3.5(\text{EN}_\text{F} - \text{EN}_\text{I})^2 = 16(1.32) + 3.5(1.32)^2 = 27\%$$

377. The charges are 21.2% of the purely ionic IF or ±0.212 *e*.

378. The dipole moment is $\mu = qr$, where q is the charge. The charge is less than that predicted for a purely ionic species ($\mu_{\text{predicted}}$). It is necessary to determine $\mu_{\text{predicted}}$ from % Ionic Character = $\frac{\mu_{\text{obs}}}{\mu_{\text{predicted}}} \times 100\%$, and the bond length from $\mu_{\text{predicted}} = qr$, where $q = 1.6022 \times 10^{-19}$ C. Rearranging and combining these gives

$$r = \frac{\left[\frac{\mu_{\text{obs}}}{\%\text{ Ionic Character}} \times 100\%\right]}{q} = \frac{\left[\frac{0.888\text{ D}}{11\%} \times 100\%\right]}{1.6022 \times 10^{-19}\text{ C}}\left(\frac{3.335641 \times 10^{-30}\text{ C m}}{1\text{ D}}\right)$$

$$= 1.7 \times 10^{-10}\text{ m}$$

379. The equation to determine the field strength is $E = \frac{e}{4\pi\varepsilon_0 r^2}$, where e is the basic unit of charge, and ε_0 is permittivity of free space. This equation gives

$$E = \frac{e}{4\pi\varepsilon_0 r^2} = \frac{(1.602 \times 10^{-19}\text{ C})}{4\pi(8.854 \times 10^{-12}\text{ C}^2\text{J}^{-1}\text{ m}^{-1})(3.5 \times 10^{-10}\text{ m})^2}\left(\frac{\text{V}}{\text{J A}^{-1}\text{ s}^{-1}}\right)\left(\frac{\text{C}}{\text{A s}}\right)$$

$$= 1.18 \times 10^{10}\text{ V m}^{-1}$$

380. The relationship is $\mu_{\text{ind}} = 4\pi\varepsilon_0\alpha E$, with $4\pi\varepsilon_0 = 4\pi(8.854 \times 10^{-12}\text{ C}^2\text{J}^{-1}\text{m}^{-1}) = 1.11 \times 10^{-10}\text{ C}^2\text{ J}^{-1}\text{ m}^{-1}$. This relationship gives

$$\mu_{\text{ind}} = 4\pi\varepsilon_0\alpha E$$

$$= (1.11\times10^{-10}\text{C}^2\text{J}^{-1}\text{ m}^{-1})(2.48\times10^{-30}\text{m}^3)(1.18\times10^{10}\text{V m}^{-1})$$

$$= (3.248\times10^{-30}\text{C}^2\text{m J}^{-1})\left(\frac{\text{J A}^{-1}\text{ s}^{-1}}{\text{V}}\right)\left(\frac{\text{A s}}{\text{C}}\right)\left(\frac{\text{D}}{3.3356\times10^{-30}\text{ C m}}\right) = 0.974\text{ D}$$

381. It is possible to determine the ion-induced dipole energy from the relationship $E_{\text{i-id}} = -\frac{1}{2}(\mu_{\text{ind}}E)$. This relationship and the information in the problem lead to

$$E_{\text{i-id}} = -\frac{1}{2}(\mu_{\text{ind}}E)$$

$$= -\frac{1}{2}[(1.76\text{ D})(1.18 \times 10^{10}\text{ V m}^{-1})]\left(\frac{3.3356 \times 10^{-30}\text{ C m}}{\text{D}}\right)\left(\frac{\text{J}}{\text{V C}}\right)$$

$$= -3.46 \times 10^{-20}\text{ J}$$

382. The relationship to determine the energy is $E_{\text{d-id}} = -\frac{\alpha\mu^2}{(4\pi\varepsilon_0)^2 r^6}$, where ε_0 is permittivity of free space. This relationship leads to

$$E_{\text{d-id}} = -\frac{\alpha\mu^2}{4\pi\varepsilon_0 r^6}$$

$$= -\frac{(2.48 \times 10^{-30}\ \text{m}^3)(1.2\ \text{D})^2}{(4\pi(8.854 \times 10^{-12}\ \text{C}^2\text{J}^{-1}\text{m}^{-1}))(3.5 \times 10^{-10}\ \text{m})^6}\left(\frac{3.3356\times 10^{-30}\ \text{C m}}{\text{D}}\right)^2$$

$$= -1.9 \times 10^{-22}\ \text{J}$$

383. When the atoms come into contact, the distance (r) between them is twice the radius or 2 $(2.02 \times 10^{-10}$ m$) = 4.04 \times 10^{-10}$ m. The general relationship to determine the dispersion energy between atoms A and B is $E_{\text{disp}} = -\frac{3}{2}\left(\frac{\alpha_A\alpha_B}{r^6}\right)\left(\frac{I_A I_B}{I_A + I_B}\right)$. Because both A and B are krypton, $I_A = I_B = I$ and $\alpha_A = \alpha_B = \alpha$. Combining terms gives $E_{\text{disp}} = -\frac{3}{2}\left(\frac{\alpha^2}{r^6}\right)\left(\frac{I^2}{2I}\right) = -\frac{3}{4}\left(\frac{\alpha^2 I}{r^6}\right)$. Using the final form of the equation gives

$$E_{\text{disp}} = -\frac{3}{4}\left(\frac{\alpha^2 I}{r^6}\right) = -\frac{3}{4}\left[\frac{(2.48 \times 10^{-30}\ \text{m}^3)^2(2.24 \times 10^{-18}\ \text{J})}{(4.04 \times 10^{-10}\ \text{m})^6}\right] = 2.38 \times 10^{-21}\ \text{J}$$

384. The Debye equation is applicable in this situation. This equation is $\left(\frac{\varepsilon_r - 1}{\varepsilon_r + 2}\right)\left(\frac{M}{\rho}\right) = \left(\frac{N_A}{3\,\varepsilon_0}\right)\left(\alpha + \frac{\mu^2}{3\,kT}\right)$. This equation simplifies to the Clausius–Mossotti equation when the molecule has no permanent dipole moment (μ). The Clausius–Mossotti equation is $\left(\frac{\varepsilon_r - 1}{\varepsilon_r + 2}\right)\left(\frac{M}{\rho}\right) = \left(\frac{N_A}{3\,\varepsilon_0}\right)(\alpha)$, where M is the molar mass, ε_0 is permittivity of free space, and N_A is Avogadro's number. Rearranging the Clausius–Mossotti equation and entering the appropriate values gives

$$\alpha = \left(\frac{\varepsilon_r - 1}{\varepsilon_r + 2}\right)\left(\frac{M}{\rho}\right)\left(\frac{3\varepsilon_0}{N_A}\right)$$

$$= \left(\frac{2.6 - 1}{2.6 + 2}\right)\left(\frac{7.613 \times 10^{-2}\ \text{kg mol}^{-1}}{126.32\ \text{kg m}^{-3}}\right)\left(\frac{3(8.854 \times 10^{-12}\ \text{C}^2\ \text{N}^{-1}\ \text{m}^{-2})}{6.022 \times 10^{23}\ \text{mol}^{-1}}\right)$$

$$= 9.2 \times 10^{-39}\ \text{C}^2\ \text{m N}^{-1}$$

385. The general relationship is $E_{\text{dd}} = -\frac{2\mu_a\mu_a}{4\pi\varepsilon_0\varepsilon_r r_0^3}$, which rearranges and reduces to $\mu = \sqrt{\frac{4\pi\varepsilon_0 r^3 E_{\text{dd}}}{2}}$, when both molecules are the same ($\mu_a = \mu_b$). (In this equation, ε_0 is permittivity of free space.) This equation gives

$$\mu = \sqrt{\frac{4\pi\varepsilon_0 r^3 E_{\text{dd}}}{2}} = \sqrt{\frac{4\pi(8.854 \times 10^{-12}\ \text{C}^2\ \text{J}^{-1}\ \text{m}^{-1})(3.7 \times 10^{-10}\ \text{m})^3(3.77 \times 10^{-21}\ \text{J})}{2}}$$

$$\times\left(\frac{\text{D}}{3.3356 \times 10^{-30}\ \text{C m}}\right) = 0.977\ \text{D}$$

Chapter 17: Kinetic Theory of Gases

386. The equation is $v_{rs} = \sqrt{\frac{8kT}{\pi\mu}}$, where k is the Boltzmann constant, T is the temperature, and μ is the reduced mass ($\mu = \left(\frac{1}{m_1} + \frac{1}{m_2}\right)^{-1} = 3.34 \times 10^{-27}$ kg^{-1}). Entering the values into the equation,

$$v_{rs} = \sqrt{\frac{8kT}{\pi\mu}} = \sqrt{\frac{8(1.381 \times 10^{-23}\ \text{J K}^{-1})(298\ \text{K})}{\pi(3.34 \times 10^{-27}\ \text{kg})}\left(\frac{\text{kg m}^2/\text{s}^2}{\text{J}}\right)} = 1{,}770\ \text{m s}^{-1}$$

387. The equation is $v_{mp} = \sqrt{\frac{2RT}{M}}$, where R is the gas constant, T is the temperature, and M is the molar mass (32.0×10^{-3} kg mol^{-1}). Entering the values gives

$$v_{mp} = \sqrt{\frac{2RT}{M}} = \sqrt{\frac{2(8.3145\ \text{J mol}^{-1}\ \text{K}^{-1})(298\ \text{K})}{32.0 \times 10^{-3}\ \text{kg mol}^{-1}}\left(\frac{\text{kg m}^2/\text{s}^2}{\text{J}}\right)} = 393\ \text{m s}^{-1}$$

388. The equation is $v_{ms} = \sqrt{\frac{8RT}{\pi M}}$, where R is the gas constant, T is the temperature, and M is the molar mass (32.0×10^{-3} kg mol^{-1}). Entering the values gives

$$v_{ms} = \sqrt{\frac{8RT}{\pi M}} = \sqrt{\frac{8(8.3145\ \text{J mol}^{-1}\ \text{K}^{-1})(298\ \text{K})}{\pi(32.0 \times 10^{-3}\ \text{kg mol}^{-1})}\left(\frac{\text{kg m}^2/\text{s}^2}{\text{J}}\right)} = 444\ \text{m s}^{-1}$$

389. The equation is $v_{rms} = \sqrt{\frac{3RT}{M}}$, where R is the gas constant, T is the temperature, and M is the molar mass (32.0×10^{-3} kg mol^{-1}). Entering the values gives

$$v_{rms} = \sqrt{\frac{3RT}{M}} = \sqrt{\frac{3(8.3145\ \text{J mol}^{-1}\ \text{K}^{-1})(298\ \text{K})}{32.0 \times 10^{-3}\ \text{kg mol}^{-1}}\left(\frac{\text{kg m}^2/\text{s}^2}{\text{J}}\right)} = 482\ \text{m s}^{1}$$

390. The relationship to determine the fraction is $F(\Delta v) = 4\pi v^2 \left(\frac{m}{2\pi kT}\right)^{3/2} e^{\left(-\frac{mv^2}{2kT}\right)}$, where m is the mass of an oxygen molecule, Δv is the velocity range (10 m s^{-1}, in this case), and k is the Boltzmann constant. To simplify the calculation, it may be simpler to calculate the value of $\left(\frac{m}{2kT}\right)$ separately as

$$\left(\frac{m}{2kT}\right) = \left(\frac{5.314 \times 10^{-26}\ \text{kg}}{2(1.381 \times 10^{-23}\ \text{J K}^{-1})(298\ \text{K})}\left(\frac{\text{J}}{\text{kg m}^2/\text{s}^2}\right)\right) = (6.46 \times 10^{-6}\ \text{s}^2\ m^{-2})$$

Combining this information gives

$$F=\frac{4\pi v^2}{\Delta v}\left(\frac{\mathrm{m}}{2\pi kT}\right)^{3/2} e^{\left(-\frac{mv^2}{2kT}\right)}$$

$$=\frac{4\pi v^2}{\Delta v}\left(\frac{6.46\times10^{-6}\ \mathrm{s^2\ m^{-2}}}{\pi}\right)^{3/2} e^{(-(6.46\times10^{-6}\ \mathrm{s^2\ m^{-2}})v^2)}$$

$$=\frac{4\pi(482\ \mathrm{m\ s^{-1}})^2}{10\ \mathrm{m\ s^{-1}}}\left(\frac{6.46\times10^{-6}\ \mathrm{s^2\ m^{-2}}}{\pi}\right)^{3/2} e^{(-(6.46\times10^{-6}\ \mathrm{s^2\ m^{-2}})(482\ \mathrm{m\ s^{-1}})^2)}$$

$$=1.92\times10^{-4}$$

391. The average time between collisions is $\Delta t=\frac{\lambda}{v}$. Using the information in the problem gives

$$\Delta \mathrm{t}=\frac{\lambda}{v}=\frac{7.10\times10^{-8}\ \mathrm{m}}{482\ \mathrm{m\ s^{-1}}}=1.47\times10^{-10}\ \mathrm{s}$$

392. A simplified form for the calculation of the probability density is $f(v_x)=\left(\sqrt{\frac{M}{2\pi RT}}\right)(e^{-Mv_x^2/2RT})$, where M is the molar mass and R is the gas constant. Using the information from the problem, and solving by parts, gives

$$f(v_x)=\left(\sqrt{\frac{M}{2\pi RT}}\right)(e^{-Mv_x^2/2RT})$$

$$=\left(\sqrt{\frac{32.0\times10^{-3}\ \mathrm{kg\ mol^{-1}}}{2\pi(8.3145\ \mathrm{J\ mol^{-1}\ K^{-1}})(298\ \mathrm{K})}\left(\frac{\mathrm{J}}{\mathrm{kg}\ m^2/\mathrm{s}^2}\right)}\right)(e^{-Mv_x^2/2RT})$$

$$=(1.424\times10^{-3}\ \mathrm{s\ m^{-1}})\left(e^{-(32.0\times10^{-3}\ \mathrm{kg\ mol^{-1}})(225\ \mathrm{kg}\ m^2\ \mathrm{s^{-2}\ mol^{-1}})^2/2RT\left(\frac{\mathrm{kg\ m^2/s^2}}{\mathrm{J}}\right)}\right)$$

$$=(1.424\times10^{-3}\ \mathrm{s\ m^{-1}})\left(e^{-(1{,}620\ \mathrm{kg}\ m^2\ \mathrm{s^{-2}\ mol^{-1}})/2(8.3145\ \mathrm{J\ mol^{-1}\ K^{-1}})(298\ \mathrm{K})\left(\frac{\mathrm{kg\ m^2/s^2}}{\mathrm{J}}\right)}\right)$$

$$=1.03\times10^{-3}\ \mathrm{s\ m^{-1}}$$

393. The difference in velocities is small; therefore, it is possible to make the simplification that follows and enter the appropriate values.

$$\int_{225.0}^{225.5} f(v)\,dv\approx f(v_x)\Delta v=(1.03\times10^{-3}\ \mathrm{s\ m^{-1}})\ (0.5\ \mathrm{m\ s^{-1}})=5\times10^{-4}$$

394. The collision diameter (collision cross section) of nitrogen (or other diatomic gases) comes from the relationship $d=\sqrt{\frac{5kv_{ms}}{6\pi\sqrt{2}\ \kappa}}$, where k is the Boltzmann constant. Incorporating the information from the problem gives

$$d=\sqrt{\frac{5kv_{ms}}{6\pi\sqrt{2}\ \kappa}}=\sqrt{\frac{5(1.381\times10^{-23}\ \text{J K}^{-1})\ (475\ \text{m s}^{-1})}{6\pi\sqrt{2}\ (0.0261\ \text{J m}^{-1}\ \text{s}^{-1}\ \text{K}^{-1})}}=2.17\times10^{-10}\ \text{m}$$

395. The collision diameter (cross section) of xenon (or other monatomic gases) comes from the relationship $d=\sqrt{\frac{mv_{ms}}{3\sqrt{2}\ \eta}}$, where m is the mass of a xenon atom (2.18×10^{-25} kg). Incorporating the information from the problem gives

$$d=\sqrt{\frac{mv_{ms}}{3\sqrt{2}\ \eta}}=\sqrt{\frac{(2.18\times10^{-25}\ \text{kg})\ (210\ \text{m s}^{-1})}{3\sqrt{2}\ (2.10\times10^{-5}\ \text{kg m}^{-1}\ \text{s}^{-1})}}=7.17\times10^{-10}\ \text{m}$$

396. It is possible to determine the collision cross section from the relationship $d=\sqrt{\frac{5\sqrt{\pi mkT}}{16\pi\eta}}$, where k is the Boltzmann constant. Entering the appropriate values into this equation gives

$$d=\sqrt{\frac{5\sqrt{\pi mkT}}{16\ \pi\ \eta}}=\sqrt{\frac{5\sqrt{\pi(2.18\times10^{-25}\ \text{kg})(1.381\times10^{-23}\ \text{J K}^{-1})(273\ \text{K})\left(\frac{\text{kg m}^2/\text{s}^2}{\text{J}}\right)}}{16\pi\ (2.10\times10^{-5}\ \text{kg m}^{-1}\ \text{s}^{-1})}}$$

$$=4.90\times10^{-10}\ \text{m}$$

397. The equation for the collision frequency is $z=\sqrt{2}\ \rho\pi d^2v_{ms}$. Entering the appropriate values into the equation gives

$$z=\sqrt{2}\ \rho\pi d^2v_{ms}=\sqrt{2}\ (2.43\times10^{25}\ \text{m}^{-3})\pi(4.09\times10^{-10}\ \text{m})^2(628\ \text{m s}^{-1})$$

$$=1.13\times10^{10}\ \text{s}^{-1}$$

398. The equation for the collision frequency is $Z=\left(\frac{1}{\sqrt{2}}\right)\rho^2\pi d^2v_{ms}$. Entering the appropriate values into the equation gives

$$Z=\left(\frac{1}{\sqrt{2}}\right)\rho^2\pi d^2v_{ms}$$

$$=\left(\frac{1}{\sqrt{2}}\right)(2.43\times10^{25}\ \text{m}^{-3})^2\pi(4.09\times10^{-10}\ \text{m})^2(628\ \text{m s}^{-1})\left(\frac{\text{mol}}{6.022\times10^{23}}\right)$$

$$=2.29\times10^{11}\ \text{mol m}^{-3}\ \text{s}^{-1}$$

399. The equation for the mean free path is $\lambda = \frac{1}{\sqrt{2}\,\rho\pi d^2}$. Entering the appropriate values gives

$$\lambda = \frac{1}{\sqrt{2}\,\rho\pi d^2} = \frac{1}{\sqrt{2}\,(2.43\times10^{25}\ \text{m}^{-3})\pi(4.09\times10^{-10}\ \text{m})^2} = 5.54\times10^{-8}\ \text{m}$$

400. The equation for the viscosity of a hard sphere gas is $\eta = \left(\frac{5\pi}{16}\right)\left(\sqrt{\frac{kT}{\pi m}}\right)\left(\frac{m}{\pi d^2}\right)$, where k is the Boltzmann constant. Entering the appropriate values into this equation gives

$$\eta = \left(\frac{5\pi}{16}\right)\left(\sqrt{\frac{kT}{\pi m}}\right)\left(\frac{m}{\pi d^2}\right)$$

$$= \left(\frac{5\pi}{16}\right)\left(\sqrt{\frac{(1.381\times10^{-23}\ \text{J K}^{-1})(298\ \text{K})}{\pi(2.66\times10^{-26}\ \text{kg})}\left(\frac{\text{kg m}^2/\text{s}^2}{\text{J}}\right)}\right)\left(\frac{2.66\times10^{-26}\ \text{kg}}{\pi(4.09\times10^{-10}\ \text{m})^2}\right)$$

$$= 1.10\times10^{-5}\ \text{kg m}^{-1}\ \text{s}^{-1}$$

401. At 1.00 atm and 273 K, a mole of an ideal gas occupies 22.4 L ($2.24\times10^{-2}\ \text{m}^3$). Dividing the volume by the number of atoms in a mole and taking the cube root gives the average separation of the molecules (3.33×10^{-9} m). Finally, dividing the average separation by the collision diameter determines the multiple of the collision diameter (8.14).

402. Using the ideal gas equation $P = \frac{nRT}{V}$, where n is the number of moles, R is the gas constant, and V is the volume, gives

$$P = \frac{nRT}{V} = \frac{\left[(1\ \text{atom})\left(\frac{1\ \text{mol}}{6.022\times10^{23}\ \text{atoms}}\right)\right](0.08206\ \text{L atm mol}^{-1}\ \text{K}^{-1})(2.7\ \text{K})}{(m^3)}$$

$$\times\left(\frac{101325\ \text{Pa}}{1\ \text{atm}}\right)\left(\frac{10^{-3}\ \text{m}^3}{1\ \text{L}}\right) = 4\times10^{-23}\ \text{Pa}$$

403. The equation is $v_{\text{ms}} = \sqrt{\frac{8RT}{\pi M}}$, where R is the gas constant, T is the temperature, and M is the molar mass ($1\times10^{-3}\ \text{kg mol}^{-1}$). Entering the values gives

$$v_{\text{ms}} = \sqrt{\frac{8RT}{\pi M}} = \sqrt{\frac{8(8.3145\ \text{J mol}^{-1}\ \text{K}^{-1})(2.7\ \text{K})}{\pi(1\times10^{-3}\ \text{kg mol}^{-1})}\left(\frac{\text{kg m}^2/\text{s}^2}{\text{J}}\right)} = 2\times10^{2}\ \text{m s}^{-1}$$

404. The equation for the collision frequency is $z = \sqrt{2}\,\rho\pi d^2 v_{\text{ms}}$, where ρ is the number density ($1\ \text{m}^{-3}$). Entering the appropriate values into the equation gives

$$z = \sqrt{2}\,\rho\pi d^2 v_{\text{ms}} = \sqrt{2}\,(1\ \text{m}^{-3})\pi(1\times10^{-10}\ \text{m})^2(2\times10^{2}\ \text{m s}^{-1}) = 9\times10^{-18}\ \text{s}^{-1}$$

405. The equation for the mean free path is $\lambda = \frac{1}{\sqrt{2}\ \rho\pi d^2}$, where ρ is the number density (1 m^{-3}). Entering the appropriate values gives

$$\lambda = \frac{1}{\sqrt{2}\ \rho\pi d^2} = \frac{1}{\sqrt{2}\left(1\ m^{-3}\right)\pi\left(1\times10^{-10}\ m\right)^2} = 2\times10^{19}\ m$$

406. The threshold energy for a reaction is $E_0 = E_a - \frac{RT}{2}$, where E_a is the activation energy, R is the gas constant, and T is the temperature.

$$E_0 = E_a - \frac{RT}{2} = (191\ kJ\ mol^{-1}) - \frac{(8.3145\ J\ mol^{-1}\ K^{-1})(700.0\ K)}{2}\left(\frac{1\ kJ}{10^3\ J}\right) = 188\ kJ\ mol^{-1}$$

407. Using gas-collision theory, the equation for the rate constant is $k = (2\times10^3)N_A P\left(\sqrt{\frac{\pi RT}{M}}\right)\sigma^2 e^{-(E_0/RT)}$, where N_A is Avogadro's number, R is the gas constant, T is the temperature, and M is the molar mass (0.127912 kg mol^{-1}). Using the given information and solving by parts gives

$$k = (2000)N_A P\left(\sqrt{\frac{\pi RT}{M}}\right)\sigma^2 e^{-(E_0/RT)}$$

$$= (2000)N_A P\left(\sqrt{\frac{\pi RT}{M}}\right)\sigma^2 e^{-[(1.88\times10^5\ J\ mol^{-1})/(8.3145\ J\ mol^{-1}\ K^{-1})(700.0\ K)]}$$

$$= (2000)N_A P\left(\sqrt{\frac{\pi RT}{M}}\right)(3.5\times10^{-10}\ m)^2 e^{-[32.30]}$$

$$= (2000)N_A P\left(\sqrt{\frac{\pi\left(8.3145\ J\ mol^{-1}\ K^{-1}\right)\left(700.0\ K\right)}{0.127912\ kg\ mol^{-1}}\left(\frac{kg\ m^2/s^2}{J}\right)}\right)(1.149\times10^{-33}\ m^2)$$

$$= (2000)(6.022\times10^{23}\ mol^{-1})(1)\left(\sqrt{1.429\times10^5\ m\ s^{-1}}\right)(1.149\times10^{-33}\ m^2)$$

$$= 5.2\times10^{-4}\ M^{-1}\ s^{-1}$$

408. The equation to determine the speed of sound is $v_s = \sqrt{\frac{C_p RT}{C_v M}}$, where R is the gas constant and M is the molar mass. Combining the given information yields

$$v_s = \sqrt{\frac{C_p RT}{C_v M}} = \sqrt{\frac{(97\ J\ mol^{-1}\ K^{-1})(8.3145\ J\ mol^{-1}\ K^{-1})(298\ K)}{(85.2\ J\ mol^{-1}\ K^{-1})(0.146\ kg\ mol^{-1})}\left(\frac{kg\ m^2/s^2}{J}\right)}$$

$$= 140\ m\ s^{-1}$$

409. The equation is $J_N = \frac{\Delta wN}{MtA}$, where N is Avogadro's number and M is the molar mass of aluminum. Entering this information into the equation gives

$$J_N = \frac{\Delta wN}{MtA} = \frac{(2.85 \times 10^{-5}\ \text{kg})(6.022 \times 10^{23}\ \text{mol}^{-1})}{(26.98 \times 10^{-3}\ \text{kg mol}^{-1})(3600\ \text{s})(7.9 \times 10^{-6}\ \text{m}^2)} = 2.2 \times 10^{22}\ \text{m}^{-2}\ \text{s}^{-1}$$

410. The equation is $P_{vap} = J_N\sqrt{2\pi mkT}$, where k is the Boltzmann constant and m is the mass of an atom (4.48×10^{-26} kg for aluminum). Entering the appropriate values into the equation and solving by parts gives

$$P_{vap} = J_N\sqrt{2\pi mkT}$$

$$= \left[J_N\sqrt{2\pi(4.48\times10^{-26}\,\text{kg})(1.381\times10^{-23}\,\text{J K}^{-1})(1460\ \text{K})\left(\frac{\text{kg m}^2/\text{s}^2}{\text{J}}\right)}\right]\left(\frac{\text{Pa}}{\text{kg/m s}^2}\right)$$

$$= \left[(2.2\times10^{22}\ \text{m}^{-2}\ \text{s}^{-1})\sqrt{(5.676\times10^{-45}\ \text{kg}^2\ \text{m}^2\ \text{s}^{-2})}\right]\left(\frac{\text{Pa}}{\text{kg/m s}^2}\right) = 1.7\ \text{Pa}$$

Chapter 18: The Rates of Chemical Reactions

411. In this case, the rate law will depend on the concentration of one reactant ([A]), the order of the reaction (n), and the rate constant (k). Combining this information gives

$$\text{Rate} = k[\text{A}]^n$$

412. The relationship is $d\xi = \frac{1}{x_i}(dn_i)$.

413. The rate of a reaction depends upon the extent of reaction ($d\xi$) and upon the change in time (t). This is

$$\frac{d\xi}{dt} = \frac{1}{x_i}\left(\frac{dn_i}{dt}\right)$$

414. The rate of conversion is the change in the number of moles per change in time. Using the information from the problem gives

$$\frac{d\xi}{dt} = \frac{0.010\ \text{mol I}_2}{0.20\ \text{s}} = 0.050\ \text{mol I}_2\ \text{s}^{-1}$$

415. The rate of conversion is the change in the molarity of moles per change in time or $(1/V)$ times the rate of conversion. The square brackets ([ ]) refer to the concentration (molarity). Using the information from the problem gives

$$\frac{d[\mathrm{I_2}]}{dt} = \left(\frac{1}{V}\right)\left(\frac{d\xi}{dt}\right) = \left(\frac{1}{0.500\ \mathrm{L}}\right)(-0.050\ \mathrm{mol\ I_2\ s^{-1}}) = -0.10\ \mathrm{mol\ I_2\ L^{-1}\ s^{-1}}$$

The negative sign indicates that there is a loss of iodine.

416. The rate for hydrogen will be the same as the rate for iodine because the coefficients are the same. The rate for hydrogen iodide will be positive because HI is forming and the numerical value will be double that of HI since the HI coefficient is double the I_2 coefficient.

417. The rates will be the reciprocal of the coefficient times the change in concentration (d[ ]) over the change in time (dt). Reactants are negative and products are positive. The relative rates are

$$-\frac{d[\mathrm{N_2}]}{dt} = -\frac{1}{3}\frac{d[\mathrm{H_2}]}{dt} = \frac{1}{2}\frac{d[\mathrm{NH_3}]}{dt}$$

418. The relationship between the equilibrium constant ant the rate constants is $K_c = \frac{k_f}{k_r}$. Rearranging this equation and entering the appropriate values gives

$$k_r = \frac{k_f}{K_c} = \frac{2.4 \times 10^{-1}\ \mathrm{s^{-1}}}{1.8 \times 10^{-3}} = 1.3 \times 10^{2}\ \mathrm{s^{-1}}$$

419. The equation for the rate constant under these conditions is $k = N_A \pi d_{12}^2 \sqrt{\frac{8k_BT}{\pi\mu}}$, where N_A is Avogadro's number and k_B is the Boltzmann constant. Entering the values into this equation and solving by parts gives

$$k = N_A \pi d_{12}^2 \sqrt{\frac{8k_BT}{\pi\mu}} = (6.022 \times 10^{23}\ \mathrm{mol^{-1}})\pi(5.25 \times 10^{-10}\ \mathrm{m})^2 \left[\sqrt{\frac{8k_BT}{\pi\mu}}\right]\left(\frac{10^3\ \mathrm{L}}{\mathrm{m^3}}\right)$$

$$= (5.214 \times 10^5\ \mathrm{m^2\ mol^{-1}})\left[\sqrt{\frac{8(1.381 \times 10^{-23}\ \mathrm{J\ K^{-1}})(298\ \mathrm{K})}{\pi(5.30 \times 10^{-26}\ \mathrm{kg})}\left(\frac{\mathrm{kg\ m^2/s^2}}{\mathrm{J}}\right)}\right]\left(\frac{10^3\ \mathrm{L}}{\mathrm{m^3}}\right)$$

$$= 2.32 \times 10^{11}\ \mathrm{L\ mol^{-1}\ s^{-1}}$$

420. The one form of the integrated rate law for a first-order reaction involving one component is $\ln\frac{[A]_0}{[A]_t} = kt$. Rearranging the equation and entering the values gives

$$\ln [A]_t = \ln [A]_0 - kt = \ln [1.00]_0 - (25.0\ \mathrm{s^{-1}})(0.0125\ \mathrm{s}) = -0.3125$$

$$[A]_t = 0.732\ \mathrm{M}$$

421. The one form of the integrated rate law for a second-order reaction involving one component is $\frac{1}{[A]_t} - \frac{1}{[A]_o} = kt$. Rearranging the equation and entering the values gives

$$\frac{1}{[\mathrm{A}]_t} = \frac{1}{[\mathrm{A}]_o} + kt = \frac{1}{1.00\ \mathrm{M}} + (25.0\ \mathrm{M}^{-1}\ \mathrm{s}^{-1})(0.0125\ \mathrm{s}) = 1.31\ \mathrm{M}^{-1}$$

$$[\mathrm{A}]_t = 0.761\ \mathrm{M}$$

422. The one form of the integrated rate law for a zero-order reaction involving one component is $[\mathrm{A}]_0 - [\mathrm{A}]_t = kt$. Rearranging the equation and entering the values gives

$$[\mathrm{A}]_t = [\mathrm{A}]_0 - kt = 1.00\ \mathrm{M} - (25.0\ \mathrm{M\ s}^{-1})(0.0125\ \mathrm{s}) = 0.69\ \mathrm{M}$$

423. The half-life of a first-order reaction is given by $t_{1/2} = \frac{0.693}{k}$. Entering the value of k gives

$$t_{1/2} = \frac{0.693}{k} = \frac{0.693}{25.0\ \mathrm{s}^{-1}} = 0.0277\ \mathrm{s}$$

424. The half-life of a second-order reaction is given by $t_{1/2} = \frac{1}{k[\mathrm{A}]_0}$. Entering the values of k and $[\mathrm{A}]_0$ gives

$$t_{1/2} = \frac{1}{k[\mathrm{A}]_0} = \frac{1}{(25.0\ \mathrm{M}^{-1}\ \mathrm{s}^{-1})(1.00\ \mathrm{M})} = 0.0400\ \mathrm{s}$$

425. The half-life of a zero-order reaction is given by $t_{1/2} = \frac{[\mathrm{A}]_0}{2k}$. Entering the values of k and $[\mathrm{A}]_0$ gives

$$t_{1/2} = \frac{[\mathrm{A}]_0}{2k} = \frac{1.00\ \mathrm{M}}{2(25.0\ \mathrm{M\ s}^{-1})} = 0.0200\ \mathrm{s}$$

426. The activation energy for the reverse reaction is the activation energy of the forward reaction minus the enthalpy change or 100 kJ mol^{-1}. (This may be easier to see using a reaction coordinate diagram.)

427. Entering the values into the rate law gives

$$\mathrm{Rate} = k[\mathrm{NO}]^2[\mathrm{Cl}_2] = (5.7\ \mathrm{M}^{-2}\ \mathrm{s}^{-1})(0.50\ \mathrm{M})^2(0.75\ \mathrm{M}) = 1.1\ \mathrm{M\ s}^{-1}$$

428. The equation for the rate constant under these conditions is $k = 4\pi N_A(D_1 + D_2) R_{12}f$, where N_A is Avogadro's number and f is the electrostatic factor (1 for uncharged species). Using this relationship and solving by parts gives

$$k = 4\pi N_A(D_1 + D_2)R_{12}f$$

$$= 4\pi(6.022 \times 10^{23}\ \mathrm{mol}^{-1})[(4.9 \times 10^{-9} + 4.9 \times 10^{-9})\mathrm{m}^2\ \mathrm{s}^{-1}]R_{12}f$$

$$= 4\pi(6.022 \times 10^{23}\ \mathrm{mol}^{-1})[(9.8 \times 10^{-9})\mathrm{m}^2\ \mathrm{s}^{-1}](5.0 \times 10^{-10}\ \mathrm{m})(1)\left(\frac{10^3\mathrm{L}}{\mathrm{m}^3}\right)$$

$$= 3.7 \times 10^{10}\ \mathrm{L\ mol}^{-1}\ \mathrm{s}^{-1}$$

429. Assuming the reacting species are approximately the same size, it is possible to estimate the rate constant from the relationship $k = \frac{8RT}{3\eta}$, where R is the gas constant. Entering the values into this relationship gives

$$k = \frac{8RT}{3\eta} = \frac{8(8.3145\ \text{J mol}^{-1}\ \text{K}^{-1})(273\ \text{K})}{3(7.00 \times 10^{-4}\ \text{kg m}^{-1}\ \text{s}^{-1})}\left(\frac{\text{kg m}^2/\text{s}^2}{\text{J}}\right)\left(\frac{\text{L}}{10^{-3}\ \text{m}^3}\right)\left(\frac{\text{mol/L}}{\text{M}}\right)$$

$$= 8.65 \times 10^9\ \text{M}^{-1}\ \text{s}^{-1}$$

430. If the reaction is diffusion controlled, then $k = 4\pi R^*(D_A + D_B)\, N_A$, where N_A is Avogadro's number. Rearranging this equation and entering the appropriate values and conversions gives

$$R^* = \frac{k}{4\pi(D_A + D_B)N_A} = \frac{1.76 \times 10^{10}\ \text{M}^{-1}\ \text{s}^{-1}}{4\pi[(2.72 + 2.72) \times 10^{-9}\ \text{m}^2\ \text{s}^{-1}](6.022 \times 10^{23}\ \text{mol}^{-1})}$$

$$\times \left(\frac{\text{M}}{\text{mol L}^{-1}}\right)\left(\frac{10^{-3}\ \text{m}^3}{\text{L}}\right) = 4.28 \times 10^{-10}\ \text{m}$$

431. The general form for the rate law described in this problem is Rate $= k[\text{A}]^1[\text{B}]^1$, where the square brackets refer to the molarities of the substances. Rearranging the rate law and entering the appropriate values gives

$$k = \frac{\text{Rate}}{[\text{A}]\,[\text{B}]} = \frac{2.75\ \text{M s}^{-1}}{[1.25 \times 10^{-5}\ \text{M}]\,[1.25 \times 10^{-5}\ \text{M}]} = 1.76 \times 10^{10}\ \text{M}^{-1}\ \text{s}^{-1}$$

432. The relationship between the activation energy and the enthalpy of activation is $E_a = \Delta H^{\ddagger} + 2RT$, where R is the gas constant. Rearranging this equation and entering the appropriate values gives

$$\Delta H^{\ddagger} = E_a - 2RT = 23.7\ \text{kJ mol}^{-1} - 2(8.3145\ \text{J mol}^{-1}\ \text{K}^{-1})(425\ \text{K})(1\ \text{kJ}/10^3\ \text{J})$$

$$= 16.6\ \text{kJ mol}^{-1}$$

433. Radioactive decay processes are classic examples of first-order kinetics. The one form of the integrated rate law for a first-order reaction is $\ln\frac{[\text{A}]_0}{[\text{A}]_t} = kt$, where $[\text{A}]_0$ is the initial amount (assumed to be the current decay level), $[\text{A}]_t$ is the amount after the elapse of time, and t is the time between $[\text{A}]_0$ and $[\text{A}]_t$ (the age of the sample). Rearranging this equation and entering the appropriate values gives

$$t = \frac{\ln\dfrac{[\text{A}]_0}{[\text{A}]_t}}{k} = \frac{\ln\dfrac{[8.05 \times 10^6\ \text{dis g}^{-1}\ \text{y}^{-1}]_0}{[4.00 \times 10^5\ \text{dis g}^{-1}\ \text{y}^{-1}]_t}}{1.21 \times 10^{-4}\ \text{y}^{-1}} = 2.48 \times 10^4\ \text{y}$$

Chapter 19: The Kinetics of Complex Reactions

434. Radioactive decay processes follow first-order kinetics. The half-life of a first-order process is $t_{1/2} = \frac{\ln 2}{k}$. Rearranging this equation and entering the values gives

$$k = \frac{\ln 2}{t_{\frac{1}{2}}} = \frac{\ln 2}{1.41 \times 10^{10}\ \text{y}} = 4.92 \times 10^{-11}\ \text{y}^{-1}$$

435. The fraction will be the amount of radium divided by the original amount of thorium. The amount of radium is the quantity produced minus the amount decaying to actinium. The relationship will be $F = \frac{[\text{Ra}]}{[\text{Th}]} = \left(\frac{k_{\text{Th}}}{k_{\text{Ra}} - k_{\text{Th}}}\right)(e^{-k_{\text{Th}}t} - e^{-k_{\text{Ra}}t})$.
Using this relationship gives

$$\begin{aligned} F &= \left(\frac{k_{\text{Th}}}{k_{\text{Ra}} - k_{\text{Th}}}\right)(e^{-k_{\text{Th}}t} - e^{-k_{\text{Ra}}t}) \\ &= \left(\frac{4.92 \times 10^{-11}\ \text{y}^{-1}}{(0.121\ \text{y}^{-1}) - (4.92 \times 10^{-11}\ \text{y}^{-1})}\right)(e^{-(4.92 \times 10^{-11}\ \text{y}^{-1})(3.0\ \text{y})} - e^{-(0.121\ \text{y}^{-1})(3.0\ \text{y})}) \\ &= 1.24 \times 10^{-10} \end{aligned}$$

436. The relationship is $\ln\frac{AB_0}{A_0B} = (A_0 - B_0)kt$. The slope is equal to $\frac{\ln\frac{AB_0}{A_0B}}{t}$; therefore, $k = \frac{\text{slope}}{(A_0 - B_0)}$. This information leads to

$$k = \frac{\text{slope}}{(A_0 - B_0)} = \frac{-5.27 \times 10^{-4}\ \text{s}^{-1}}{(0.00486 - 0.00980)\text{mol L}^{-1}} = 0.107\ \text{L mol}^{-1}\ \text{s}^{-1}$$

437. The gas-collision theory relationship is $k = (2 \times 10^{-3})(N_A)\left(\sqrt{\frac{\pi RT}{M}}\right)\sigma^2 e^{-E_a/RT}$, where N_A is Avogadro's number and R is the gas constant. Entering the appropriate values into this relationship gives

$$k = (2 \times 10^{-3})(N_A)\rho\left(\sqrt{\frac{\pi RT}{M}}\right)\sigma^2 e^{-E_a/RT}$$

Solving by parts:

$$k = (2 \times 10^{-3})(6.022 \times 10^{23}\ \text{mol}^{-1})(1)\left(\sqrt{\frac{\pi RT}{M}}\right)\sigma^2 e^{-E_a/RT}$$

$$k = (1.204 \times 10^{21}\ \text{mol}^{-1})\left(\sqrt{\frac{\pi RT}{M}}\right)\sigma^2 e^{-(1.91 \times 10^5\ \text{J mol}^{-1})/[(8.3145\ \text{J mol}^{-1}\ \text{K}^{-1})(667\ \text{K})]}$$

$$\times(1.204 \times 10^{21}\ \text{mol}^{-1})\left(\sqrt{\frac{\pi RT}{M}}\right)\sigma^2 e^{-(1.91 \times 10^5\ \text{J mol}^{-1})/[(8.3145\ \text{J mol}^{-1}\ \text{K}^{-1})(667\ \text{K})]}$$

$$k = (1.204 \times 10^{21}\ \text{mol}^{-1})\left(\sqrt{\frac{\pi RT}{M}}\right)\sigma^2(1.10 \times 10^{-15})$$

$$k = (1.324 \times 10^{6}\ \text{mol}^{-1})\left(\sqrt{\frac{\pi RT}{M}}\right)(3.5 \times 10^{-10}\ \text{m})^2$$

$$k = (1.324 \times 10^{6}\ \text{mol}^{-1})\left(\sqrt{\frac{\pi(8.3145\ \text{J mol}^{-1}\ \text{K}^{-1})(667\ \text{K})}{(127.9\ \text{g mol}^{-1})}}\right)(1.2 \times 10^{-19}\ \text{m}^2)$$

$$k = (1.589 \times 10^{-13}\ \text{m}^2\ \text{mol}^{-1})\left(\sqrt{136.2\ \text{J g}^{-1}\left(\frac{10^3\ \text{g}}{1\ \text{kg}}\right)\left(\frac{\text{kg m}^2/\text{s}^2}{\text{J}}\right)}\right)\left(\frac{1\ \text{L}}{10^{-3}\,\text{m}^3}\right)$$

$$k = 5.86 \times 10^{-8}\ \text{L mol}^{-1}\ \text{s}^{-1}$$

438. In general, $K = \frac{k_1}{k_{-1}}$. Rearranging and entering the values gives

$$k_{-1} = \frac{k_1}{K} = \frac{2.2 \times 10^4\ \text{L mol}^{-1}\ \text{s}^{-1}}{1.0 \times 10^{-4}} = 2.2 \times 10^8\ \text{L mol}^{-1}\ \text{s}^{-1}$$

439. The equation for the relaxation time is $\tau = \frac{1}{k_1 + k_{-1}[A_{eq} + B_{eq}]}$, where A_{eq} is the equilibrium concentration of the hydrogen ion, B_{eq} is the equilibrium concentration of the hydroxide ion, and $A_{eq} = B_{eq} = 1.0 \times 10^{-7}$ M. Solving the ratio of k_1 to k_{-1} for k_1 gives $k_1 = (1.8 \times 10^{-16})k_{-1}$. Substituting into the relaxation time equation gives

$$\tau = \frac{1}{(1.8 \times 10^{-18})k_{-1} + k_{-1}[A_{eq} + B_{eq}]} = \frac{1}{k_{-1}[1.8 \times 10^{-16} + A_{eq} + B_{eq}]}$$

Rearranging

$$k_{-1} = \frac{1}{\tau[1.8 \times 10^{-18} + A_{eq} + B_{eq}]} = \frac{1}{(3.6 \times 10^{-5}\ \text{s})[(1.8 \times 10^{-16}\ \text{M}) + 2(1.0 \times 10^{-7}\ \text{M})]}$$

$$= 1.4 \times 10^{11}\ \text{M}^{-1}\ \text{s}^{-1}$$

Finally, $k_1 = (1.8 \times 10^{-16})k_{-1} = (1.8 \times 10^{-16})\ (1.4 \times 10^{11}\ \text{M}^{-1}\ \text{s}^{-1}) = 2.5 \times 10^{-5}\ \text{M}^{-1}\ \text{s}^{-1}$

440. When there data are limited, a modified version of the Arrhenius equation is useful. This equation is $\ln\frac{k_1}{k_2} = \frac{E_a}{R}\left(\frac{1}{T_2} - \frac{1}{T_1}\right)$, where R is the gas constant. Rearranging this equation and entering the values gives

$$E_a = \frac{R\left(\ln\frac{k_1}{k_2}\right)}{\left(\frac{1}{T_2} - \frac{1}{T_1}\right)} = \frac{(8.3145\ \text{J mol}^{-1}\ \text{K}^{-1})\left(\ln\frac{1.07 \times 10^{-3}\ \text{s}^{-1}}{1.08 \times 10^{-4}\ \text{s}^{-1}}\right)}{\left(\frac{1}{402\ \text{K}} - \frac{1}{427\ \text{K}}\right)} = 1.31 \times 10^5\ \text{J mol}^{-1}$$

441. It is best to solve this problem graphically. The plot will be $y = \ln k$ and $x = 1/T$. The graph should give a straight line with $E_a = -R(\text{slope})$, with R being the gas constant. The slope of the graph is –16.4; therefore $E_a = -\ (8.3145\ \text{J mol}^{-1}\ \text{K}^{-1})(-1.64 \times 10^4)$ $= 1.61 \times 10^5\ \text{J mol}^{-1}$.

442. If the activation energy is 0, then $k = Ae^{-E_a/RT}$ becomes $k = A$. The value of A (the pre-exponential factor) comes from $A = \frac{4\pi(r_{ES})(D_E + D_S)N_A}{1000}$, where N_A is Avogadro's number. This equation leads to

$$A = k = \frac{4\pi(r_{ES})(D_E + D_S)N_A}{1000}$$

$$= \frac{4\pi(5 \times 10^{-10}\ \text{m})[(0.29 + 6.73) \times 10^{-6}\ \text{cm}^2\ \text{s}^{-1}](6.022 \times 10^{23}\ \text{mol}^{-1})}{1000}$$

$$\times \left(\frac{0.01\ \text{m}}{1\ \text{cm}}\right)^2 \left(\frac{1\ \text{L}}{10^{-3}\ \text{m}^3}\right) = 3 \times 10^6\ \text{L mol}^{-1}\ \text{s}^{-1}$$

443. Rearranging the equation given in the problem and entering the appropriate conversion factors gives

$$\text{A} = \frac{k}{e^{-E_a/RT}} = \frac{4.62 \times 10^{-7}\ \text{s}^{-1}}{e^{-(129\ \text{kJ mol}^{-1})\left(\frac{10^3\ \text{J}}{1\ \text{kJ}}\right)/[(8.3145\ \text{J mol}^{-1}\ \text{K}^{-1})(344\ \text{K})]}} = 1.79 \times 10^{13}\ \text{s}^{-1}$$

444. An approximation of the entropy of activation comes from $\Delta S^{\ddagger} = R\left(\ln \frac{Ah}{k_B T}\right)$, where R is the gas constant, h is Planck's constant, and k_B is the Boltzmann constant. Using this approximation and entering the values gives

$$\Delta S^{\ddagger} = R\left(\ln \frac{Ah}{k_B T}\right) = (8.3145 \text{ J mol}^{-1} \text{ K}^{-1})\left(\ln \frac{(1.79 \times 10^{13} \text{ s}^{-1})(6.63 \times 10^{-34} \text{ J s})}{(1.381 \times 10^{-23} \text{ J K}^{-1})(344 \text{ K})}\right)$$
$$= 7.61 \text{ J mol}^{-1} \text{ K}^{-1}$$

445. The intercept of a Lineweaver–Burk plot is $1/V_{max}$; therefore,

$$V_{max} = \frac{1}{\text{intercept}} = \frac{1}{1.18 \times 10^{-2} \text{ M}^{-1} \text{ s}} = 84.7 \text{ M s}^{-1}$$

446. The slope of a Lineweaver–Burk plot is K_M/V_{max}. From this relationship and the information in the problem,

$$K_M = (\text{slope})\ V_{max} = (75.5 \text{ s})\ (84.7 \text{ M s}^{-1}) = 6.39 \times 10^{3} \text{ M}$$

447. On an Eadie–Hofstee plot, V_{max} is equal to the intercept; therefore, $V_{max} = 8.56 \times 10^{-5}$ M s^{-1}.

448. On an Eadie–Hofstee plot, K_M is equal to the negative of the slope; therefore, $K_M = 6.52 \times 10^{-3}$ M.

449. In this case, it is possible to determine the rate of the reaction from the relationship Rate $= \frac{1}{2}\, k_3\, [\text{E}]_0$, where $[\text{E}]_0$ is the initial amount of enzyme. Using this relationship gives

$$\text{Rate} = \frac{1}{2}\, k_3\, [\text{E}]_0 = \frac{1}{2}\left(3.7 \times 10^{5} \text{ s}^{-1}\right)\left[\frac{0.050 \text{ g}}{52{,}000 \text{ g mol}^{-1}}\right]_0 = 0.18 \text{ mol s}^{-1}$$

450. The Arrhenius equation is useful in the form $\ln \frac{k_1}{k_2} = \frac{E_a}{R}\left(\frac{1}{T_2} - \frac{1}{T_1}\right)$, where R is the gas constant. Rearranging this equation and entering the values gives

$$\ln k_1 = \frac{E_a}{R}\left(\frac{1}{T_2} - \frac{1}{T_1}\right) + \ln k_2$$
$$= \frac{(1.0 \times 10^{5} \text{ J mol}^{-1})}{(8.3145 \text{ J mol}^{-1} \text{ K}^{-1})}\left(\frac{1}{(427 \text{ K})} - \frac{1}{(437 \text{ K})}\right) + \ln(1.0 \times 10^{-3}) = -6.263$$

$k_1 = 1.9 \times 10^{-3}$ s^{-1} (This is nearly double.)

451. The general form for a rate law for this reaction is Rate = $k[I^-]^m[ClO^-]^n[OH^-]^p$, where k is the rate constant, the terms in brackets refer to the concentrations of the different species, and the exponents are the orders for the different species. The first step in determining the rate law is to determine the individual orders. Examining the different experiments in pairs where the concentration of only one reactant changes is the simplest approach. In the case of the iodide ion, use experiments 4 and 5, then for the hypochlorite ion use experiments 1 and 2, and for the hydroxide ion use experiments 1 and 3. For both the iodide ion and the hypochlorite ion, doubling the concentration doubles the rate; therefore, the order for each of these components is 1. However, in the case of the hydroxide ion, doubling the concentration halves the rate; therefore, the rate is –1. This leads to the rate law

$$\text{Rate} = k[I^-][ClO^-][OH^-]^{-1}$$

452. Rearranging the rate law gives $k = \frac{\text{Rate}}{[I^-][ClO^-][OH^-]^{-1}}$. Entering the values gives

$$k = \frac{\text{Rate}}{[I^-][ClO^-][OH^-]^{-1}} = \frac{1.2 \times 10^{-2}\ \text{M s}^{-1}}{[0.0020\ \text{M}][0.010\ \text{M}][0.10\ \text{M}]^{-1}} = 60\ \text{s}^{-1}$$

453. This problem combines the Arrhenius equation ($k = Ae^{-E_a/RT}$) and the half-life equation for first-order reactions ($t_{1/2} = \frac{\ln 2}{k}$). Combining these equations gives $\frac{\ln 2}{t_{1/2}} = Ae^{-E_a/RT}$, where R is the gas constant. Rearranging this equation and entering the appropriate values gives

$$T = \frac{-E_a}{R \ln\left[\frac{\ln 2}{A\, t_{1/2}}\right]} = \frac{-8.0 \times 10^4\ \text{J mol}^{-1}}{(8.3145\ \text{J mol}^{-1}\ \text{K}^{-1}) \ln\left[\frac{\ln 2}{(3.0 \times 10^{12}\ \text{s}^{-1})\ (3600\ \text{s})}\right]} = 260\ \text{K}$$

Chapter 20: Macromolecules

454. The important equation is $X = (1 - p)p^{1-p}$. Entering the values gives

$$X = (1 - p)p^{1-p} = (1 - 0.90)\ (0.90)^{1-0.90} = 0.099$$

The mole fraction is a unitless quantity.

455. The important equation is $w = iX(1 - p)$. Entering the values gives

$$w = iX(1 - p) = 25\ (0.099)(1 - 0.90) = 0.25$$

The weight fraction is a unitless quantity.

456. Do not forget, while the molar mass of the amino acid is 75.0 g mol^{-1}, the formation of the polymer is a condensation reaction expelling an H_2O molecule (18.0 g mol^{-1}) leaving a molar mass of the monomer (M_0) of 57.0 g mol^{-1}. The key equation is $\bar{M}_n = \frac{M_0}{1-p}$, which rearranges to

$$p = 1 - \frac{M_0}{\bar{M}_n} = 1 - \frac{57.0\ \text{g mol}^{-1}}{6.30 \times 10^3\ \text{g mol}^{-1}} = 0.991$$

457. The important relationship is $\bar{X}_n = \frac{1}{1-p}$. Entering the values from the problem gives

$$\bar{X}_n = \frac{1}{1-p} = \frac{1}{1-0.991} = 1.11 \times 10^2$$

458. Do not forget, while the molar mass of the amino acid is 75.0 g mol^{-1}, the formation of the polymer is a condensation reaction expelling an H_2O molecule (18.0 g mol^{-1}) leaving a molar mass of the monomer (M_0) of 57.0 g mol^{-1}. The important relationship is $\bar{M}_{\text{m}} = M_0\left(\frac{1+p}{1-p}\right)$. Entering the values gives

$$\bar{M}_{\text{m}} = M_0\left(\frac{1+p}{1-p}\right) = (57.0\ \text{g mol}^{-1})\left(\frac{1+0.991}{1-0.991}\right) = 1.26 \times 10^4\ \text{g mol}^{-1}$$

459. The mass of each repeating unit (–CF_2–) is 50.0 g mol^{-1} and the number of chain units $= N = \frac{2.0 \times 10^5\ \text{g mol}^{-1}}{50.0\ \text{g mol}^{-1}} = 4.0 \times 10^3$.

The important equation is $(\bar{r}^2)^{1/2} = N^{1/2}l$. Entering the values gives

$$(\bar{r}^2)^{1/2} = N^{1/2}l = (4.0 \times 10^3)^{1/2}(156\ \text{pm}) = 9.9 \times 10^3\ \text{pm}$$

460. The mass of each repeating unit (–CF_2–) is 50.0 g mol^{-1}, and the number of chain units $= N = \frac{2.0 \times 10^5\ \text{g mol}^{-1}}{50.0\ \text{g mol}^{-1}} = 4.0 \times 10^3$.

The important equation is $(\bar{r}^2)^{1/2} = (2N)^{1/2}l$. Entering the values gives

$$(\bar{r}^2)^{1/2} = (2N)^{1/2}\,l = [2(4.0 \times 10^3)]^{1/2}(156\ \text{pm}) = 1.4 \times 10^4\ \text{pm}$$

461. The important relationship is $\frac{\left(\frac{\eta}{\eta_0}\right) - 1}{c}$. Using the information from the problem gives

$$\frac{\left(\frac{\eta}{\eta_0}\right) - 1}{c} = 1{,}250\ \text{cm}^3\ \text{g}^{-1} = \frac{0.050}{c}$$

$$c = 4.0 \times 10^{-5}\ \text{g cm}^{-3}$$

462. Using the information from the problem gives the following relationship, where R is the gas constant

$$M = \frac{RTS}{D(1 - v\rho)}$$

$$= \left(\frac{(8.314 \text{ J mol}^{-1} \text{ K}^{-1})(298 \text{ K})(2.06 \times 10^{-13} \text{ s})}{(1.25 \times 10^{-10} \text{ m}^2 \text{ s}^{-1})(1 - (7.49 \times 10^{-4} \text{ kg}^{-1} \text{ m}^3)(9.968 \times 10^2 \text{ kg m}^{-3}))} \right)$$

$$\times \left(\frac{\left(\frac{\text{kg m}^2}{\text{s}^2} \right)}{\text{J}} \right) \quad M = 16.1 \text{ kg mol}^{-1}$$

463. The important relationship is $\bar{M}_n = \frac{\sum n_i M_i}{\sum n_i}$. Using the information from the problem gives

$$\bar{M}_n = \frac{\sum n_i M_i}{\sum n_i} = \left(\frac{28\%}{100\%} \right)(1.80 \times 10^4 \text{ g mol}^{-1}) + \left(\frac{37\%}{100\%} \right)(2.40 \times 10^4 \text{ g mol}^{-1})$$

$$+ \left(\frac{35\%}{100\%} \right)(1.25 \times 10^4 \text{ g mol}^{-1}) = 1.8 \times 10^4 \text{ g mol}^{-1}$$

464. The appropriate equation is $M = \frac{RTS}{D(1 - \bar{v}\rho)}$, where R is the gas constant. Entering the appropriate values gives

$$M = \frac{RTS}{D(1 - \bar{v}\rho)} = \frac{(8.3145 \text{ J mol}^{-1} \text{ K}^{-1})(293 \text{ K})(7.1 \times 10^{-13} \text{ s})}{(4.0 \times 10^{-7} \text{ cm}^2 \text{ s}^{-1})[1 - (0.75 \text{ cm}^3 \text{ g}^{-1})(0.9982 \text{ g cm}^{-3})]}$$

$$\times \left(\frac{\text{kg m}^2/\text{s}^2}{\text{J}} \right) \left(\frac{1 \text{ cm}}{0.01 \text{ m}} \right)^2 \left(\frac{10^3 \text{ g}}{1 \text{ kg}} \right) = 1.7 \times 10^5 \text{ g mol}^{-1}$$

465. Rearranging the Mark Houwink equation and solving for the molar mass gives $M = \exp\left[\frac{\ln\left(\frac{[\eta]}{K}\right)}{a} \right]$. Using the equation in this form gives

$$M = \exp\left[\frac{\ln\left(\frac{[\eta]}{K} \right)}{a} \right] = \exp\left[\frac{\ln\left(\frac{78 \text{ cm}^3 \text{ g}^{-1}}{1.17 \times 10^{-2} \text{ cm}^3 \text{ g}^{-1}} \right)}{0.67} \right] = 5.1 \times 10^5 \text{ g mol}^{-1}$$

466. The key relationship is $S = \frac{MD(1-\nu\rho)}{RT}$, with R being the gas constant. Entering the appropriate information gives

$$S = \frac{MD(1-\nu\rho)}{RT}$$

$$= \frac{(1.20\times10^{4}\ \text{g mol}^{-1})(1.52\times10^{-10}\ \text{m}^2\ \text{s}^{-1})(1-(7.2\times10^{-4}\ \text{kg}^{-1}\ \text{m}^3)(9.9968\times10^{2}\ \text{kg m}^{-3}))}{(8.314\ \text{J mol}^{-1}\ \text{K}^{-1})(298\ \text{K})\left(\frac{\left(\text{kg m}^2/\text{s}^2\right)}{\text{J}}\right)\left(\frac{1000\ \text{g}}{1\ \text{kg}}\right)}$$

$$= 2.06\times10^{-13}\ \text{s}$$

467. The key relationship is $S = \left(\frac{M(1-\upsilon\rho)}{N_A 6\pi\eta}\right)\left(\frac{4\pi N_A}{3M\upsilon}\right)^{1/3}$, N_A being Avogadro's number. This equation rearranges to $M = \sqrt{162\pi^2\upsilon N_A^2\left(\frac{\eta S}{(1-\upsilon\rho)}\right)^3}$. Entering the appropriate information, and solving by parts, gives

$$M = \sqrt{162\pi^2\upsilon N_A^2\left(\frac{\eta S}{(1-\upsilon\rho)}\right)^3} = \sqrt{162\pi^2(7.2\times10^{-4}\ \text{kg}^{-1}\ \text{m}^3)(6.022\times10^{23}\ \text{mol}^{-1})^2\left(\frac{\eta S}{(1-\upsilon\rho)}\right)^3}$$

$$= \sqrt{(4.2\times10^{47}\ \text{kg}^{-1}\ \text{m}^3\ \text{mol}^{-2})\left(\frac{(0.001005\ \text{Pa s})(2.06\times10^{-13}\ \text{s})}{[1-(7.2\times10^{-4}\ \text{kg}^{-1}\ \text{m}^3)(9.9968\times10^{2}\ \text{kg m}^{-3})]}\left(\frac{\text{kg/m s}^2}{\text{Pa}}\right)\right)^3}$$

$$= \sqrt{(4.2\times10^{47}\ \text{kg}^{-1}\ \text{m}^3\ \text{mol}^{-2})\left((7.3878\times10^{-16}\ \text{Pa s}^2)\left(\frac{\text{kg/m s}^2}{\text{Pa}}\right)\right)^3}\left(\frac{10^3\ \text{g}}{1\ \text{kg}}\right)$$

$$= 1.3\times10^{4}\ \text{g mol}^{-1}$$

468. The diffusion is related to the radius through the Stokes–Einstein relation, which in one form is $D = \frac{kT}{6\pi\eta R}$, where k is the Boltzmann constant. Rearranging this equation and entering the appropriate values gives

$$R = \frac{kT}{6\pi\eta D} = \frac{(1.3807\times10^{-23}\ \text{J K}^{-1})(310\ \text{K})}{6\pi(6.915\times10^{-4}\ \text{Pa s})(1.06\times10^{-10}\ \text{m}^2\ \text{s}^{-1})}\left(\frac{\text{kg m}^2/\text{s}^2}{\text{J}}\right)\left(\frac{\text{Pa}}{\text{kg/m s}^2}\right)$$

$$= 3.10\times10^{-9}\ \text{m}$$

469. The ceiling temperature comes from the relationship $T_c = \frac{\Delta H_p{}^\circ}{\Delta S_p{}^\circ}$. Using the information from the problem gives

$$T_c = \frac{\Delta H_p{}^\circ}{\Delta S_p{}^\circ} = \frac{(-155\ \text{kJ mol}^{-1})}{(-112\ \text{J mol}^{-1}\ \text{K}^{-1})}\left(\frac{10^3\ \text{J}}{1\ \text{kJ}}\right) = 1.38\times10^{3}\ \text{K}$$

470. The equation for the diffusion coefficient is $D = \left(\frac{RT}{6\pi N_A \eta}\right)\left(\sqrt[3]{\frac{4\pi N_A}{3M\bar{v}}}\right)$, where R is the gas constant and N_A is Avogadro's number. Entering the values into this equation and solving by parts,

$$D = \left(\frac{RT}{6\pi N_A \eta}\right)\left(\sqrt[3]{\frac{4\pi N_A}{3M\bar{v}}}\right) = 1.06 \times 10^{-6}\ \text{cm}^2\ \text{s}^{-1}$$

$$= \left(\frac{(8.3145\ \text{J mol}^{-1}\ \text{K}^{-1})(293\ \text{K})}{6\pi(6.022\times10^{23}\ \text{mol}^{-1})(0.01005\ \text{P})}\right)\left(\frac{1\ \text{P}}{\text{g cm}^{-1}\ \text{s}^{-1}}\right)\left(\frac{\text{kg m}^2/\text{s}^2}{\text{J}}\right)\left(\frac{10^3\ \text{g}}{1\ \text{kg}}\right)$$

$$\times\left(\frac{1\ \text{cm}}{0.01\ \text{m}}\right)^2\left(\sqrt[3]{\frac{4\pi(N_A)}{3(M)(\bar{v})}}\right)$$

$$= (2.135 \times 10^{-13}\ \text{cm}^3\ \text{s}^{-1})\left(\sqrt[3]{\frac{4\pi(N_A)}{3(M)(\bar{v})}}\right)$$

$$= \left(\sqrt[3]{\frac{4\pi(N_A)}{3(M)(\bar{v})}}\right) = 4.965 \times 10^6\ \text{cm}^{-1}$$

$$= \left(\sqrt[3]{\frac{4\pi(6.022\times10^{23}\ \text{mol}^{-1})}{3(M)(0.75\ \text{cm}^3\ \text{g}^{-1})}}\right) = \left(\sqrt[3]{\frac{3.363 \times 10^{24}\ \text{g mol}^{-1}\ \text{cm}^{-3}}{(M)}}\right)$$

$$= \frac{3.363 \times 10^{24}\ \text{g mol}^{-1}\ \text{cm}^{-3}}{(M)} = 1.224 \times 10^{20}\ \text{cm}^{-3}$$

$$M = \frac{3.363 \times 10^{24}\ \text{g mol}^{-1}\ \text{cm}^{-3}}{1.224 \times 10^{20}\ \text{cm}^{-3}} = 2.75 \times 10^4\ \text{g mol}^{-1}$$

Chapter 21: The Solid State

471. Using the Bragg equation ($n\lambda = 2d \sin\theta$),

$$\sin\theta = \frac{n\lambda}{2d} = \left(\frac{(1)(0.1548\ \text{nm})}{2(3.35 \times 10^{-10}\ \text{m})}\right)\left(\frac{10^{-9}\ \text{m}}{1\ \text{nm}}\right) = 0.2301$$

$$\theta = 13.3°$$

472. The described arrangement is

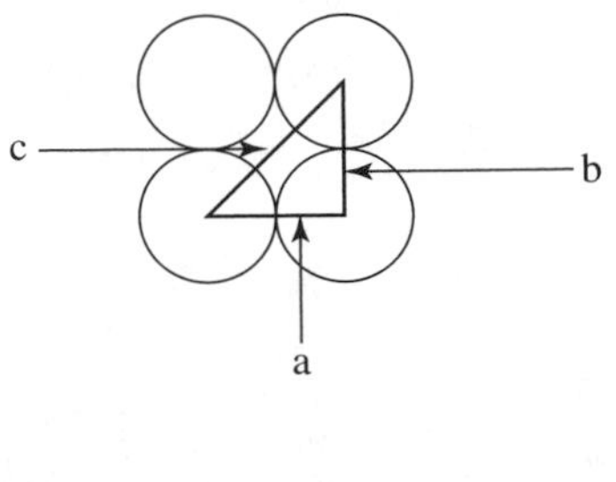

This is a square arrangement so $a = b$, and each is twice the radius (= 2). The length of c is twice the radius of the large ion plus the diameter (twice the radius) of the hole. Using the Pythagorean theorem, $a^2 + b^2 = c^2$. This gives

$$2^2 + 2^2 = c^2$$

$$8 = c^2$$

$$c = 2.828 = 2 + (\text{diameter of hole})$$

Diameter of hole = 0.828 = $2r$, so the radius is 0.414.

473. Using the information from the problem gives

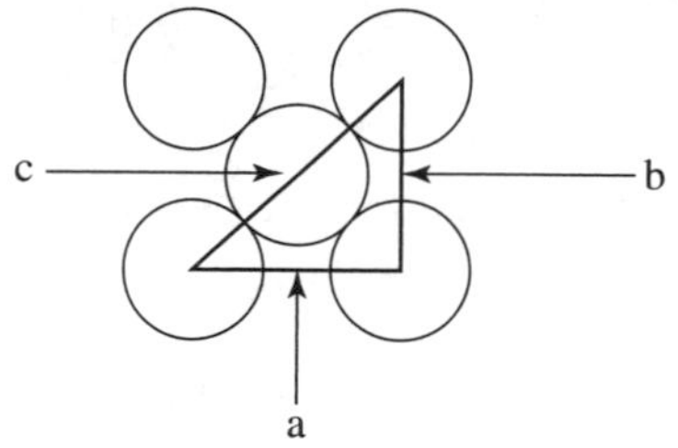

The unit cell edge ($a = b$) is

$$\sqrt[3]{\left(\frac{\text{cm}^3}{2.70\text{ g}}\right)\left(\frac{26.981\text{ g}}{\text{mol}}\right)\left(\frac{1\text{ mol}}{6.022\times10^{23}\text{ atoms}}\right)(4\text{ atoms})} = 4.05\times10^{-8}\text{ cm}$$

Using the Pythagorean theorem, $a^2 + b^2 = c^2$. With $a = b$, this gives

$$2a^2 = c^2$$

$$c = \sqrt{2}(4.05\times10^{-8})\text{cm} = 5.72\times10^{-8}\text{ cm}$$

$$\text{Radius} = c/4 = 1.43\times10^{-8}\text{ cm}$$

474. The molar volume of molybdenum is molar mass (95.94 g mol^{-1}) divided by its density. The molar volume is 9.387 $\text{cm}^3\ \text{mol}^{-1}$. The packing efficiency of a body-centered cubic lattice is 0.6802; therefore, the volume of the molybdenum atoms in the solid is (0.6802)(9.387 $\text{cm}^3\ \text{mol}^{-1}$) = 6.385 $\text{cm}^3\ \text{mol}^{-1}$. The volume of a single Mo atom is the molar volume of the atoms divided by Avogadro's number or (6.385 $\text{cm}^3\ \text{mol}^{-1}$)/(6.022 × $10^{23}\ \text{mol}^{-1}$) = 1.060 × $10^{-23}\ \text{cm}^3$. This is the volume of a sphere ($V = \frac{4}{3}\pi r^3$). Solving for the radius gives $r = 1.365\times10^{-8}$ cm.

475. The packing efficiency is the volume of the contents of the unit cell divided by the volume of the unit cell. This gives

$$\text{Packing efficiency} = \frac{\left(\frac{4}{3}\right)\pi r^3}{(a)^3} = \frac{\left(\frac{4}{3}\right)\pi r^3}{(2r)^3} = 0.52$$

476. The packing efficiency is the volume of the contents of the unit cell divided by the volume of the unit cell. This gives

$$\text{Packing efficiency} = \frac{2\left(\frac{4}{3}\right)\pi r^3}{(a)^3} = \frac{2\left(\frac{4}{3}\right)\pi r^3}{\left(\frac{4r}{\sqrt{3}}\right)^3} = 0.6802$$

477. The packing efficiency is the volume of the contents of the unit cell divided by the volume of the unit cell. This gives

$$\text{Packing efficiency} = \frac{4\left(\frac{4}{3}\right)\pi r^3}{(a)^3} = \frac{4\left(\frac{4}{3}\right)\pi r^3}{(2\sqrt{2}r)^3} = 0.74$$

478. Using the explanation given in the problem,

$$\text{Packing efficiency} = \frac{\left(\frac{4}{3}\right)(\pi)\left(r_{Cs}^3 + r_{Cl}^3\right)}{a^3} = \frac{\left(\frac{4}{3}\right)(3.14159)(174^3 + 181^3)}{(411.0)^3} = 0.676$$

479. Using the information from the problem gives

$$\left(\frac{3.1\text{ g}}{\text{cm}^3}\right)\left(\frac{(4.507 \times 10^{-8}\text{ cm})^3}{2\text{ atoms}}\right)\left(\frac{6.022 \times 10^{23}\text{ atoms}}{\text{mol}}\right) = 85\text{ g mol}^{-1} = \text{rubidium}$$

480. Using the information from the problem gives

$$N_A = \left(\frac{4\text{ atoms}}{(4.96 \times 10^{-8}\text{ cm})^3}\right)\left(\frac{\text{cm}^3}{11.3\text{ g}}\right)\left(\frac{207.2\text{ g}}{\text{mol}}\right) = 6.01 \times 10^{23}\text{ atoms/mol}$$

481. Using the information from the problem gives

$$\sqrt[3]{\left(\frac{\text{cm}^3}{3.1\ \text{g}}\right)\left(\frac{85.4678\ \text{g}}{\text{mol}}\right)\left(\frac{1\ \text{mol}}{6.022\times 10^{23}\ \text{atoms}}\right)(2\ \text{atoms})} = 4.5\times 10^{-8}\ \text{cm}$$

482. A body-centered unit cell contains two potassium atoms, which may be used to determine the mass of a unit cell. The mass of the unit cell and the density will lead to a determination of the cell volume, and the cube root of the cell volume will give the lattice constant. Combining this information gives

$$a = \sqrt[3]{\left(\frac{\text{cm}^3}{0.862\ \text{g}}\right)\left(\frac{39.10\ \text{g}}{\text{mol}}\right)\left(\frac{\text{mol}}{6.022\times 10^{23}\ \text{atoms}}\right)\left(\frac{2\ \text{atoms}}{1}\right)\left(\frac{0.01\ \text{m}}{\text{cm}}\right)^3} = 5.32\times 10^{-10}\ \text{m}$$

483. Using the information from the problem gives

$$\left(\frac{2\ \text{atoms}}{(533.3\ \text{pm})^3}\right)\left(\frac{1\ \text{pm}}{10^{-12}\ \text{m}}\right)^3\left(\frac{10^{-2}\ \text{m}}{1\ \text{cm}}\right)^3\left(\frac{1\ \text{mol K}}{6.022\times 10^{23}\ \text{atoms}}\right)\left(\frac{39.0983\ \text{g}}{\text{mol}}\right) = 0.8561\ \text{g cm}^{-3}$$

484. Using the information from the problem gives

$$\left(\frac{6.022\times 10^{23}\ \text{atoms}}{\text{mol}}\right)\left(\frac{1\ \text{mol}}{55.845\ \text{g}}\right)\left(\frac{7.87\ \text{g}}{\text{cm}^3}\right)\left(\frac{1\ \text{cm}}{0.01\ \text{m}}\right)^3\left(\frac{10^{-12}\ \text{m}}{1\ \text{pm}}\right)^3(361\ \text{pm})^3$$

$= 3.99$ atoms

→ 4 atoms

485. Using the information from the problem gives

$$\left(\frac{6.022\times 10^{23}\ \text{MgAl}_2\text{O}_4}{\text{mol}}\right)\left(\frac{1\ \text{mol}}{142.265\ \text{g}}\right)\left(\frac{3.55\ \text{g}}{\text{cm}^3}\right)\left(\frac{\text{cm}}{0.01\ \text{m}}\right)^3\left(\frac{10^{-12}\ \text{m}}{\text{pm}}\right)^3(644\ \text{pm})^3$$

$= 4.01$

→ 4 formula units

486. The equation for the Fermi energy is $E_F = (3.65\times 10^{-19})\left(\frac{N}{V}\right)^{2/3}$ eV, which gives the energy in electronvolts if the volume (V) is in cubic meters. Using this equation gives

$$E_F = (3.65\times 10^{-19})\left(\frac{N}{V}\right)^{2/3}\ \text{eV} = (3.65\times 10^{-19})\left(\frac{4}{(4.04\times 10^{-10}\ \text{m})^3}\right)^{2/3}\ \text{eV} = 5.64\ \text{eV}$$

487. The potassium unit cell contains two potassium atoms, each of which donates one conduction electron. Therefore, there are two conduction electrons in a volume of a^3. This density is equal to $\frac{N_A}{\bar{V}}$, where N_A is Avogadro's number and $\bar{V}$ is the molar volume. This information leads to

$$\frac{N_A}{\bar{V}} = \frac{2 \text{ electrons}}{(5.32 \times 10^{-10}\ \text{m})^3} = 1.33 \times 10^{28} \text{ electrons m}^{-3}$$

488. The relationship between the conduction electron density and the Fermi energy is $E_F = \left(\frac{\hbar^2\pi^2}{2\,\text{m}}\right)\left(\frac{3\,N_A}{\pi\,\bar{V}}\right)^{2/3}$, where $\hbar$ is Planck's constant divided by 2π (1.054573×10^{-34} J s), and m is the rest mass of an electron ($9.1093897 \times 10^{-31}$ kg). Entering the information into the equation gives

$$E_F = \left(\frac{(1.054573 \times 10^{-34}\ \text{J s})^2\pi^2}{2\,(9.1093897 \times 10^{-31}\ \text{kg})}\right)\left(\frac{3\,(1.33 \times 10^{28}\ \text{m}^{-3})}{\pi}\right)^{2/3}\left(\frac{\text{kg m}^2\ \text{s}^{-2}}{\text{J}}\right) = 3.28 \times 10^{-19}\ \text{J}$$

Chapter 22: Processes at Solid Surfaces

489. This problem requires the ideal gas equation plus some conversions. Beginning with $n = PV/RT$ gives

$$A = \frac{(1.00\ \text{atm})(125\ \text{mL})(6.022 \times 10^{23}\ \text{mol}^{-1})(1.3 \times 10^{-19}\ \text{m}^2)}{(0.08206\ \text{L atm mol}^{-1}\text{K}^{-1})(298\ \text{K})}\left(\frac{0.001\ \text{L}}{1\ \text{mL}}\right) = 400\ \text{m}^2$$

490. The information from the problem gives

$$\text{A} = \frac{(0.129\ \text{L g}^{-1})(6.022 \times 10^{23}\ \text{mol}^{-1})(1.62 \times 10^{-19}\ \text{m}^2)}{22.4\ \text{L mol}^{-1}} = 561\ \text{m}^2\ \text{g}^{-1}$$

491. It is necessary to begin by calculating the flux (J_N), molecules striking the surface from the relationship $J_N = \frac{PN_A}{\sqrt{2\pi MR\,T}}$, where N_A is Avogadro's number, R is the gas constant, and M is the molar mass. This relationship gives

$$J_N = \frac{PN_A}{\sqrt{2\pi MRT}} = \frac{(2.0 \times 10^{-6}\ \text{torr})(6.022 \times 10^{23}\ \text{mol}^{-1})}{\sqrt{2\pi(17.0 \times 10^{-3}\ \text{kg mol}^{-1})(8.314\ \text{J mol}^{-1}\ \text{K}^{-1})\ (298\ \text{K})}}$$

$$\times \left(\frac{1.013 \times 10^5\ \text{Pa}}{760\ \text{torr}}\right) = 9.9 \times 10^{18}\ \text{m}^{-2}\ \text{s}^{-1}$$

Multiplying by the surface area gives the total flux,

$$9.9 \times 10^{18}\ \text{m}^{-2}\ \text{s}^{-1}\ (1.00\ \text{cm}^2)\left(\frac{0.01\ \text{m}}{1\ \text{cm}}\right)^2 = 9.9 \times 10^{14}\ \text{s}^{-1}$$

The percentage of the surface covered by adsorbed molecules is

$$\left(\frac{9.9 \times 10^{14}\ \text{s}^{-1}\ (1\ \text{s})}{5.0 \times 10^{15}}\right)(100\%) = 20\%$$

492. It is necessary to begin by calculating the flux (J_N), molecules striking the surface from the relationship $J_N = \frac{PN_A}{\sqrt{2\pi MR\,T}}$, where N_A is Avogadro's number, R is the gas constant, and M is the molar mass. This relationship gives

$$J_N = \frac{PN_A}{\sqrt{2\pi MRT}} = \frac{(1.2 \times 10^{-5}\ \text{Pa})(6.022 \times 10^{23}\ \text{mol}^{-1})}{\sqrt{2\pi(32.0 \times 10^{-3}\ \text{kg mol}^{-1})(8.314\ \text{J mol}^{-1}\ \text{K}^{-1})\ (298\ \text{K})}}$$

$$= 3.2 \times 10^{17}\ \text{m}^{-2}\ \text{s}^{-1}$$

Multiplying by the surface area gives the total flux,

$$3.2 \times 10^{17}\ \text{m}^{-2}\ \text{s}^{-1}\ (1.00\ \text{cm}^2)\left(\frac{0.01\ \text{m}}{1\ \text{cm}}\right)^2 = 3.2 \times 10^{13}\ \text{s}^{-1}$$

Calculating the time (t) necessary,

$$\frac{2.0 \times 10^{15}}{3.2 \times 10^{13}\ \text{s}^{-1}} = 62\ \text{s}$$

493. The relationship to determine the flux is $J_N = \frac{PN_A}{\sqrt{2\pi MRT}}$, where N_A is Avogadro's number, M is the molar mass (3.9948×10^{-2} kg mol^{-1}), and R is the gas constant. This relationship gives

$$J_N = \frac{PN_A}{\sqrt{2\pi MRT}}$$

$$= \frac{(7.0 \times 10^{-8}\ \text{Pa})(6.022 \times 10^{23}\ \text{mol}^{-1})}{\sqrt{2\pi(3.9948 \times 10^{-2}\ \text{kg mol}^{-1})(8.3145\ \text{J mol}^{-1}\ \text{K}^{-1})(273\ \text{K})\left(\frac{\text{kg m}^2/\text{s}^2}{\text{J}}\right)}}$$

$$\times\left(\frac{\text{kg/m s}^2}{\text{Pa}}\right)\left(\frac{0.01\ \text{m}}{1\ \text{cm}}\right)^2 = 1.8 \times 10^{-11}\ \text{s}^{-1}$$

494. The equation is $k_d = \frac{P\ N_A}{(\sqrt{2\ \pi\ M\ R\ T})(\exp(\Delta H_{ads}/RT))}$, where N_A is Avogadro's number, R is the gas constant, and M is the molar mass of oxygen. Entering the values and solving by parts gives

$$k_d = \frac{PN_A}{(\sqrt{2\pi MRT})(\exp(\Delta H_{ads}/RT))}$$

$$= \frac{(3.0 \times 10^{-5}\ \text{Pa})\ (6.022 \times 10^{23}\ \text{mol}^{-1})}{\left(\sqrt{2\pi(32.0 \times 10^{-3}\ \text{kg mol}^{-1})(8.314\ \text{J mol}^{-1}\ \text{K}^{-1})\ (298\ \text{K})}\right)(\exp(\Delta H_{ads}/RT))}$$

$$= \frac{(1.8066 \times 10^{19}\ \text{Pa mol}^{-1})}{\left(\sqrt{\left(498\ \text{kg J mol}^{-2}\right)\left(\frac{\text{kg m}^2/\text{s}^2}{\text{J}}\right)}\right)\left(\exp\left(\left(-10.8\ \text{kJ mol}^{-1}\left(\frac{1000\ \text{J}}{1\ \text{kJ}}\right)\right)/(8.314\ \text{J mol}^{-1}\ \text{K}^{-1})\ (298\ \text{K})\right)\right)}$$

$$= 6.3 \times 10^{19}\ \text{m}^{-2}\ \text{s}^{-1}$$

495. There are several different forms of the Langmuir isotherm (with a variety of notations for the various constants). The following is the form used for this problem.

$$\theta = \frac{b\ P}{1 + b\ P} = \frac{V}{V_m} \quad \text{or} \quad P/V = P/V_m + 1/bV_m$$

A plot of P/V versus P will be linear with the slope = $1/V_m$ and the intercept would be $1/bV_m$. The slope is 0.01691 cm^{-3} g, and the intercept is 0.002641 atm cm^{-3} g. Therefore,

$$V_m = \frac{1}{\text{slope}} = \frac{1}{0.01691\ \text{cm}^3\ \text{g}} = 59.1\ \text{cm}^3\ \text{g}^{-1}$$

$$b = \frac{1}{V_m(\text{intercept})} = \frac{1}{(59.1\ \text{cm}^3\ \text{g}^{-1})(0.002641\ \text{atm cm}^{-3}\ \text{g})} = 6.40\ \text{atm}$$

496. The relationship is $\theta = \frac{kP}{1+kP}$. Using the information from the problem gives

$$\theta = \frac{kP}{1+kP} = \frac{(7.8 \times 10^{-3}\ \text{torr}^{-1})(175\ \text{torr})}{1+(7.8 \times 10^{-3}\ \text{torr}^{-1})(175\ \text{torr})} = 0.58$$

497. The number of molecules necessary to cover the surface is

$$\text{Molecules} = \frac{(25\ \text{g})(800\ \text{m}^2\ \text{g}^{-1})}{1.0 \times 10^{-19}\ \text{m}^2} = 2.0 \times 10^{23}\ \text{molecules}$$

Using the ideal gas equation ($PV = nRT$) to determine the volume of gas,

$$V = \frac{nRT}{P}$$

$$= \frac{(2.0 \times 10^{23}\ \text{molecules})\left(\dfrac{1\ \text{mol}}{6.022 \times 10^{23}\ \text{molecules}}\right)\left(\dfrac{0.08206\ \text{L atm}}{\text{mol K}}\right)(298\ \text{K})}{1.0\ \text{atm}} = 8.1\ \text{L}$$

498. The solution requires the Clausius–Clapeyron equation, where R is the gas constant. This equation is $\ln\left(\frac{P_1}{P_2}\right) = \frac{\Delta H_{ads}}{R}\left(\frac{1}{T_2} - \frac{1}{T_1}\right)$, which rearranges to

$$\Delta H_{ads} = \frac{R \ln\left(\dfrac{P_1}{P_2}\right)}{\left(\dfrac{1}{T_2} - \dfrac{1}{T_1}\right)}$$

Assigning variables: $P_1 = 3.20$ atm, $T_1 = 195$ K, $P_2 = 32.0$ atm, and $T_2 = 298$ K,

$$\Delta H_{ads} = \frac{(8.314\ \text{J mol}^{-1}\ \text{K}^{-1})\left[\ln\left(\dfrac{3.20\ \text{atm}}{32.0\ \text{atm}}\right)\right]}{\left(\dfrac{1}{298\ \text{K}} - \dfrac{1}{195\ \text{K}}\right)} - 1.08 \times 10^4\ \text{J mol}^{-1}$$

499. The appropriate relationship is $\Delta G_{ads} = RT \ln P$, where R is the gas constant.

$$\Delta G_{ads} = RT \ln P = (8.314\ \text{J mol}^{-1}\ \text{K}^{-1})\ (298\ \text{K}) \ln 32.0\ \text{atm} = 8.59 \times 10^3\ \text{J mol}^{-1}$$

500. Begin with $\Delta G_{ads} = \Delta H_{ads} - T\Delta S_{ads}$, which rearranges to

$$\Delta S_{ads} = \frac{\Delta H_{ads} - \Delta H_{ads}}{T} = \frac{(-1.08 \times 10^4 - 8.59 \times 10^3)\ \text{J mol}^{-1}}{298\ \text{K}} = -65.1\ \text{J mol}^{-1}\ \text{K}^{-1}$$